DEPRAVED AND DISORDERLY

DEPRAVED AND DISORDERLY

Female Convicts, Sexuality and Gender in Colonial Australia

JOY DAMOUSI

Department of History
University of Melbourne

PUBLISHED BY THE PRESS SYNDICATE OF THE UNIVERSITY OF CAMBRIDGE
The Pitt Building, Trumpington Street, Cambridge CB2 1RP, United Kingdom

CAMBRIDGE UNIVERSITY PRESS
The Edinburgh Building, Cambridge CB2 2RU, United Kingdom
40 West 20th Street, New York, NY 10011–4211, USA
10 Stamford Road, Oakleigh, Melbourne 3166, Australia

First published 1997

Printed in Hong Kong by Colorcraft

Typeset in New Baskerville 10/12 pt

National Library of Australia Cataloguing in Publication data
Damousi, Joy, 1961– .
Depraved and disorderly: female convicts, sexuality and
gender in colonial Australia.
Bibliography.
Includes index.
ISBN 0 521 58323 3.
ISBN 0 521 58723 9 (pbk.).
1. Women convicts – Australia – History. 2. Women convicts –
Australia – social conditions – History. 3. Penal colonies – Australia –
History. 4. Sex role – Australia – History. 5. Australia –
History – 1788–1851. I. Title.
364.37409944

Library of Congress Cataloguing in Publication data
Damousi, Joy, 1961–
Depraved and disorderly: female convicts, sexuality and gender in
Colonial Australia/Joy Damousi.
p.   cm.
Includes bibliographical references and index.
1. Women prisoners – Australia – History – 19th century.
2. Criminals – Rehabilitation – Australia – History – 19th century.
3. Women prisoners – Australia – Sexual behaviour. I. Title.
HV9873.D36 1997
364.374'099409034–dc21   96–46423

A catalogue record for this book is available from the British Library

ISBN 0 521 58323 3 hardback
ISBN 0 521 58723 9 paperback

For Michaela Richards
1961–1993

Contents

Conversions

Length
1 inch = 25.4 mm
1 foot = 30.5 cm
1 mile = 1.61 km

Volume
1 pint = 568 mL
1 cup = 250 mL

Mass
1 ounce (oz) = 28.3 g
1 pound (lb) = 454 g

Acknowledgments

I am indebted to the Australian Research Council, which made the research for this project possible with the generous assistance of several grants. I also wish to thank the staff at the Archives Office and State Library in both Tasmania and New South Wales, who were extremely helpful in locating sources.

This book developed out of various discussions with many people. I owe an enormous debt to the generosity and support of Lyndal Ryan and Deborah Oxley, two of the leading scholars in the field of convict women's history. During the course of my research, Lyndal Ryan pointed me to sources and offered important suggestions when reading parts of the manuscript, while Deborah Oxley has been unconditional in her encouragement and interest in the project. This text is built on and informed by their insights and their scholarship.

I was privileged to benefit from the valuable comments of various readers. Paul Collins enthusiastically shared his encyclopedic knowledge of convict history. Philip Harvey read the penultimate manuscript with precision and care. Robert Reynolds generously shared his vast expertise on theory, directed me to references and enthusiastically discussed many ideas with me, which have shaped much of my thinking. Stuart Macintyre helped me to refine my arguments and his support continues to sustain my writing. I am particularly grateful to Lyndal Roper for her pertinent suggestions, sharp insights and warm encouragement.

I have been assisted by many others along the way. Phillipa McGuinness embraced the concept for the book and kindly offered much needed guidance, advice and reassurance. Sally Nicholls's editing skills are formidable and her suggestions vastly improved the text. John Hirst was enthusiastic at the beginning of the project, and suggested some directions I could pursue. David Goodman, David Philips, Chips

Sowerwine, Patrick Wolfe, and Charles Zika kindly directed me to references from their specialist areas and took an enthusiastic interest in my research from which I have greatly benefited.

My interstate trips to Sydney, Hobart and Canberra were enhanced by the warm hospitality and good cheer of James Campbell, Emma Grahame, Guy Fitzroy, Peter Langmede, Christine Owen, Henry Reynolds, Sue Rickard, Penny Russell, Marion K. Stell, Mary Spongberg and Elizabeth Walsh.

Other friends were supportive in different respects. I owe a unique debt to Katie Holmes—critic and supporter—who commented on the manuscript with erudition and who provided a much valued and dearly cherished friendship.

In many and varied ways, Verity Burgmann, Ann Curthoys, Patricia Grimshaw, Susan Magarey, Marilyn Lake, Jill Matthews, Judith Smart, Shurlee Swain and Christina Twomey have been central in sustaining and nourishing my intellectual pursuits. I also thank Julie Brown, Pauline Brightling, Georgine Clarsen, Jenny Dawson, John Dillane, Sarah Ferber, Rose Lucas, Carmel Reilly, David Shugg and Julie Wells for always being there. I am deeply appreciative to Ann Turner, who, in ways both subtle and profound, has been a source of inspiration through her nurturance, her creativity and her passions.

Finally, this book is dedicated to Michaela Richards who showed a rare courage in giving so generously of herself.

When quoting, I have been faithful to the original documents, idiosyncratic spelling and all. Similarly, I have used the spellings of people's names as they appeared in the source material.

Introduction

In May 1822, twenty-five convict women were removed from the female prison in Parramatta, New South Wales, and sent to the government settlement at Emu Plains at the foot of the Blue Mountains. Governor Sir Thomas Brisbane, who, during his five-year reign, aspired to reform rather than simply punish convicts, believed light field work in a rural environment would be more conducive to reform than the overcrowded conditions in the prisons and the vagaries of private service. 'It had occurred to me', he recalled, 'that a certain number of women might be usefully employed in light field work, such as hand-weeding, pulling of Corn, scutching of flax, and other occupations, as might thereafter render them more useful members of Society, if they should become Settlers' wives, and more beneficial to their health than being crowded in the Factory'. He hastened to add that at the time of the experiment he 'gave the strictest orders to the Superintendent and those acting under him to prevent all improper intercourse between the men and women, and to employ them separately under different Overseers'.[1] The Emu Plains project was a part of Brisbane's vision to reduce the expense of the colony and to make it self-sufficient. This was a concern which extended to the female prisons, where the coarse woollen cloth made by the prisoners had sold so well that the prison had, over a three-year period, recorded a profit.[2]

The Emu Plains experiment received little attention until 1825, when allegations were made that women had been selected from the prison, 'for the express purpose of being prostituted at Emu Plains'. It was claimed that 'convict men were allowed the use of the women' and that the women demanded 'rations for such favours'. The men, it was said, 'lived by plunder', and were violent to the women 'to gratify their lust'. In consequence, 'women were in a dreadful state of disease, and complained of this treatment'.[3]

1

Brisbane ordered a public inquiry into the allegations against him, and he fiercely denied them. He claimed that he had carefully monitored the settlement, and was left with 'favourable impressions of the morality and propriety of the measure of women being sent to Emu Plains'. If he had heard or known of any 'illicit intercourse taking place between the men and the women at Emu Plains, I should immediately have withdrawn the women from Emu Plains', he claimed, and 'severely punished those responsible'. Although he admitted that two women became pregnant, and were returned to the factory, these women did marry the fathers of the children and other women who had volunteered to be transferred had also married men they had met at the settlement.[4]

Those who testified before the inquiry agreed with the governor that there had been no ill practice. James Kinkhorn, the assistant superintendent, stated that he had never 'heard of any promiscuous intercourse being permitted between the men and women, much less of any women being compelled to submit to the embraces of the men'. The assistant surgeon, James Mitchell, reported that the 'women appeared to be clean and orderly . . . and pleased with the general good order and cleanliness of the whole establishment'. Donald McLeod, a magistrate at Parramatta, stressed the success of the settlement in reforming the women. Of the thirty-two women in total who were sent to Emu Plains, 'twenty-three are married and are living with their husbands'.[5] The findings of the inquiry would have no doubt satisfied all parties, for it absolved government officials of any wrongdoing by conveniently finding the behaviour of the women to be the cause of the disturbances. The inquiry found that while there had been illicit relations between the convict women and men, these relationships had been 'voluntary and were initiated by the women'.[6]

This dispute about promiscuity and sexuality, productive and reproductive labour, oppression and autonomy, points not only to issues that concerned colonial authorities in relation to convict women, but also highlights some of the key themes that have shaped convict women's history. The scandal at Emu Plains would have affirmed the view of some historians that convict women could not escape whoredom. Others would argue that, as was the case at Emu Plains, marriage gave women protection and the means to move beyond their situation.

There is no doubt that women were in an exposed and vulnerable position. Of the 160,000 or so convicts transported during the period of transportation to Australia from Britain between 1788 and 1868, only about 25,000 were women. The focus of this book is on the period from the 1820s to the 1840s, during which time transportation of convicts to Australia reached its peak. All convicts were sentenced for seven years, fourteen years, or for life. Most of the women were condemned for a seven-year term.[7] The discussion centres on New South Wales where transportation ceased in 1840, but there are comparisons made to Van Diemen's Land, which became independent from NSW in 1825.[8] Although there was a flow of free immigrants to the colonies throughout this period, there remained a striking gender imbalance. It was no surprise that what was deemed sexual impropriety was an ongoing source of concern for the authorities.

This work inevitably draws on the insights of earlier studies but its purpose is to shift the debate away from earlier discussions of the positive or negative experiences of convict women and the essence of their morality because such discussions have narrowed the focus to questions of the origins of convicts.[9] In the Emu Plains incident, for instance, unlike earlier discussions, we are concerned with how ideas about masculinity, femininity, and sexuality are shaped and defined and how convict women dealt with their relationships with the convict men and their commanders in order to be autonomous and create a space for themselves.

My aim is to ask different questions of Australia's convict period by focusing on the ways in which cultural meaning is shaped, and on the nature of relationships. In doing this, a central purpose is to make gender and sexual difference the basis of cultural analysis, rather than simply 'adding' women to the narrative.

One way in which we can analyse these issues is to consider cultural symbols or signs of the nineteenth century as a way of understanding the meanings of particular representations and relationships. Towards this end, this book explores the expression of, and relationships between, masculinity, femininity, the body, sexuality, motherhood, fatherhood, cleanliness, order, identity, race, play, resistance, and space. But more importantly, it also attempts to consider the range of meanings attached to these categories at particular times within colonial society. The challenge for historians, argues Joan Scott, is to identify 'which symbolic representations are invoked, how, and in what contexts'.[10]

It is not enough, however, to isolate meaning or cultural signs. They are, of course, historically determined and are contingent on those moments at which they assume meaning.[11] It would be impossible to read cultural signs in any meaningful way without historicising them—without an attention to context, and to the process of their construction.

The period from 1820 to the 1840s is particularly interesting; it was during these two decades that several developments occurred that considerably altered the colonies of New South Wales and Tasmania. First, under the rule of Governors Darling, Gipps and Arthur a series of reforms was introduced which restructured the forms of punishment and the way power was exercised. The surveillance and systematic forms of discipline espoused by Arthur and Darling during the 1820s made this society one in which its inhabitants were subject to the closest scrutiny under the microscope of the state. Their vision of a new order which shaped the reforms these governors introduced meant that the nature of protest and resistance inevitably also changed.

Second, in the specific context of the experience of convict women, the establishment of the female factories during this period and the systematic allocation of women from these factories to domestic service redefined the exchange between the convict and free settler and provided a set of different conditions for the intersection of gender, sexuality and femininity. Third, the establishment of the orphan schools threw into sharp relief the place of the child in this society. In analysing the ways in which convict and Aboriginal women were institutionalised, the meanings, expectations and understanding of these children can be scrutinised. And fourth, it was during this period that free immigrants began arriving in the colony in significant numbers. Prior to 1820, those defined as 'free' mainly comprised medical and judicial officials, government bureaucrats and their wives and children. With an increasing number of free immigrants entering the colony, and many convicts becoming free during the 1820s and 1830s there was a profound transition in the composition of the population and in the nature of relationships.

There are a number of broad themes to develop within this context, the organising principle being the significance of sexual difference for the maintenance and disturbance of social order. One important perspective from which to analyse these dynamics is the discussion of purity and pollution, which is a constant theme in contemporary accounts of convict men and women. An examination of this discussion not only points to the ways in which these concepts shaped understandings of femininity, masculinity and sexuality, but also illuminates the ways in which male observers constructed their own sense of themselves as white, male and middle class in relation to convict women. In other words, in focusing on language as the medium of self-representation,[12] terms such as 'pollution' and 'purity' reveal the way in which convict women became a particularly potent site of sexual anxiety. Unlike Aboriginal women, who could be dismissed as alien, convict women were the threat from within. There was both a fear and fascination with the unsettling power of the 'other'—in terms of gender and class—embodied in convict women and also in the projection of male sexuality in the eroticisation of these women.

We may also turn to points of resistance, or agency, which differ from conventional notions, such as laughter and play. Whereas resistance has been perceived in particular terms, usually through unified action,[13] such definitions did not often apply to convict women. For women, vociferous laughter and play—dancing, chanting and playing tricks—undermined the exercise of power. Laughter and play within this culture at this time by women was more than 'unseemly in polite company': it undermined the exercise of power.[14] Children, too, adopted particular behaviour that could not easily be included within common perceptions of convict protest, which were driven by notions of justice and liberty. Sulking, for example, amongst girls in the orphan schools was a form of withdrawal and a behaviour that was difficult to punish. The regularity of children sulking in school is in contrast to how children are commonly presented as passive victims of schools of industry that socialised and moulded them.

Another broad theme that has been considered from a range of viewpoints in historical accounts is punishment. Some have focused on whether it was harsh or lenient, effective or ineffective, while others have asked whether the camaraderie of the prison was better or worse for women than the outside world of a penal colony. However, a consideration of the meanings of one form of humiliating punishment—that of headshaving—can direct our attention elsewhere. It can illuminate how hair was central to the convict woman's sense of feminine self and to her femininity, an identity that was challenged when she moved between the inside and outside worlds. The shift in identity from that of 'bound' to 'free' is also interesting to pursue here. In applications by convicts and free for the release of their children from the orphan schools we can analyse how that shift also brings about different understandings of 'fatherhood', 'motherhood' and 'childhood'.

'Abandonment' and 'displacement' are other metaphors to which we could point to highlight these themes of cultural anxiety and gender. This is particularly apparent in the applications by men to place their children in the orphan schools after their mothers had fled. Concern about the 'abandoning mother', the 'wandering mother' and the 'orphan' all suggest an unease about the gender order. The 'wandering life' was often conflated with freedom of choice, especially in sexuality, but unlike men, who often promoted fear, envy and pity, for women, the sentiments aroused were invariably anger and resentment. The perceptions of 'motherhood', in particular, point to ambiguity and contradiction for while on the one hand convict women were encouraged to reproduce, they were also despised as mothers of the emerging free population.

Finally, historians have to date focused primarily on the establishment of boundaries and borders, considerations obviously central to a study of penal societies. But I am interested in those moments of transgression that highlighted understandings of sexuality, masculinity and femininity. In this society, we can see this particularly in three situations: within the spatial economy on convict ships, in the towns and on the public streets when convict women intruded upon them, and in the movement of convict women between the inside and the outside of female prisons. On convict ships, for instance, we can point to how the tension and fluidity between the public and the private spaces illuminate the ways in which gender and sexuality shaped relationships on these ships.

In 'reading the signs'[15]—of headshaving, of moments of laughter and play, of the language of pollution, purity and abandonment, of the inside/out nature of the prisons and the spatial economy on ships and within the towns, of the perception of convict women as savage and the 'other', of the 'abandoning' and 'wandering mother' and of the 'orphan'—we can broaden our understanding of colonial culture.

Attention to these categories can further illuminate the moments which crystallise understandings of sexual difference. It can also point to the ways in which the social order was at once undermined and sustained, not only through social control, but also in the intersection of language, movement, sexuality and gender. The aim in attempting to capture the tensions within this society at this time would be to challenge the certainty and closure implied in some of the discussions in earlier convict histories. The purpose is twofold: first, to reassess and to analyse the nature of relationships, the meanings of particular forms of punishment, power and resistance and the forging of sexual, racial and gendered identities; second, is to identify the nature of cultural anxiety during this period, which was expressed through notions of gender and sexual disorder, race and class dynamics.

This book begins with the convict women's voyages out to Australia and looks at their subsequent journey. It considers the punishments they endured and their recalcitrant acts of resistance. But it is also concerned with the fate of their children and their status as mothers; the vagaries of marriage and the shift to being free, all of which show us how anxiety about gender and sexuality was a dynamic element in colonial culture.

PART ONE

Sexuality, Punishment and Resistance

Part One is an examination of four areas in colonial society where certain relationships forged particular sexual, racial and gendered identities, which illustrate how anxiety about gender, race and sexuality was manifested and expressed by convict women and by the male officials who attempted to contain them.

In Chapter One, on board the convict ships, we can see how the confined space on these ships created anxiety about sexual order and disorder and how these dynamics defined a particular relationship between the ships' surgeons and the convict women. Mutiny and rebellion on these ships carried sexual meaning as women came to be defined as the agents of disorder.

This theme of disorder is further developed in Chapter Two. Once ashore, we trace how the presence of convict women on the colonial landscape came to represent an anxiety about the polluted nature of women's sexuality, thus unsettling masculine self-control. The racial implications of discussions of convict women are explored as a means of understanding how white, ruling-class, masculine identity was shaped *vis-à-vis* convict women's difference. In Chapters One and Two, the themes of looking and seeing, sensory delight and deprivation are also pivotal in these interactions.

The different avenues of resistance available to convict women are considered in Chapter Three. These are analysed in terms of how resistance assumed different meanings for men and women, especially in terms of the expression of convict women's desire and pleasure. As in the previous two chapters, women's recalcitrance was framed by a concern about both heterosexual and homosexual female sexuality.

The feminine convict self comes into further focus with the examination of headshaving and its impact on convict women's femininity. The

7

violent response to this punishment suggests the tensions within women's identity in moving from inside to outside the walls of the prison.

Three issues underline these sections. These chapters are bound by considerations of the body as the place where cultural meanings are inscribed. Convict women's bodies are central to discussions of sexuality, eroticisation and disorder in Chapter Two and in the symbolism of head-shaving in Chapter Four. The disruptive presence of women's bodies within a particular space of the ship and in the public space beyond the prison walls is explored in Chapters One and Three respectively.

The intersections between masculinity, femininity and sexuality are another theme which shapes and connects these chapters. This inter-relationship is evident in Chapter One in the paternalistic relationships forged between convict women and surgeons; in the eroticisation and fear of women's sexuality discussed in Chapter Two; in expectations of particular behaviour and in the transgressive quality of women's sexuality in Chapter Three; and in the masculinisation of women through head-shaving in Chapter Four.

Finally, a concern with racial cleanliness underpins these discussions. The comparison between convict women and Aboriginal women is explored in discussions on sexuality in Chapter Two, but notions of cleanliness, order and racial concerns are also prevalent in the opinions expressed by surgeons.

In Part One, the dynamics of gender, race and sexuality are con-flated to suggest the ways in which certain identities and cultural mean-ings were shaped within the context of nineteenth-century British colonialism.

CHAPTER 1

Chaos and Order
Gender, Space and Sexuality on Female Convict Ships

Chaos and Order

In May 1820, the convict ship *Janus*—a whaling vessel—sailed into Port Jackson from Cork, after a voyage of 150 days. To the outside observer, the trip seemed uneventful. There were two deaths reported, certainly not an alarming number by nineteenth-century standards. Some convict ships lost many more of their inhabitants through illness or shipwreck, although only 2 per cent of convict women who travelled died on the voyage out.[1] Of the 105 convict women who were on board, only one had died, which reflects the remarkably low mortality rate at this time, for just under 99 per cent of the women transported from 1816 to 1829 survived the voyage.[2] The other casualty was the Surgeon-Superintendent James Creagh, who died off the Tasmanian coast. But it was not for these deaths that the *Janus* gained notoriety and became the subject of an investigation before a Bench of Magistrates soon after its arrival in Sydney in July 1820. Following the discovery that many of the female convicts on the *Janus* were pregnant, Governor Macquarie felt it his duty to direct the Bench to investigate the circumstances surrounding their confinement. The magistrates subsequently found that 'prostitution did prevail in great degree on board the said ship' and that there was little effort made by the Captain or officers to repress or prevent its practice.[3]

The issue of controlling prostitution and monitoring the liaison between sailors and female convicts remained a constant source of anxiety on board ship. Nothing had prepared the women for such a voyage. In England and Ireland women prisoners were brought by wagon from country and city gaols and herded on to small ships or hulks. Their bodies and souls were attended to while they waited for the ship that was to launch them, anywhere from three to five months later, to an unimaginable place.[4] They were medically examined to ascertain their ability to cope with the physical demands of the voyage ahead and were lectured by Elizabeth Fry, the prison reformer and Quaker, who preached the necessity of 'abandoning their evil ways, and becoming Useful Members of Society'.[5] In their journey from prison to port, the women had had little contact with men. The opportunities available for sexual interaction on the long voyage were unprecedented.

Successive governors were alerted to the disturbances these en-counters could precipitate. In 1826, Governor Arthur expressed his alarm at the conduct of Surgeon-Superintendent Matthew Burnside, employed on the *Providence*, who had cohabited with one of the women, Julia Mills, and 'frequently allured others into his Cabin to drink. He has also in other respects conducted himself most unworthy of the trust reposed in him'. It was found that the master, John Wauchope, had 'in no way exerted himself in an earnest manner to prevent the impro-prieties'.[6] Governor Ralph Darling agreed, claiming that Burnside's behaviour was 'extremely unbecoming his character, as a Married Man'.[7] Earlier, Barron Field, Judge of the Supreme Court, had responded to Governor Macquarie's request for details on this matter on board the *Lord Melville*, on which he had sailed. Field despaired, claiming that 'to prevent connexion between the women and the seamen would . . . be quite impossible, even if the hatches had been battened every night'. He reassured the governor that on the whole there was as little immorality as was possible when the sexes were brought together. A decent exterior had certainly been maintained, and he flattered himself that because of his high office, his presence had operated as a 'moral check'.[8]

No such public decency was attained on the *Janus*. Throughout the investigation into the disturbance on that ship, the master, Thomas Mowat, fiercely denied accusations of impropriety. He insisted that he had attempted—through his best endeavours—to monitor contact between the sailors and the women. Although he admitted at times 'it was utterly impossible for me totally to suppress the vice', he asserted that each evening hatches were fastened; the sailors were never down with the women at night and he punished the women 'on a straight waistcoat' when they misbehaved. He denied accusations that the convict woman Mary Long was a 'constant companion in his birth place'. She was a servant, he insisted, who entered his cabin only to obtain linen to wash and to mend his clothing. Ann Moore, the wife of Corporal Moore, one of the officers, supported Mowat in his interpretation of the events, claiming she never saw 'more between the Sailors and female Convicts, excepting seeing them walk about the Decks'.[9] Bars and gratings were placed securely at night, and Mowat, she asserted, 'always checked the seamen, when they were Speaking to the women'.

But these pleas of innocence were not wholeheartedly supported by those who travelled with them. The most vitriolic and damning testimonies came from the two Catholic priests on board. The Reverend Philip Connolly claimed there were 'two or three women often, indeed Constantly, in the captain's Cabin'. Sailors took their partners from the prison room and prostitution was carried on, according to Connolly, 'to a most shameful extent'. The security was poor: hatches could not be kept down, the locks were bad and sailors could access the prisoners' berth. According to Connolly, Mowat was not serious about imposing order: his comments 'appeared to me to be making play'. The 'women were as determined to communicate with the sailors, as the men themselves were', and if the surgeon attempted to punish any of them 'he was only laughed at'. Such disorder, concluded Connolly, 'was a matter of great concern'.[10]

John Joseph Therry concurred with his fellow priest. Therry asserted that the 'utmost prevalence of vice' prevailed and there was 'criminal intercourse between the sailors and the female convicts'. While he sympathised with the captain that if he were too severe with the sailors the crew would mutiny, Therry believed discipline had not been established on board, and much of the 'crime and disorder' could have been curtailed.[11]

Mary Long, who confessed to being pregnant to Captain Mowat, claimed that she did not know of any prisoner being let out of the prison after the lock-down hour. She did not know of the women being down in the sailors' berth and when she was in the captain's berth, it was commonly and publicly known. Lydia Eldsen, who was pregnant to the chief mate, John Hedges, claimed she was not certain whether several of the women were out of the prison during the night and could not say either way. The surgeon did not attempt to prevent the movement of sailors, she said, although he implored them to be more circumspect when coming up and down from the sailors' berth, but Eldsen claimed that she 'went up and down openly [and] the other women did the same'. Long later claimed that the surgeon-superintendent had lived with Ellen Connelly before he died, and a number of women had lived with the sailors during the course of the journey.[12]

The final testimony came from Jacob Pistor, the master boat builder in the Sydney dockyard. Having examined the ship a fortnight after its arrival, he concluded that the *Janus* was 'fitted up a great deal better than female convict ships usually were . . . sufficient to prevent any communication between the sailors and the prisoners in their Births'.[13] Despite Macquarie's determination to repress such 'flagrant dereliction of Duty for the future', these incidents on the *Janus* were neither unique to that ship nor uncommon.

Examining the convict ship as a way of exploring gender relationships has not yet been considered by historians. Charles Bateson's study of convict ships, first published in 1959, is the most comprehensive and detailed work on the subject. This and other works, like Babette Smith's *A Cargo of Women*, are concerned with details of the physical conditions on the ships, rather than the relationships and representations which are shaped within its boundaries. While both of these works consider convict women's experience on various voyages out to Australia, neither is informed by a gendered perspective, which includes how ideas and practices were shaped about masculinity, femininity and sexuality. Greg Dening's study of the *Bounty* considers the social space and the symbolic environment of the ship, but he is not concerned specifically with the dynamics of the female convict ship.[14]

What we see on these ships—as was evident on the *Janus*—is a concern with order and potential chaos in the interaction between what we can delineate as 'public' and 'private' spaces. On all convict ships, the public was the realm of order, rationality, control, regimentation and routine. But on female convict ships, private space became the arena of chaos and disorder, unsettling the imperatives of efficiency, order and rank through sexual promiscuity. On these ships the private space was also an invisible realm, which made it even more insidious. The imperative of looking and seeing, hiding and exposing became a part of the intersection between public and private spaces. This demarcation between the two was not, nor is it ever, so clear: these spatial boundaries intersected, overlapped and shaped each other. Furthermore, such a confined and isolated space accentuated sexual anxiety. The fluidity between these boundaries meant that the private space unsettled, undermined and at times disrupted the rigid boundaries which defined the public order. The public violation of what was deemed decent and decorous on the ship became an important issue in these testimonies. The unsettling force of the hidden, unseen realm of sexuality in creating potential disorder was an underlying tension, despite the efforts of the captain to deny its occurrence.

This interaction between public (order) and private (chaos) and the need to contain disruption through invisibility and seclusion—sensory deprivation—became central to the upholding of decency on the *Friendship*. The question of looking and observing became a key dynamic in how sexuality was contained. The transport ship *Friendship*, commanded by Andrew Armett, arrived in Sydney in January 1818 carrying 97 convict women, four fewer than when the ship sailed from England in July 1817. Its inhabitants had experienced a 'tedious passage which produced scurvy and very considerable debility and sickness among the Convicts and crew'. On its arrival, Macquarie received a letter from the surgeon,

Peter Cosgreave, who reported that there had been a 'very indecent and licentious intercourse' between the officers and crew and the women convicts, despite the efforts of the captain and surgeon to curtail such behaviour. Attempts to repress or prevent the 'highly reprehensible conduct' had had little effect but to produce a 'constant jarring' between them and the crew. Indeed, for Armett, the private space where sexual liaisons took place became not only the source of disorder and chaos, but a place that he attempted to keep hidden, out of public view. Despite his efforts, such behaviour impacted upon and shaped the public domain of the ship. He reminded his crew of the 'consequence that was likely to result from their meddling with the Convicts, being considered as the Cargo', but a 'spirit of great insubordination and mutiny seemed to exist, originating from the restraint of Prostitution'. When all the officers and crew were implicated, it was 'useless to Contend [the] matter'. Armett gave instructions to his crew and officers to have no intercourse whatsoever with the convicts on board. He was aware that women hid in the officers' berth, but he begged the officers

> not to adopt the System of prostitution in my sight. I said 'do not let me see it, it is directly contrary to my orders'. I never saw anything indecent myself, but my Orders as to the intercourse with the women were I believe Violated by every Man in the ship.

Armett concluded that if there was any liaison 'it was done in the most private and secret way possible as I never saw anything of it myself'. While the private realm remained invisible, it unsettled the public domain on the ship, as Armett attempted to discipline his crew and tried to curtail the potential of a mutiny.

In his letter to Governor Macquarie, Cosgreave suggested the need for a 'private' realm as a place for disorder, so that its influence on the efficient running of the ship could be controlled. 'The Women constantly lived in the Men's births', he claimed, 'and the officers took off the Hatches at Night to let up others for themselves and for such as wanted them'. While he observed that prostitution was 'universal in the ship', he too asserted 'he too never saw any improper act between the women and the men'. Cosgreave claimed he embarked on the ship with every expectation that there would be no complications. He communicated with the chief mate, 'lately Married', 'from whom I had every reason to expect a cordial Co-operation in the discharge of my duty', officers 'who had been strongly recommended and members of a religious society'. With such company, he had 'entertained every hope of [them] complying with [my] orders', at least 'to succeed so far as to preserve the bounds of decency'. Instead, Cosgreave found himself having to punish 'every act of profligacy' even when the 'Effrontery of the aggressors was considerably increased'.

Others confirmed that there had been such activity. Ann Barfoot, a passenger, reported that William Hicks, the chief officer, removed the hatches between eleven and one in the night and let the women down in the morning. Thomas Walker, the deputy assistant commissary general, reported that the captain had resigned to stating that if the men and women got together he could not help it: he could not be awake at all times. Walker testified in the defence of Hicks, claiming that he did his duty with 'utmost zeal and assiduity' in attempting to extinguish the lights in the women's compartment when they had been seen 'at unseasonable hours'. William Cordeaux stated that the captain did not care about prostitution, unless it was visible, and 'done under his own Eye'. Cordeaux insisted that 'there was no public violation of decency and decorum in the ship'.[15]

To be sure not all female convict ships carried such experiences. As the historian John West notes, 'of vessels remembered for their pollution, the *Friendship* and the *Janus* are distinguished'.[16] But in both these incidents, promiscuity unsettled the public order of the ship and, as we shall see, the potential for sexual disorder remained a constant source of anxiety. Attempts were made to render it invisible, to obliterate the private, but this only served to heighten existing tensions. As Dening notes, the 'social contract of a total institution is to be public. The personal in such a contract is disturbing. The personal creates ambivalences and blurs the boundaries between control and protection'.[17] Within this context, women were considered to be the agents of disorder.

John Haslem, appointed surgeon to the *Mariner* in 1816, noted that the convict men became 'more thoroughly corrupted' from intimacy with convict women.[18] West perpetuated this view when he observed that on the *Janet Shore* 'the persuasion of the women accomplished what the male prisoners rarely attempted, and when on their voyage to the colonies have never been able to effect. The soldiers and sailors, seduced by their caresses, seized the vessel, and having shot the captain and the chief officer, steered into a South American port'.[19] In an inquiry into the events on the *Elizabeth*, in 1828, John Vincent, the assistant chaplain, formally laid charges against J. H. Hughes, the surgeon on board. Vincent accused Hughes of preventing him from administering his service. More offensively, it was the 'open and barefaced violation of common decency', the 'intercourse between the seamen and convicts . . . [which had] been carried out on . . . the voyage to scandalous lengths', to which he objected. Here, again, it was the visibility of promiscuity that was most offensive. Women roaming during the night throughout the ship unsupervised and the convict women seen in the rooms of officers meant that 'Mrs. Vincent and myself have passed four months and a fortnight, during the most favourable season for a voyage, and with fine weather . . . [on] nothing better than a floating brothel'.[20]

While not all observers formulated such a damning opinion of convict women, the elements of chaos and disturbance were commonly identified as features of their behaviour. 'The general character and conduct of the prisoners', wrote Surgeon-Superintendent Thrasycles Clarke in 1830, 'were such as might be expected from the lowest class of society'.[21]

This image has gained currency in the writings of several historians who have argued that the journey out for women was so corrupting that it demoralised them. Their association with criminals for a period of eight months degraded them, and the chances of a convict woman reaching her destination undebauched, according to this view, were extremely slim.[22] Others have argued that liaisons between convict women and the ship's crew in fact were harmonious and that the trip across the seas improved their health. Babette Smith observes that on the *Princess Royal* in 1829 'although there was probably some promiscuity the men and women settled into pairs as the voyage progressed'.[23] Phillip Tardif notes that despite 'the rigours of a long sea voyage . . . the fresh sea air seemed to breathe new life into the majority of women'. He claims that by 'the time land was sighted, they were physically and mentally rejuvenated'.[24]

The discussion concerning the voyage from Britain to Australia has centred on whether women's experience was better or worse than that of their male counterparts, or whether the voyage had a corrupting or rejuvenating impact on them. Rather than dwell on these perspectives, which cast women's experiences as either positive or negative, I want to emphasise how sexual practice unsettled the interaction between public and private space on these ships and how visibility and seclusion were an important part of this interaction. I want to stress the way in which women dealt with the relations of power in different ways to men, in order to be autonomous and to create a space for themselves.

The relationship between private as disordered and public as ordered space is central to the interactions which took place on female convict ships. Nineteenth-century ideas about the public and private have been considered in the realm of ideology and the formation of the colonial state,[25] but the interaction between these realms beyond the level of ideology, and on the particular institution of the ship, has yet to be considered. As Greg Dening and others have noted, ships are entirely public institutions: sailors are without space of their own, and private space is the preserve of those who occupy a privileged position within the ship's hierarchy. Within this framework, he argues, 'the personal' creates ambiguities and is disturbing.[26]

What happened to this spatial arrangement when convict women intruded into the quintessentially masculine culture of these ships? Space, as Doreen Massey has argued, embodies 'by its very nature . . . power and symbolism, a complex web of relations of domination and subordination'.[27] On female convict ships, public and private spaces were redefined as private space became sexualised. It is for this reason that mutiny and rebelliousness amongst women were defined on the ship in sexual terms: the potential for disruption differed in nature and scope to that of male convicts.

When considering these issues, it is important to note that by the time the *Janus* had sailed in 1820, convict women were more rigidly supervised on the ships and endured a more structured daily routine than those who sailed during the pre-1816 phase of transportation. On the *Lady Juliana*, for instance, which sailed in 1789, the authorities had not provided female convicts with materials so they could sew or work. It was up to the captain to bring linen on board so the women could make shirts on the voyage, but this was not official policy.[28] This was in contrast to the regimented daily routine introduced after about 1817, which included specific instructions about the labour to be performed by convict women and the times when these duties were to be undertaken. Surgeon-Superintendent William Elyard records in 1821 that on the *John Bull* convicts would be on the decks at 6 a.m., breakfast would be served at 8 a.m., and by 9 a.m. their beds would be up and the prison cleaned. Women would then be employed in sewing or washing. At 2 p.m. they would be fed, then work again in the afternoon and by 7 p.m. he would muster the convicts to their beds and ensure they were safely locked up for the night.[29] Convict women would certainly have had more opportunity to enter into sexual liaisons with the officers and seamen during the earlier transportation phase, when their daily activities were not so rigidly structured.

Changes in the design of convict ships also need to be noted if we are to understand how sexual interaction within these confined spaces also changed over time. On the earlier ships that carried convicts, the prison occupied the third deck, within a space 75 feet long and 35 feet in length. There were also four rows of one-storey high cabins. In 1817, this design was altered and the prison was divided into three separate compartments. Surgeon Peter Cunningham describes this sort of prison on the ships during the 1820s:

> Two rows of sleeping berths, one above the other extend on each side of the between-decks, each berth being 6 feet square, and calculated to hold four convicts, everyone thus possessing 18 inches space to sleep in . . . Strong wooden stanchions, thickly studded with nails, are fixed round the fore and main hatchways, between decks, in each of which is a door with three padlocks, to let the convicts out and in and secure them at night.[30]

There was also a particular need on female convict ships for three or four compartments to be separated from the prison, to be used for confinement.

Another important issue was the gender balance within these confined areas. It wasn't until after 1811 that the segregation of male and female convicts became the norm. Up until that time, there were mixed as well as single-sex ships. Between 1801 and 1810, for instance, of the twenty-nine convict ships which arrived in Sydney, ten carried both men and women, while seven carried women only and twelve carried only male convicts. After 1811, only two ships carried men and women: the *Archduke Charles* in 1813 and the *Francis and Eliza* in 1815.[31] After 1815 ships no longer carried both male and female convicts.[32] The numbers of convict women who travelled on the ships varied dramatically. In 1827 the *Persian* carried 60 women—the lowest number of women to be carried to Sydney—while in 1852 the *Sir Robert Seppings* transported 220 women. Of the trips made to Hobart, which began in 1818, a mere 30 women disembarked from the *Maria* in 1818, while 260 landed on the *Blackfriar* in 1851. Between 1801 and 1853, the average number of convict women who travelled on these ships to Sydney was approximately 135, while it was slightly more, at 144 per trip, to Hobart.[33]

Changing modes of punishment that were introduced and implemented over time also affected the ways in which convict women dealt with their predicament. From the 1820s punishment was 'less injurious' to convicts' health. Women's punishment changed from floggings and wearing irons, to solitary confinement on bread and water.[34] These changes would have altered the ways in which women could move and occupy the spaces on these ships.

Judging by reports in the surgeons' journals, the interaction between public and private spaces differed on male convict ships. It was largely through theft, fighting, or overt 'mutinous behaviour' that public order on the ship was unsettled. These were not sexualised activities, although there is no doubt homosexual liaisons were a source of disorder within an all-male environment. Surgeon William Rae listed amongst the general rules to be followed on his ship *Eliza*: 'no man to get into the apartment of the Boys nor the Boys into that of men'. But homosexual disturbance was not perceived in the same way, and it was theft which was identified more commonly as disruptive. This is clear from another of Rae's rules, which he also noted in 1822:

> Whenever [a convict] is found guilty of Robbing or Theft shall have his back placarded with *Thief* and be kept in . . . Irons for the rest of the voyage; and whoever is found guilty of fighting, gambling . . . will suffer twenty-four hours solitary confinement upon bread and water or such other Punishment as the case deserves.[35]

Richard Naylor was 'punished in the most exemplary manner' for 'attempting to steal' from boxes on board the ship. Earlier during the voyage, Richard Childs was found guilty of stealing from Joseph Bates. The surgeon noted that as 'this crime is likely to be such a cause of evil and disturbance during the voyage . . . the offender [was] punished with one dozen and a half lashes and held out as an example to others if found guilty of a similar offence'. After about six months at sea, the petty thefts had become so prevalent that the surgeon ordered 'all money to be given up to the Chief mate of the ship'. In his concluding remarks, Rae claimed that the 'number of chests and packages in the prison belonging to the Prisoners allowed a constant excitement to Theft and Robbery'.

Similarly, for disobedience, insolence and 'mutinous' conduct the prisoner remained in irons and handcuffs, landing 'in the same state at the place of his destination'.[36] Mutterings of mutinous intent evoked a harsh punishment, as John Elinhurst discovered, when he made claims that 'if there were 10 or 12 of his mind' he 'would take the ship'.[37] Fighting and using disrespectful language could also earn severe punishment. Henry Flanagan, for instance, was handcuffed 'for exciting dissatisfaction among the convicts, and for unbecoming language and conduct towards the Boatswain of the Prison without any cause whatever'. Andrew Keogh was similarly admonished and handcuffed for being 'very abusive' to Sergeant Clancey upon opening the prison door.[38] Within the context of a public institution like a ship, as Dening notes, 'trust that the little property personally owned was safe was critical for every man on board'. Stealing was an age old crime and 'extravagant' punishment for stealing from shipmates was tolerated by the men.[39] Through a consideration of these incidents we can see how space was organised differently on male and female convict ships. As we will see, the sexualised element on female ships also determined the ways in which mutiny and rebellion were understood.

Mutiny and Rebellion

In item 13 of the *Instructions for Surgeons-Superintendents and Masters on Board Convict Ships*, published in 1838, it was stipulated that if a surgeon was appointed to a ship with female convicts, he was to use

> his utmost endeavours to prevent their prostitution with the Officers, Pass-
> engers or Crew; shewing a good example himself in this particular, and not
> failing to report to the governor any instance of improper intercourse with
> the women which may be detected.

In the same set of instructions convicts were to be allowed on deck as 'much as possible', consistent with safety, but surgeons were to be 'on guard against any attempt at mutiny amongst them, taking precautions to prevent any surprise, especially during the time of divine service, or at any other time when considerable numbers are on Deck'.[40] While there was no connexion made in these instructions between the two items, clearly, mutiny and disorder came to carry different meanings for male and female convicts. For women, notions of disorder were conceived in sexual terms and a particular form of surveillance was undertaken accordingly. Women's presence was objectified and sexualised on these ships in a space inhabited by men. Robert Espie was acutely attuned to the need to keep a sharp eye out for sexual disorder. A veteran of six voyages to Australia, he was familiar with the potential for such disorder. As the surgeon-superintendent on the *Lord Sidmouth* between August 1822 and March 1823, he noted in September 1822 that while he was

> happy to be able to remark that the women generally are most orderly disposed, indeed I shall not have thought from all I have heard of the ungovernable character of female convicts that those [we] have be so easily managed—it is quick to add that [I] cannot spare one hour from looking after them otherwise a breach of the last article of my instructions would . . . take place, but hitherto I have nothing to complain of on the part of the sailors taking liberties with the women.[41]

In October, he proudly reported that he had observed 'no proper liberties . . . towards the women, but this is mainly owing to my own vigilance'. His surveillance had been so careful, that he reported there 'is no appearance of any intercourse between the women [and] sailors nor do I apprehend there will be any during the passage but this is only to be depended on while they are well looked after'. While he had observed 'advances of a licentious nature between the crew and the women . . . this could never be if I were not constantly to attend to every regulation(s)'. He concluded his journal with the observation that convict women 'constantly require to be looked after and particularly to [keep them] from contact with the sailors—this can only be done by . . . checking all appearances of intimacy before the ship leaves England, directing the master to discharge any sailor who may show a disposition this way, which I in two or more instances did to his no small annoyance'. He was pleased, however, to have got 'rid of so troublesome a charge having been kept constantly in the alert during the period'.[42]

William Elyard, too, was conscientious in his surveillance. He 'observed some intimacy' between the convicts and one of the officers and requested him 'not to take liberties with the convicts', stating that he expected 'he would not interfere with them'. Although surgeons were careful to monitor heterosexual activity, homoerotic acts were not as easily regulated. Elyard noted the disturbance when, in November 1821,

'Margaret Brennan [got] out of her bed and went to Mary King's bed . . . her son called her . . . several times to return—went to Mary King's bed after her when Rose McDonald insisted on Margaret Brennan going to her own bed and pushed her and the boy away'.[43] The surveillance of potential sexual activity was a task adopted by surgeons on female convict ships.

Women negotiated this type of surveillance in different ways. Their resistance included using improper language, quarrelling and being boisterous, behaviour not effectively adopted by men, who were hopelessly restricted in their movement because of their irons. Women could move freely on the decks. William Anderson, surgeon on the *City Of Edinburgh* throughout 1828, reported that the women had 'perfect liberty at all times to come on the deck from 8 o'clock [in the morning] to sunset and this no doubt had its effects in keeping them in good health and buoyant spirits'.[44] The movement of male convicts was far more restricted with usually two groups of about 50 to 75 convicts being allowed out for about five hours each.[45] Disobedience had different meanings for men and women, and because of the difficulty of punishing women, they had broader scope for disruption. 'It required much management', concluded Joseph Hughes, the surgeon-superintendent on board the *Elizabeth*, 'to prevent jealousies and quarrels lest any preference might be understood'. He was disgusted by their 'waste destruction of clothes, Building and Blankets deplorable throwing them overboard to our very face—and shortly after becoming ill for want of the same thro cold'. He concluded that while he had secured their 'esteem and goodwill in my medical capacity', in other respects, they had been 'slothful, dirty disposed with a most lamentable recklessness of character unconquerable'.[46]

To be sure, the surgeons were fearful of mutiny in a more conventional sense similar to the threat presented by male convicts. In November 1821, Elyard charged Biddy Lummy, Eliza Wilson and Jane Mitchell with holding committees and 'forming mischief and mutiny' and of being 'dangerous, malignant and undermining'. He gave orders to all convicts that they have no communication with these women and that if any committee were assembled, they would be flogged. There was also fear of disturbance when he heard the convicts 'make use of mutinous language', referring to the talk about the mutiny on the *Lady Jane*. He confined them, but they insisted that 'they had no mutinous intentions'. But women's 'protests' were perceived within different parameters to those of men and their physical freedom allowed them these options for rebellion. Before the *John Bull* departed, the women refused to eat the food served to them. They threw away the oatmeal, which had been boiled with water and sugar for breakfast. A week later, Elyard reported that they had stolen 'a bag of bread [and] before the officers could get below they had scattered it about between the docks'. They also complained about the provisions, but on examination he 'found the complaint unnecessary: bread tho' brown good and sweet'.[47]

Physical attacks and quarrels were not unusual. Thomas Reid noted with frustration in his *Two Voyages to New South Wales and Van Diemen's Land* that he was forced to contain the passions of two convict women, Sarah Downes and Elizabeth Cheatham, who were fighting, both being 'intoxicated and furiously riotous', determined to murder one another.[48] To a young prisoner reformer like Reid, such behaviour would have confirmed his belief that transportation was a brutal and irrational means of improving the character of prisoners. A close associate of Quaker and prisoner activist Elizabeth Fry, he 'regarded transportation with repugnance' and made only two voyages in his capacity as surgeon-superintendent.[49] Others took action that Reid had resisted. In August 1821, Elyard reported that on the *John Bull* he had punished Mary Downs with a collar around her neck 'for assaulting Matilda Brown and for making a second attack upon her in the presence of myself, and the Captain'. Jane Mitchell was a particularly quarrelsome and noisy prisoner. Elyard confined her in hospital with a collar on for about an hour and a half. Jane Hamilton similarly was confined after being quarrelsome and riotous. During the course of another evening, Elyard found the convicts 'quarrelsome and riotous', threatening them with a severe flogging in the morning if they continued such behaviour.[50] It was not only convict women who were recalcitrant and boisterous on board the ships. Morgan Price noted that in terms of the frequent use of abusive language and fighting, free women could be as badly behaved as the prisoners. On board his ship he had 'found considerable more trouble with the free settlers than the convicts'. Price placed one free woman, who was making use of 'most abusive language', in the prison.[51]

Whereas the key disturbance on male ships related to theft, disorder on female ships was characterised in terms of this recalcitrant behaviour. In October 1822, Espie reported that he had handcuffed Elisabeth Kinsey and Mary Brown together and put them in the coal hole 'for abusive and mutinous conduct, and disturbing the peace of the ship'. At dark, he released them, but kept them handcuffed together throughout the night. Sarah Gordon was placed in solitary confinement for making a disturbance while the clergymen were at prayers. This woman, Espie concluded, 'is an abandoned character and I think the worst on Board'. Espie remained cautious noting one Sunday that he 'served no wine today in consequence of the noisy and disorderly conduct of the women last Sunday after its issue'.[52] Like Espie, Elyard, on the *John Bull* during the latter half of 1821, was aware of the need to 'prevent any communication with the seamen' and was forced to curtail 'disturbances' by convict women. He reported the absence of Margaret Finlay, Ann Anderson and Mary Ryan, and later found Ryan 'hid away all day with Mr. Wise 2nd officer . . . with whom she had been drinking—as she was at this time intoxicated, nor would she have come then had I not prevented anyone from taking her bed below for her—and finding she could not escape she came forward and confessed—after mustering and seeing all to their beds locked up for the night'. On another occasion, on mustering the convicts Elyard missed some of them and 'procuring a light found . . . Margaret Finlay . . . with Seamen and Ellen Keenan and Mary Brady in the Cook's Kitchen'. Ryan was implicated again when she and Mary Moran had gone missing at the 6 p.m. mustering. It was discovered that they had 'secreted themselves among men' and he had them put in irons and confined all night to 'prevent any communication with the men'.[53]

Women challenged the boundaries that circumscribed their behaviour in different ways to men. Their disturbance was perceived in sexual terms and understood in relation to middle-class expectations of feminine behaviour, such as passivity, docility and subservience. Surgeons devised various ways of dealing with this disorder. Some exercised their full powers by inflicting punishment, while others developed a paternalistic relationship, which allowed the women to have some autonomy and to empower themselves.

Paternalism

The complex intersection of public and private space meant that different types of relationships evolved between the surgeon-superintendents and convict women. Some surgeons viewed themselves as fathers to those under their command and their masculinity was shaped by a paternalistic attitude towards the women. Women often exploited this to undermine the unequal relations and in doing so created a degree of autonomy within a power structure designed to restrict them. The official arrangements that were in place were not, however, always conducive to relations between the surgeons and convicts developing in this way.

In the history of British naval expansion, it was roughly between 1816 and 1845 that stringent controls and clearer instructions were implemented on the organisation of ships. Towards the end of the eighteenth century, the rules and regulations outlined for the officers and surgeons on convict ships became more clearly defined and the prisoners were much more closely monitored. By 1820, there had been an improvement in the conditions on the ships, the voyage had become much faster and fewer deaths occurred on board.[54] The change in the role of surgeons on the ships also meant that the nature of their relations changed. It was not until the 1820s that detailed regulations for the management of prisoners were drawn up, which stipulated the precise duties of the surgeon-superintendent and meant possibly more contact with the convict women they supervised.[55]

But the surgeons did not travel alone with these women. There would usually be three officers, a master and often a mate as well. The all-male crew would include a carpenter, boatswain, ship's cook, steward, sailmaker, armourer, able and ordinary seamen, and a number of apprentices. The first influx of free immigrants did not occur until the 1820s, so they were not present on these ships until after that period. The families of the surgeons sometimes accompanied the surgeons on board although they would have had to pay for their passage.[56]

The reports written by surgeon-superintendents provide an illuminating glimpse of the ways in which gender ordered relationships on these ships. The surgeon-superintendent combined the skills of a physician, magistrate, chaplain and mentor.[57] His duties included supervising the thorough cleaning of convict quarters; issuing and supervising rations; monitoring the health of convicts; keeping convicts employed; conducting divine service; and guarding against mutiny. Together with the master he was responsible for punishments. Despite such power, the surgeon was nonetheless in an ambiguous position as mediator between the Crown and the women.

Few of the surgeons who were initially appointed had naval experience, but by the 1820s, it had become imperative to appoint naval surgeons because of their sea practice. Prior to this time, the surgeons' powers were ill-defined and once the ships had lost contact, they took little notice of instructions. It was also difficult to recruit senior and well-trained surgeons because it was not a prestigious appointment. It was not until 1814 that the status and practice of surgeons began to change. In that year, an investigation conducted by William Redfern, the leading surgeon in New South Wales, into the high mortality on convict ships, concluded that there was an urgent need for 'Skilful and Approved Medical Men', 'Men of Abilities' to be appointed to this position.[58] Redfern's report, regarded as 'one of the major Australian contributions to public health', not only recommended the need for ventilation and cleanliness on the ships, but, more significantly, outlined the need for surgeons' duties to be more clearly defined.[59] Although very few medical catastrophes occurred after this system was introduced, naval surgeons were generally not well regarded as most of them were either novices, or unable to obtain jobs in their profession on shore although they were more professional than the earlier contracted surgeons.[60] The journals, which they were obliged to keep throughout the journey, provide details of the daily routine on convict ships, medical documentation of the condition of convict women and, usually, a description of the voyage.

William Elyard was not unusual in forming a paternalistic relationship
with the women who sailed with him on the *John Bull*. He lectured them
when they had committed a crime, and delivered sermons about the evils
of prostituting themselves to the sailors. On the conclusion of the voyage
in 1821, the women kissed his hand and cheek. The way in which Elyard
reprimanded convict women was similar to the way children were
punished. In August 1821 he wrote that in the hospital there was

> quarrelling among the Convicts who were making use of very infamous
> language. I went into the Prison and reprimanded the parties concerned and
> threatened them with severe punishment if such language was again made use
> of—they promised I should hear no more of it and I sent them on deck.

In another incident, while serving breakfast at 8 a.m., 'Ellen Nolan [was]
brought from confinement', Elyard remonstrated with her, 'holding out
to her the consequences of premeditated revenge—she promised not to
interfere in future and she was then discharged'. Elyard could also be
protective of the women under his command. One Sunday during divine
service, he placed those he considered 'requiring reproof, in the most
conspicuous place'. He brought Mary Ryan and Mary Moran both in
irons and placed them

> close before me with the rest, and gathering all the convicts, Passengers and
> children around me I performed the church service and read to them a
> religious tract on interference and another on chastity and endeavoured to
> point out to them the consequence that must result from their disobeying my
> orders against prostituting themselves to the Seamen . . . It grieved me to see
> women in Irons and after church . . . [I released them] . . . from irons.

He admonished prisoners and cautioned 'the whole of the women not
to have connexion with the Seamen'. Ellen Keenan, who had insulted
and dared the Captain to confine her, had been put into the coal hole
with a collar on. Later that day, after 'having promised to be more circumspect in her language for the future' she was released from confinement. In a similar incident, after finding Jane Moore 'amongst the men'
and threatening to punish her with a severe flogging, he repeatedly
cautioned her not to prostitute herself, and she promised not to again.
He confined Ellen Rourke 'for being noisy and quarrelsome when prom-
ising to be quiet, discharged her to bed'. After having bought some snuff
at St Jago he 'gave all the Women who chose it a pinch to keep them in
good humour'.[61]

This practice of lecturing convict women and eliciting a promise from
them to be better behaved may have been particular to Elyard's relationship with these women, but even the sterner Espie released Sarah Boland

and Elizabeth Marden, whom he had handcuffed for fighting, 'on a promise of better behaviour'.[62] The surgeon on the *Henry Wellesley*, William Leyson, admitted that he considered 'the tranquillity of mind . . . most essential to bodily health', and allowed the convict women 'on deck from an early time of the morning', and 'to amuse themselves, by running about, dancing, or in any innocent way whenever the duty of the ship would admit it'.[63] George Fairfowle, one of the best known of the surgeon-superintendents, who had made the voyage to Australia at least seven times between 1817 and 1834, had expressed similar sentiments.[64] As the surgeon on the *Sovereign*, during its voyage of March to August 1827, Fairfowle claimed that while the women were initially 'disposed to be disorderly', in the course of eight or ten days, by admonition and steady punishment, 'they learned that an offence would not lightly be passed over, and that perseverance in improper conduct invariably tended to their own discomfort'. But Fairfowle was not autocratic perhaps because, having already made the trip four times, he came to believe this was the most effective means to maintain order. He reported that 'cheerful and innocent amusements among themselves were encouraged, and provided the songs were not licentious, singing was permitted until 8 o'clock except on Sundays and Thursdays, when I provided more serious employment'.[65] Indeed, women sang hymns that many of them, 'having been trained to it in Newgate, did with considerable taste and melody' and it 'became a pleasant duty', rather than an 'irksome task'. While making no claims that such activity actually reformed these women, they were, he believed, 'taught to preserve some degree of decency and even decorum in both minds and gestures, which was something gained'. This practice took two hours of their time, and rather than be 'inclined to quarrel or to play mischievous tricks on each other', it 'occupied their minds, and was thus conducive to health, order and regularity'.[66]

Other surgeons developed a similar relationship with convict women. Peter Cunningham had travelled widely as a navy surgeon and had seen service in Spain, East Indies, and North and South America. A veteran of five trips to New South Wales between 1819 and 1828, he earned a reputation as a surgeon who was particularly concerned with the welfare of the convicts for whom he was responsible. Of the 750 convicts who passed through his care on convict transports, only three had died.[67] This attention to their well-being was reflected in his delight in their play; on one of his voyages, several women 'danced several times weekly in the evenings throughout the voyage, kept singing for an hour or two every night . . . and had occasionally regular concerts and masquerades . . . dressed out in their gayest plumage . . . they would prolong the frolic till bedtime'.[68]

Thomas Reid, who believed the women could be reformed through moral instruction, was often chivalrous and protective of them, maintaining a belief in feminine purity. He noted in one of his journal entries that 'this morning a woman, who conducted herself throughout the voyage with exemplary propriety, solicited my protection against the insulting abuse and infamous threats of two of the sailors, which she declared had been quite unprovoked'. Reid took it upon himself to protect some of these women against some of the 'ruffians' who would have been 'more destructive to females in their circumstances, than a pack of wolves would have been'. He despaired at the contamination of ideal 'feminine virtue'—an idealisation which could be viewed as controlling—which needed to be better protected and cherished amidst such moral corruption. This instance is unusual in that it is the men who are identified as a source of disorder by provoking the women.

Reid soon discovered, however, how some convict women could negotiate these relationships. Ann Newton seemed to have lost her 'disposition to licentious romping and careless expressions' when she began to sit apart from her companions, where he noted she 'assiduously pursues her work in silence and remarkable reserve yet appearing cheerful and contented'. But it was this convict who became involved in a 'secret arrangement' made between three sailors, Newton, Ann Harwood and Anne Farrell, the women having 'concerted to accompany [the sailors] below'. Reid was disappointed with Newton, who had shown a 'strong inclination to amendment', and explained her behaviour by observing that idleness had revived her mischievous habits.[69]

For some of the surgeons, like Colin Arnott Browning, his paternalism and masculine self were influenced by a Christian pursuit to be an 'affectionate father to his long lost and prodigal offspring'.[70] In 1817, Browning was appointed a surgeon in the navy. His first voyage to Australia was as a surgeon-superintendent in 1831 on board the *Surry*, and he made six subsequent trips. A generous and kind surgeon, he used evangelical sermons to encourage prisoners to redeem themselves, and was attentive to their needs.[71] 'I look upon you', he said to those under his charge on the *Earl Grey* in 1842 'as so many members of that family to which I also belong—the offspring of our common and almighty Parent, the Creator and the Preserver of the universe'.[72] Browning drew on metaphors from evangelical Christianity about the family, the fundamental social organisation of society with the patriarch directing its members.[73] In his address to the prisoners on embarking, he claimed that

United together as one large family, not only personal but relative duties must be every moment recurring . . . Let everyone prefer his brother before himself . . . We shall have no angry and selfish contests about supposed or real personal rights and privileges; but we shall hear the language of brotherly affection.[74]

Browning's style may have been characterised by a particularly passionate zeal, but embracing convicts as his flock was not peculiar.

Other surgeons, who may not have shared Browning's reformist inclination, manipulated their parental role to achieve different ends. The masculine nature of paternalism sometimes carried sexual overtones and convict women were not reluctant to act when they believed they were being ill-treated. They could respond directly and often violently to abuse. An illustration of this was the attack of convict women on one Surgeon-Superintendent James Hall, in December 1823 on the ship *Brothers*. In the colony, Hall was notorious for his ability to be at the centre of controversy. He was accused of making false allegations regarding the Emu Plains project and became embroiled in a dispute regarding a female prisoner.[75] The events in which he was involved on board ship were no less dramatic, because of his propensity to attract trouble with convict women. Hall declared that his attitude to the female convicts was 'such as a father would adopt over his favourite children'. On the voyage of the *Mary Ann*, in 1822, he had kissed some of the young women after punishing them, if they were sorry for their sins. When queried about Hall's general behaviour, one of the convict women on the ship claimed his general conduct was like 'a father'.[76] A passenger, Richard Davis, who testified at the inquiry into the incident on the *Brothers*, observed 'that Mr. Hall conducted himself more like a Father to the female Prisoners that otherwise . . . this restraint upon the Women was necessarily put on in order to enforce due subordination and Submission on board'.[77]

While to some he may have adopted a paternalistic relationship with convict women, to others Hall had been particularly harsh in punishing them. He ordered some of them to be confined in a dungeon for six weeks, for nine days of which there was no bed to lie on, and for three weeks rations were bread and water. They were allowed on deck for only two hours. The dungeon was only six feet square, and the women were stifled for want of air. He also struck Anne Russel 'with the Handcuffs the Blood followed, and the Marks are now to be seen on her Arm'. Another source of the women's discontent was that Catherine Ryan's hair was cut off and she was handcuffed.[78] One of the officers, Mr Meach, instigated the rebellion, offering the women a bottle of rum before and after 'knocking Mr. Hall down in the Prison and jumping his Guts out'. To what extent the women were inspired by the promise of such rewards can never be known, but certainly Hall's behaviour would have incited the women to attack him violently. Some officials doubted the sincerity of his motives, and showed little sympathy. Following the inquiry, Governor Brisbane wrote to Bathurst urging him not to allow Hall to settle in New South Wales because of a doubt about his 'moral character'.[79]

The relationships that were formed between the surgeons and convict women were shaped by an interplay between masculine paternalism and an assertive femininity. This meant that the women could deal with the surgeons in ways not available to male convicts. Underlying these dynamics was a particular understanding of femininity and masculinity, which informed the ways in which punishment and order were structured and understood.

Femininity, Masculinity

A central motif on the voyage to Australia was the type of behaviour expected of convict women. Surgeons' discussion of women's bodies is a key to how they understood these women. The filth/cleanliness metaphor shaped the way convict women's femininity was perceived on board these ships, as ideas about dirt and cleanliness were directly related to ideas about social order and disorder. The juxtaposition between women's 'filth'—both metaphorically and literally—and the need for the ships to be clean and ordered is a continuing theme throughout these journals. British imperialist conquest was driven by an assertion of racial purity and sexual cleanliness. The obsession with sanitation not only served to eradicate disease, but also became an effective way of patrolling the borders of working-class women's sexuality, deemed 'contagious', 'dirty' and impure.[80]

In 1851, William B. Jones on the *Aurora* observed with the necessary degree of meticulousness the instructions regarding cleanliness, which demanded that the main 'prison decks . . . under the care of the super-intendents . . . are to attend to the cleanliness, maintain order and report any irregulation'. By this time, such fastidiousness had become an expected part of the surgeon's working day. Cleanliness was conflated with order:

> Cleanliness was the first object from dawn of day to its close, whenever practicable and this prosecuted systematically both in person and also in the various compartments of the ship disseminating the solution of the Chloride of lime liberally . . .[81]

Joseph Hughes, writing on the *Elizabeth* in 1827, drew a more direct parallel between the 'filth' of women and disorder on ships when he reported, with great indignation, that

> owing to the extremely filthy disposition of the women and their reckless character, choosing rather to live in their Dirt, than be clean . . . the decks of Prisons have required washing with plenty of Ablution, instead of the more salutary custom of scraping . . . even this washing, was and is effected with con-siderable trouble, leaving out abuse and the foulest language . . . all in toler-able health considering so various and depraved a set of women, many worn out with former debaucheries poverty and chronic diseases.[82]

Cleanliness was stipulated as a crucial requirement on the ships for the 'health and comfort both of the convicts and passengers'.[83] In the instructions to surgeons, it was stated that patients with 'infectious disorders' were to be received into hospital. They were to be cleaned and their clothing washed in boiling water, or fumigated, to prevent the possibility of infection.[84] But it was assumed that this level of cleanliness was difficult to achieve for convict women, because they were of a 'polluted' and 'disordered' disposition. Peter Leonard, on the *Atwick* in 1837–38, wrote that the preservation of health involved an attention 'to cleanliness and dryness in prison . . . ventilation, bodily exercise and constant mental employment'. The prison deck, water closets, and hospital were sprinkled with chloride of lime three times a week, generally at night after the prisoners had gone to bed, as a means of fumigation. A bathing tub was placed on the quarter deck. 'Every facility', Leonard reported, 'was afforded the convicts by numerous washing days to have their inner clothing kept at all times thoroughly clean'. Leonard noted that the condition of the majority of convicts was good, but some were in a most 'filthy' condition, being women of 'intemperate habits and irregular mode of life'.[85] Joseph Hughes related the difficulty of maintaining a high degree of cleanliness in convict women to their depravity, and to their 'former debaucheries, poverty and chronic diseases'. As he reported on Christmas Day in 1827, 'I cannot describe in sufficient terms the proneness to *filth* and their *savage disposition* to revenge and they thwart all attempts to keep them clean . . .'.[86] Twice a week, George Fairfowle on the *Sovereign* would inspect the women and children to see 'that their hair was combed and their persons linen and stockings were clean'.[87]

The relationship between cleanliness, order and femininity—as suggested by Hughes' reference to 'savage'—was comprehended within the broader ideology of race and ethnicity and its relationship to empire and imperialism. Edward Ford Bromley, surgeon on the *Surry*, 1832–33, concluded in his report that

> The great difficulty I experienced among the Irish prisoners was a rooted dislike to every kind of cleanliness, which it was difficult to eradicate. Beyond this their general conduct was as good as could be expected from such a class of people.[88]

The condition of Irish women was given particular attention when they were found to be carrying a disease. William Hamilton, on board the *Elizabeth* in 1818, noted that a woman from Cork had been 'labouring under contagious diseases'. William Jones, on the *Aurora*, reported that one of his patients, Jane McGregor, 'is of Scotch birth, has been [of] respectable and mild quiet disposition . . . opposite to the rest of her sex from the same quarter of the world on board'. But broader generalisations about convict women were more common. For Thrasycles Clarke, on the *Kains*, the overcrowding on the ships produced not only 'a spirit of devilishness', but also 'diseases dangerous in character and difficult to treat in so dense a population'.[89]

Syphilis was the most enduring inscription of the disorder and 'pollution' of convict women's bodies, irrespective of their nationality. On board the *Aurora*, Jones wrote that Eliza Williams was a prostitute who had 'syphilitic diseases' in the 'worst form' and it was 'with the greatest difficulty that she can articulate, and the odour that emanates from her breath, and person is of so disgusting a nature, that sickens every one, her skin is cold . . . pulse feeble; appetite not bad'.[90] Venereal disease was a condition that required the discharge of the prisoner back to prison, because it was considered a 'depraved state of health'.[91] Another woman who boarded Jones's ship was 'labouring under secondary syphilis in the worst form . . . the offensive state she was in . . . was most obvious'.[92] While convict male ships similarly required attention to cleanliness, the conflation of their sexuality with the need for purification and sanitation was absent.

Women's bodies needed different attention on the ships to that of male convicts when they became pregnant, gave birth and managed their children.[93] Many surgeons believed that children at the breast should not have been included on board the ships. In the 1820s, children under the age of seven were permitted to accompany their mothers, but nursing mothers were not allowed to be transported until their babies were weaned.[94] Women's physicality—displayed in breastfeeding and pregnancy—would also have determined what was seen on the ship and what was hidden. Breastfeeding in public was not considered acceptable and was publicly concealed. Travelling on the *Kains*, Clarke claimed that 'children ought not to be embarked on such a voyage as this, until old enough to be weaned fairly, to have been weaned sufficiently long to have forgotten the Breast'. He noted that there were three children under six months of age sent on board with their mothers, and although the regulations stated that women were not to be sent on board with children at the breast, this didn't prevent it from happening. Certainly many surgeons felt that infants on board ship put particular strain on the surgeons. Jones noted the arrival of 'no less than 14 infants at the Breast of these—two very sickly, one died, and another—lived only 13 days after its birth'. William Anderson was similarly unimpressed, noting in 1828 that six children at their mothers' breast (whose provisions were 'scanty') had boarded the *City of Edinburgh*.[95]

These negatively presented statistics, however, do not take account of those women who were extremely protective of their children. Jones claimed that Jane McGregor was provided with her principal happiness by her adult daughter, who accompanied her. Children also died at birth: Emma Williams, a 'delicate female . . . [of] extremely small size', did not live.[96] More often, the surgeons recorded stories of mothers who were violent towards their children. In November 1821, some of the female convicts on board the *John Bull* reported to the surgeon-superintendent, William Elyard, that Jane Hamilton had been beating her child and had threatened to murder it. Elyard recorded the incident and the action he took after the women requested him to save the child. He 'found Mary Day had forcibly taken the child from her—the head had been cut with a half a pint Tin Pot and was bleeding very much—took the child into the Hospital, stopped the Hemorage and dressed the head—then left the child to the care of Jane Burne the nurse'.[97] Elyard confined Hamilton and put the child under the care of Rose Rickey, the school mistress. He instructed Rickey not to allow 'the mother to see or speak to the child, as she had been in the habit of teaching the child to swear . . . whenever she had been offended by any person she had always beaten and ill treated the child'.

Ideas about femininity and order were not only emphasised in relation to motherhood and cleanliness. Punishment, too, was coded with gendered meanings. Headshaving evoked a particularly hostile response and proved to be a most effective form of punishment in the female factories of the colonies. It shamed women and stripped them of their feminine qualities. Espie reported in November 1822 that he had punished Racheal Davis and Elizabeth Hartwell for 'boisterous and outrageous conduct' by shaving their heads. 'This mode of punishment', he claimed, 'seems to be the only thing they regard'. While flogging of women ceased in 1817 some of the surgeon-superintendents were not afraid to challenge ideas about conventional punishment for men and for women. After several futile attempts to discipline the women on the *Elizabeth*, Espie finally resorted to corporal punishment by taking a 'good, stout, piece of rope [and] whipped them most soundly over the arms legs and back and this ws continued . . . til have conquered every refractory spirit among them . . .'.[98]

Other activities shaped ideas about their womanhood. It was assumed that idleness would lead to mutinous behaviour. Women were expected to undertake needlework, washing, attend school and divine service. The reports of some of the surgeons suggest that they aspired to recreate a tranquil bourgeois ideal. Morgan Price notes that 'children are daily at school and the women employed in Knitting stockings . . . Beds are brought on Deck every morning after the decks are washed'. On board the *Aurora*, washing was done on Tuesdays and Fridays. Two women from each mess were to wash the clothes of the mess. Prisoners were appointed to classes for instruction in reading and writing. Schooling took place either below or above deck (according to the state of the weather) and the children joined in with the women. Divine service was performed every Sunday morning.[99] A typical day on the *Lord Sidmouth* in October 1822 was as follows: 'Prisoners constantly employed throughout the day at their patchwork—school going well under the care of the pastor. Women washing their clothes during the forenoon'.[100] Elyard noted that the convicts were 'employing themselves in any way they could find'. This involved reading religious publications and mending their clothes. But women did not always follow such prescriptions. Women were often not attentive at Bible service and used the Bible pages to paper their curls.[101] Smoking was common amongst convict women and attempts were made to curtail its practice on the ships. This was done for safety reasons, but the deprivation of tobacco was perceived as a form of punishment.[102] Elyard reported that he detected

> Mary Dorons with a lighted Rag and Pipe of tobacco for the purpose of smoking after being locked up took them from her and after telling her the result of fire occurring in the night threw the pipe . . . overboard, then mustered all to their beds . . .

Mary Hinds was similarly detected with a 'lighted rag and nutmeg grater used to carry fire below for the purpose of smoking after being locked up: reprimanded her'.[103]

Paternalism was not the only form of masculinity being played out in these interactions. Ideals of middle-class masculinity were often hypocritically espoused by those who could not themselves conform to such ideals. Sailors were often punished severely for their contact with convict women. William Leyson on *Henry Wellesley* noted that he had the chief mate discharged, because his

> pertinacity in holding improper intercourse with the Prisoners had become exceedingly vexatious, as independent of having detected a prisoner in bed with him who had been abstracted from the prison at night by breaking the roundhouse locks. I had every reason to believe that the bad behaviour of several of the Prisoners arose from this contempt of all authority.[104]

John Brown, the captain's steward, was flogged after 'having occasioned a disturbance between Ellen Keenan and Ellen Clarke' and confined to the quarter deck, so as to have no communication with the women on Elyard's ship.[105] This was a practice maintained from the early voyages. Surgeon Arthur Bowes Smyth, writing in 1787, noted in his journal that, after being found with convict women, the second mate was removed from the ship.[106] Sailors were often humiliated for their behaviour.

Dening has observed the theatre of punishment on ships and the aloofness with which it was administered.[107] The emasculation of convict men and other men was also part of this performance as the lashings of sailors served to reduce and diminish them. As William Rae observed, punishment by the lash was held out as an example to others.[108] It was not only convicts or officers whose punishment was made into a spectacle. A sailor, a carpenter and a boy were caught with women and 'drumd out . . . wt. the Rogue's March playing before them and the Boy had petticoats put upon him, they had all of them their hands tyed behind 'em'.[109]

On the *Elizabeth* in 1836, Robert Espie wrote in frustration that 'I had fairly imagined I know how to manage convict women having had two ships of that sort before, but for some cause or other I most decidedly did not succeed to my own satisfaction in this last ship . . .'. During the trip he had turned his 'time and attention' to punishing the women, by 'corporal punishment . . . solitary confinement cutting their hair etc etc but these trifles only invited them to go [to] greater lengths'.[110] When convict women crossed the boundaries of what were deemed to be public and private realms in the confined space of a convict ship, this sort of behaviour carried different meanings from those of male convicts. Disorder and rebellion were sexualised. Unlike Espie, some of the surgeons allowed the convict women to negotiate their relations with the men on the ships, relations which were inevitably defined by particular nineteenth-century understandings of masculinity and femininity. These ideas and expectations were to shape relations between convict women and ruling-class men, once they were ashore.

The confined, claustrophobic space of a convict ship, situated in the vast expanse of ocean, accentuated the sexual tensions between the women and their commanders. Within the microcosm of colonial society, the boundaries that would govern convict women's behaviour were even more restrictive and the disobedient actions of the women even more pronounced.

CHAPTER 2

'Depravity and Disorder'
The Sexuality of Convict Women

The Polluting of Parramatta

In his public tract on 'sexual disorder', *An Answer to Certain Calumnies*, published in 1826, Samuel Marsden, Anglican clergyman, magistrate and member of the board of management of the Parramatta Female Factory, explored the link between convict women's sexuality and their 'polluting' of the town of Parramatta. One cause of corruption, he wrote in a letter to Governor Macquarie in 1815, was the behaviour of male convicts. But a second, more insidious, cause of the moral and political decline of Parramatta and its neighbourhood 'is the miserable state of the female convicts in the service of the Crown, and employed at the Government factory'.[1]

The expansion of Parramatta coincided with the presence of convict women in its public spaces. Prior to Governor Macquarie's arrival in New South Wales in 1810, the town largely consisted of a number of huts scattered over the area, which had been established under Governor Arthur Phillip's command during the 1790s. By 1802 there had been some growth with the establishment of 180 houses inhabited by free men and government officials. But it was with Macquarie's arrival in the colony that the town's architecture was transformed. Parramatta began to flourish as several public buildings were installed. The orphan school and the hospital were erected in 1818,[2] and ten years later the *Sydney Gazette* noted that the town was 'improving in point of respectable and capacious buildings'.[3]

The one blemish on the town was the presence of convict women. On arrival in the colonies, women were issued with new clothing, their details were recorded and they were taken to the prisons.[4] Until a female prison was established in the 1820s, convict women would be given employment, but were left largely to look after themselves. In 1804, Governor King instructed that the two rooms on the upper floor of the existing gaol in Parramatta be used to confine female convicts. But the conditions were overcrowded and by 1818, there were 200 women attempting to obtain sixty places. Those who could not find a place there would either secure accommodation in Parramatta, or cohabit and trade as prostitutes.[5]

It was no wonder that convict women used sex as a commodity to survive, given the high demand for their services not only as servants and mistresses, but also as prostitutes. Some commentators were sympathetic to the fact that many were forced to rely on male protection and that prostitution was a lucrative option available to them. Navy surgeon Peter Cunningham observed that because in many instances women were led astray by men, their offences should be viewed more 'with an eye of pity than of anger'. Reform rather than punishment should be the objective.[6] Women were exposed in this way because they were in a minority, although the ratio between men and women did narrow. In 1820, for instance, the ratio of convict males to convict females was 9:1; by 1835 this had declined to 7:1.[7]

In Parramatta, women under 'disciplinary confinement' were locked up in the evenings in the factory, while others were left out after hours— either to seek accommodation in the town, or sleep in outbuildings. They were forced into prostitution or theft in order to obtain money to cover the cost of accommodation in the town.[8] Convict women thus had a visible presence in the public space of Parramatta, a presence that came to symbolise disorder. During the nineteenth century, such perceptions of women in the city landscape were common as women's congregation in public streets was often associated with social instability.[9]

In an attempt to obtain a more effective asylum for convict women, Samuel Marsden argued that the release of these women on the streets was dangerous. This was not only because of their drunkenness and loitering, but because of the ways in which their sexual deviance and their 'pollution' were 'contaminating' the town, by inhabiting the male public domain. 'During the night', he wrote, 'these women spread them-selves through all the town and neighbourhood of Parramatta, and some are glad to cohabit with any poor, wretched man who can give them shelter for the night'. The conflation of deviant sex, disease and filth pervades his writing on convict prostitutes, whose 'vices have rendered them loathsome to the better part of society'. More importantly, they had polluted the urban landscape, as the public vices of abandoned females become the 'grand source of moral corruption, insubordination, and disease, and spreads its pestilential influence throughout the most remote parts of the colony'.[10] The town, then, was being affected by these convict women, whose 'vices' threatened its tranquillity. Marsden defined the sexuality of convict women through the notion of social disorder. His use of filth and disease as metaphors for this disorder suggests his own anxiety about what their sexuality represented. For Marsden these women were the embodiment of disease, representing anarchy and social disintegration, to be both feared and controlled.[11]

Arriving in the colony in 1794, Marsden became a leading advocate of the need for convicts to marry and procreate within marriage in order to eliminate the 'vice, idleness and depravity' amongst convict women. 'Nothing would ameliorate the situation of the female prisoners so much as matrimony', he confidently asserted in 1807. Without matrimony, women would continue to lead a 'vagrant, wandering, idle, vicious life to the end of their days' and the 'rising generation will be brought up in . . . vice'.[12] In his roles of chaplain and magistrate, Marsden became embroiled in several disputes regarding the relationship between the Church and the State during his long residency in the colony, which ended with his death in 1838. An evangelical zeal characterised his attempts to convert convicts and informed the way he preached on the immorality of women.[13] Some convict women agreed with Marsden for the need for marriage, but they did so for different reasons. Women believed that it could provide protection and an escape from destitution. Too many discovered, however, that this was not the case and violence, assault and abuse within marriage were common.[14] Establishing a female prison was for Marsden the panacea as such an institution would employ convict women, remove them from promiscuity and temptation and 'restore these wretched exiles to society'. A prison would also contain women's bodily filth.

The boundaries of the body, it was assumed, could not be separated from other social and cultural boundaries. Bodily filth and disease as a metaphor for disorder and disintegration has a long history, and led to deviance being understood through the language of pollution and pestilence during the nineteenth century. The symbolism of pollution revealed a fear and anxiety about the mapping of the existing social order.[15] The perceived existence of 'dirt' amongst convict women suggested social chaos. Such views about pollution, dirt and cleanliness informed the views about marriage as a depollutant, as a state of purity and morality, which could contain female sexuality.

James Mudie, a marine lieutenant and colonial magistrate, made similar observations of the contaminating and polluting nature of the sexuality of convict women in his 1837 publication, *The Felonry of New South Wales*. Mudie was notorious for his harsh treatment of convicts. He believed that they could only be disciplined by severe punishment[16] and he became well known for his malevolent attitude towards them. Mudie's inhumanity precipitated a series of altercations with Governor Bourke, who he believed was lenient towards convicts. After several quarrels and a series of failed political manoeuvres, Mudie left NSW in disgust, determined to wreak revenge on those he believed had damaged his reputation.[17] It was with this unforgiving fury that he unleashed *The Felonry of New South Wales*. Despite the caution we should therefore exercise in analysing this text, it is nonetheless revealing for its use of particular metaphors. Mudie had reserved his most vitriolic criticism for convicts and during the course of investigations into transportation in 1837, was scathing of them. 'I never know an instance', he asserted, 'of any female convict coming out that I would consider a fair character'.[18] Their language, he asserted in *The Felonry*, 'would pollute the eyes cast upon it in writing'. Moreover,

> Their open and shameless vice must not be told. Their fierce and untameable audacity would not be believed. They are the pest and gangrene of the colonial society—a reproach to human nature—and lower than the brutes, a disgrace to all animal existence.[19]

Convict women's sexual deviance was conflated with a festering sore on society, disorder and subhuman behaviour. Mudie discussed a common theme, the ways in which convict women crossed the boundary that separated the human from the animal. This perception of convict women's 'savagery' was also enthusiastically promoted and sensationalised by the press. 'On Sunday evening', reported the *Hobart Town Courier* in June 1832,

> as Skinner the assistant chief constable was putting a woman into the watchhouse, she turned upon him with the ferocity of a tigress, seized his arm with her teeth, and bit off about a pound of flesh and muscle, which with the piece of his jacket and shirt, she masticated and swallowed with much apparent *gout*.[20]

Using similar animal metaphors, the surgeon Peter Cunningham observed that when convict women's passions were unleashed, the effect was catastrophic. The

> wild buoyancy of their dispositions being bridled by the severe restraints imposed upon them, they were like wanton colts loosened from the stall when they landed, and, in the fulness of their delight on being at last freed from the galling yoke, broke out into all manner of extravagancies.[21]

The use of disease, infection, filth, pollution—as well as savagery—as metaphors for social and political problems also informed commentaries on the London poor. Contemporary writers in Britain like Dickens,

Engels, Mayhew and Chadwick similarly conflated filth with social and moral disorder.[22] The poor were defined as a 'festering mass', who produced a 'miasma', which could carry across geographical and social boundaries and infect respectable society. While contagion depended on physical contact, miasma was invisible, unknown. Prostitutes had been the focus of such discussion, where they had been identified as the source of disease, contaminating society. Sexual deviancy was described through the language which evoked infection and pollution.[23] In a similar way, the convict woman's body represented this social 'disorder' through filth and pollution. Brothels were described by the *Sydney Gazette* as 'sinks of lewdness', which 'stalk forth drunkedness, robbery and murder'.[24] In these understandings of convict women, the bodily boundaries of animal and human were blurred and identified as a source of disorder. But it was when sexual boundaries collapsed that an even greater fear was aroused.

Why were convict women considered agents of such chaos and disorder within this society? Certainly, they were seen to perpetuate social chaos because of their sexual assertiveness and autonomy, which was labelled sexual deviance. But what did it mean to challenge the boundaries of the feminine ideal by being sexually active or adopting behaviour more acceptable for men, such as drunkenness? Why was this behaviour perceived as a threat to the social order, beyond its implicit challenge to understandings of femininity during this period?

In order to examine these questions, we need to explore sexual difference not only from a cultural viewpoint, but from the point of view of the psyche. This is not to deny the importance of cultural ideas about masculinity and femininity. The men in the military and the navy carried ideas to the colonies about domesticity, which shaped their knowledge about gender. During the mid-nineteenth century, respectability formed the basis of their attitude towards convict women. By cohabiting with men, these women were deemed prostitutes, and their intemperance repulsed British authorities.[25] The prescriptions of masculine and feminine behaviour were well defined. Bourgeois masculinity at this time was cast in terms of restraint, discipline and self-control, although lascivious activity was assumed to be an acceptable part of male sexuality.[26] As military men of 'drill and guard', governors such as Macquarie and Darling agreed with such views. Marriage was to Macquarie 'the natural destiny of women and of men' and on his marriage to his first wife, he wrote that he would live more 'regularly, temperately and traditionally' than he had done as a bachelor, no doubt as a result of having contracted venereal disease. For Macquarie, qualities of heroism, honour, duty, loyalty and camaraderie were central to his masculine self.[27] Darling also aspired to a high sense of duty. Eliza Darling and her husband shared the virtues of moral and religious instruction for women and self-control for men.[28] By the late eighteenth century, British ideas about the feminine had come to be understood in terms of a passivity, subservience, dependence and fragility. Unlike a century earlier, when women were deemed to possess sexual desire,[29] by the time transportation was fully under way, women were not expected to be sexually active, and it was believed that their sexual feelings could only be expressed through love in marriage. The middle-class ideal was that wives were to be virtuous and respectable. The concept of female sexuality allowed little place for desire and pleasure, being expressed in terms of women's reproductive capacity.[30] The family was the site of stability and morality; particular sexual acts outside marriage were considered sinful.[31] Women were to embody the highest moral standards. As the guardians of public morality, indulgences like alcoholism debased femininity.

The outspoken and controversial Lady (Jane) Franklin reinforced such ideas. Franklin shared the views regarding convict reform that preoccupied penologists of the day regarding convict women's sexual immodesty.[32] In 1841 she was inspired by the prisoner reformer Elizabeth Fry to form the shortlived Tasmanian Ladies Society for the Reformation of Female Prisoners.[33] But she remained stern in her convictions in regard to the flagrant disregard by convict women for particular standards of femininity. In 1839, she recorded in her journal that:

> I entirely differed from the opinions which I believe were generally entertained by the Govt. officers connected with the Convict Dept. as to the management of women—that I thought nothing could be more vicious in itself, so mischievous to the Community & so derogatory to the sex in general as the prevailing idea that women were incapable of being objects of punishment & that marriage without any reference to their conduct was the best [illegible word] for all their disorders.[34]

As Governor George Gipps reiterated in 1841: 'there is nothing in the whole catalogue of crime, so thoroughly revolting as drunkedness in a woman; there is no object of disgust or horror that offends the sight of God or man, so entirely as a drunken woman'.[35]

Many of the men who sailed to the colonies believed in these views. As we have seen, Samuel Marsden was one of the chief proponents of such opinions. But the rhetoric of social prescription did not always instruct sexual practice and many of Marsden's contemporaries kept convict mistresses. Travelling to a remote and distant colony completely dislocated and reordered the world they had known. It was also not uncommon for those in the colonial services to take advantage of the sexual opportunities that the British Empire opened for them. The widespread practice of prostitution and the opportunities for homosexuality within the vast domain of the British colonies were evidence of an inextricable link between empire and sexuality.[36]

Several military and naval officers of a particular generation, like William Balmain, David Collins, Charles Grimes, George Johnston, D'Arcy Wentworth and Philip Gidley King, had convict mistresses and King, Collins and Balmain fathered children by them. These men, born in the 1750s, and 1760s, had not inherited the views of passive female sexuality and femininity, which were to define later Victorian attitudes and deny women's sexual passions. By the beginnings of the nineteenth century, there had 'been a gradual shift from the earlier view of women as sexually voracious towards the innocence and passivity of Victorian sensibility'.[37] Before 1815, it had been accepted that several convict women accompanied soldiers or officers as their mistresses.[38] Macquarie had approved a number of pardons for this purpose. In 1812, he noted that he had issued more free pardons than anticipated, 'in order to enable a number of women who had lived for many years with and had children by soldiers of the 102d regiment to marry those men and accompany them home'.[39] Some, like David Collins, flaunted convention by openly displaying his liaisons. While his wife remained in England he had three convict mistresses over a number of years and several illegitimate children. He was clearly attracted to young women (there was a twenty-year difference in his second liaison and almost a forty-year difference in his third) and to those of different class origins.[40]

The 'excess' passion and sexual deviancy of convict women compromised men's masculine control and sexual restraint. The notorious case of Lieutenant Ralph Clark indicates how men of his ilk espoused conventional views but could not, in practice, uphold them. Clark was commissioned as a Second Lieutenant of Marines in 1779 and was appointed to the 6th Company to sail to Australia. In his journal, written between 1787 and 1792, convict women occupy a pivotal place in his narrative. As previously discussed, the lack of surveillance and discipline of convict women on the ships in the period before 1817 allowed for closer contact between the convicts and their commanders. Clark referred to them as 'damned whores', adding it was their lack of 'morality', abusive language, sexual licence and recalcitrance that disgusted him, and caused him to refer to them as 'a disgrace to ther Whole Sex'. In 'all the course of my days I never hard Such exspertions come from the Mouth of human being', Clark wrote in July 1787, after Elizabeth Barber, a convict woman, had abused the doctor on board. Her sexual assertiveness repulsed him, as she desired an officer to 'come and kiss her C . . . for he was nothing but a lousy Rascal as we Wair all'. It was such behaviour that elicited his description of her as a 'brute'. Such assertiveness, and the women's pleasure inspired further disgust, and he referred to four of the women he caught in the 'men's place', as 'D . . . d troubelsem whores'. Clark declared that he 'would rather have a hundered more men than to have a Single Woman . . . I hope in the ships that ever I May goe in hereafter there may not be a Single Woman'. He was relieved when the women aboard his ship were replaced by sheep at Cape Town: 'I think we will find [the sheep] much more agreeable ship mates than [the women] were'.

And yet, even for Clark, this repulsion embodied both a fascination and a temptation. 'A good God what a Seen of Whordome is going on there in the womans camp', he wrote in February 1788, 'no Sooner has one man gone in with a woman but a nother goes in with her'. But he was aware of being tempted himself:

> I hope Almighty will keep me free from them as he has heather to done but I need not be affraid as I promised you my Tender Betsey I will keep my word with you—I never will have any thing [to do with] any woman whatever except your Self my dear wife.

The contrasts of femininity—of the whore and the virgin—are pervasive throughout his journal. Clark was unforgiving because he compared convict women to his wife, Alicia, 'the most tender best and Beautifulest of her sex'. He idealised and adored her, describing her as 'the best of woman kind'.[41] She represented the ideal wife: moral, virtuous, pure and sexless, a fantasy that was further pronounced by the sexual behaviour of the convict women who surrounded him. Like so many of his contemporaries, however, Clark did succumb to sexual temptation. In July 1791 Mary Branham, a 20-year-old convict woman, bore him a daughter while they were at Norfolk Island. In November, they accompanied Clark when he sailed for Sydney.

In their scrutiny of convict women's behaviour, military and naval officers joined the surgeons, who, as we have seen, were also quick to comment. The surgeon, John White, on the female transport *Charlotte*, also understood femininity in terms of the difference between the virgin and the whore. A widely travelled surgeon, whose service took him to India and the West Indies, in 1787 he recorded in disgust that:

> the desire of the women to be with the men was so uncontrollable that neither shame (but indeed of this they had long lost sight) nor the fear of punishment could deter them from making their way through the bulkheads to the apartments assigned to the seamen.[42]

White understood femininity within these extremes. He noted the different behaviour of women in Rio de Janeiro and Cape Town where the *Charlotte* stopped en route to Botany Bay. 'The ladies at the Cape are lively, good natured, familiar and gay', he observed,

The habits and customs of the women of this place are extremely contrasted to those of the inhabitants of Rio de Janeiro. Among the latter a great deal of reserve and modesty is apparent between the sexes in public. Those who are disposed to say tender and civil things to a lady, must do it by stealth, or breathe their soft sighs through the lattic work of a window or grates of a convent.

On the other hand, he continues, at the Cape, 'if you wish to be a favourite with the fair, as the custom is, you must in your own defence . . . *grapple* the lady, and paw her in a manner that does not partake in the least of gentleness'. Amongst these women, 'a kiss ravished now and then in the most public manner . . . is not only pleasing to the fair one, but even to her parents'. Although White found this conduct 'rough and uncouth' these ladies did not 'overstep the bounds of virtue'. In contrast to such descriptions of these 'ladies', convict women were 'wretches' who suffered from a 'depravity [in] their hearts' because of the 'promiscuous intercourse . . . taking place between them and the seamen and marines'.[43] Like his counterpart Clark, White nonetheless weakened to these temptations. In 1793, he had a child with a convict, Rachel Turner.[44]

Sexuality, Pollution and Disorder

The unsettling impact of convict women therefore needs to be considered beyond a threat to colonial respectability. As we can see in the comments made by Marsden and Mudie, and earlier, in the behaviour of Clark and White, underlying contemporary judgements by these establishment men was, first, a fear of female sexuality, of its assertiveness, power and danger. 'The females are far from coy', noted one observer in 1832.[45] The public expression of convict women's desire, pleasure and potential for sexual activity was perceived not only as a social threat but was also a challenge to the psychic layers of masculine desire and self-control. We can glimpse this through the language used to represent the sexual disorder of these women.

During the early nineteenth century in Australia, attention was drawn to sexuality through a 'sex panic'. In Britain, ideas about sexuality were 'hardening' and femininity 'was evolving into a passionless maternity or weak sensuality, only roused by men's actions'.[46] Efforts were made to control changes in sexual behaviour and there were warnings of the dangers of non-conformity, which was a menace to social order and 'polluted' the community and body politic.[47] The connection made between female sexuality and social catastrophe was not exclusive to the nineteenth century, but featured in other historical moments. Women were the source of 'disorder' according to the writings of Rousseau during the seventeeth century. According to Rousseau, the basis lay in their sexual passion, because women were unable to subdue and sublimate their sexual desires in the same way as men. In order to contain such 'disorderliness' sexual segregation was necessary although it would not cure the disorder of women. The idealisation of the family and motherhood provided the vehicle for restraining the 'disorder', as the cult of domesticity promoted cleanliness and purity. Here, too, the 'dirty', 'polluting' woman was a most revolting creature and the source of 'disorder'.[48] Elements of this ideology had similarly informed discussions on female sexuality and witchcraft a century earlier. The root of social disorder was perceived to be demonic female lust, which, again, had to be contained. Representations of witchcraft were linked to the contemporary discourse of a fear of sexuality, moral cleansing and a 'fascination with the erotic'.[49] This connection between cleansing, purity, pollution and the erotic is also an explicit one in writings on convict women.

The metaphors of 'pollution' and 'dirtiness'—those used by Marsden and Mudie—are central to the way in which convict women's sexuality was framed. Both male and female convicts' bodies were perceived to be 'polluted'. The contaminating influence of convictism was a commonly expressed fear especially in debates on transportation—primarily by free immigrants who were anxious to establish a new identity for the colonies.[50] But it was the female who was perceived as having a sexed body. The perception of the female body as polluted and disease-ridden was not only inextricably linked to deviance and social order, but it also became the focus for sexual anxiety. The only white males who were described in such terms at this time were homosexual convicts.

This association of 'dirt' with 'disorder' is a revealing one. According to Mary Douglas, there is a cultural link between them, where the rituals of cleanliness aim to contain this threat of chaos as purity is perceived to imply order, structure and discipline. Some pollutions, she argues, 'are used as analogies for expressing a general view of the social order'. Dirt is deemed offensive, against order, and efforts to eliminate it suggest attempts to 'organise the environment'. Ideas about contagion and purification reflect the anxiety about social disorder and order.[51]

When historians have discussed these issues, they have not considered the use of terminology and what that may suggest about the unsettling nature of women's sexuality in psychic terms, but, rather, have asked questions about the accuracy or otherwise of characterisations of convict women as 'whores'. Portia Robinson, Babette Smith, Monica Perrott and Annette Salt are intent on rescuing those convict women who were not 'dissolute' and 'abandoned', but who 'succeeded' in becoming 'respectable' citizens. Convict women who had 'failed' to seize the economic opportunities offered by a fledgling colonial society were those who had 'destroyed their chances', rebelled when it was 'more prudent to remain meek' and their futures were in large part shaped by the 'character of the women themselves'. In these women's studies, it is argued that many convict women acted in ways which 'jeopardised their future' because it was the reliable, honest, hard-working convict women, the 'steady sober women' who became respectable members of the community.[52] Robinson, for example, is intent on illustrating the ways in which convict women lived lives that were 'at least outwardly honest', because they became the 'pioneer family' women of Australia.[53]

This focus on whether convict women did 'succeed' in becoming respectable citizens, or whether they remained 'dissolute' all of their lives, is based on a notion of success measured in terms of the creation of a bourgeois nuclear family. In this approach, the convict woman is blamed for failing to achieve such an ideal, while the wider forces that shaped her life continue to go unexamined. This attention to individual material success also narrows the range of issues we can explore in relation to punishment and protest as well as to sexuality, for it detracts from the power relations that shaped gendered identities in colonial society. We need to look at the 'obsessive interest in feminine sin' that Michael Sturma identifies in writings by ruling-class men[54] in order to move the focus beyond these binaries and illuminate the meaning to these men of the spectacle of convict women.

We also need to understand the repulsion and fascination, as well as the fear these women unleashed. They were forbidden and unknown. The fear of difference meant that they were perceived as the 'other' in both class and gender terms. Both fear and fascination are reflected in two responses of men to convict women: the way in which convict women's collectivity unsettled many male commentators, and, in the projection of male sexuality in the eroticisation of convict women. If identity is shaped through language and through perceptions of the 'other', then by analysing these expressions of fear and fascination, we can consider how these men defined themselves in relation to the 'other' of convict woman along class, race and gender lines. It was the convict women's promiscuity that offended bourgeois respectability. Not only disdain but also anxiety characterised this response to convict women. The vocabulary of pollution, contamination and disorder needs to be comprehended within this framework of fear and fascination.

We can see these issues coalesce in the discussion relating to the reform of convicts. The testimonies to the inquiry into the state of the Colony of New South Wales, undertaken by Commissioner John Bigge in 1821 to examine the laws, regulations, judicial and ecclesiastical institutions, revenue and trade of the penal colony, are revealing for another way in which convict women's sexuality was presented as a source of pollution and disorder. Those who testified to the inquiry expressed the view that convicts needed to be separated from the free population. Robert Lowe, editor of the *Sydney Gazette*, wrote to Bigge in 1821 asserting that convicts employed in 'agricultural occupations' were more likely to reform, because in the

> Town of Sydney . . . where large bodies of these People are congregated together, their old habits are kept alive by the influence of bad example . . . whereas when they become detached . . . under sober and industrious Masters . . . these unfortunate Characters, have opportunity for reflection, being then removed from the Source of iniquity & I am confident that reform amongst such, is by no means unfrequent, which I think is not the case amongst the convicts retained in the Capital . . .[55]

Others who testified to the Bigge inquiry agreed with this mode of reform. Archibald Bell argued that such segregation was 'conducive to religious and moral habits and most likely to promote a legitimate and well disposed population', while the pastoralist John Macarthur wrote forcefully of the pollution of the towns and potential of the country to reform:

> When Men are engaged in rural occupations their days are chiefly spent in solitude—they have much time for reflection and self examination, and they are less tempted to the perpetration of crimes than when herded together, in Towns, amidst a mass of disorders and vices.[56]

One crucial dimension of this was the insidious influence of convict women and their 'vices'. Marsden was not the only contemporary commentator to use the language of infection to draw attention to the unsettling influence convict women had on the social, political and sexual landscape they inhabited. Macarthur, well known for his anti-convict sentiments,[57] recommended that women particularly be employed 'in situations remote from Towns', 'where there would be consequently less excitement and less opportunity to indulge their vicious propensities, than when herded together in large putrifying masses, working, or more properly speaking, idling in an ill-conducted manufactory'. Macarthur claimed to have avoided going into the town, where the 'lower classes are reported to be disorderly'.[58] George Hammersley expressed a particularly alarmist view of the potential disorder presented by convict women. For Hammersley, allowing convict women to 'run rampant' meant that the 'cloathes and Provisions in his majesty's stores; or in the rich man's cellar, or in the poor man's cottage; are all under the influence of these women; and are easily obtained by them'.[59]

A further contradiction was that, although convict women were valued for their reproductive capacity, they were also perceived as a danger to coming generations, because the fear of promiscuity was expressed through notions of 'contagion' and 'contamination'. These were images that also informed discussions of urban life in nineteenth-century Britain.[60] Lachlan Macalister, a JP, claimed that 'Nothing can be more baneful than the employment of convict women in charge of children'.[61] Peter Murdoch echoed these sentiments. Murdoch had had extensive and close contact with female convicts. He had been the superintendent of the Emu Plains experiment in 1822, and later became police magistrate at Richmond and then Oatlands in Van Diemen's Land.[62] He had employed eleven convicts on his various properties. Murdoch did not 'think anything so bad' as to have 'the character of the rising generation' in the charge of such individuals. 'I quite shudder now when I contemplate their conduct and consider that my children were under their charge.' Contamination threatened the next generation, concluded the Report from the Select Committee on Transportation of 1837:

> It can be easily imagined what a pernicious effect must be produced upon the character of the rising generation of the Australian colonies, in consequence of the children of settlers being too frequently, in their tenderest years, under the charge of such persons.[63]

The Catholic priest William Ullathorne was equally repulsed by the prospects of the coming generation being mothered by women of disrepute. A fierce critic of transportation, Ullathorne argued vehemently that the system had dismally failed to reform convicts.[64] Drawing on metaphors of contamination, he observed that 'children are cradled in vice . . . with the poison of ungodly lips'. After a stint in the female factory, they were 'again sent forth into circulation carrying with them infection to every extremity of the colony'. In Hobart, he claimed, servants were obtained directly from the ships, 'to prevent them bringing with them the contamination of the factory'.[65]

These women not only had the capacity to contaminate the next generation, but were also the destroyers of men. The earlier Select Committee on Transportation had concluded in 1812 that convict women were 'likely to whet and to encourage the vices of the men'.[66] 'Convict women are generally so depraved', asserted the pastoralist John Macarthur in his testimony to the Bigge inquiry 'and the cause of so much disorder'. Macarthur proclaimed this view more forcefully when asked whether the paucity of women in the colony created moral 'disorder'. 'In some degree it may', he replied,

> but not altogether, because I have known many instances of exceedingly well-conducted men on our own establishment, who have obtained permission to marry convict women, and from that time their character has given way altogether; the women become the instruments of corruption.[67]

Not only were convict women perceived to be disorderly, but they were apparently more difficult to control than convict men and noted for their incapacity to reform. Bigge himself was alarmed that so few measures had been taken to control and contain their 'disorder'. 'The evil consequences arising to the colony', he reported in his findings in 1822, 'from the indiscriminate association, and the unrestrained prostitution of so many licentious women, have been seriously felt by the inhabitants at large'. Action could have been taken earlier to contain their behaviour:

> The complaints in the colony respecting the misconduct of the female convicts, of their disobedience, and of their immoral connections . . . must have pointed at the want of accommodation in the colony, and punishment of the female convicts, as the natural source of these evils.[68]

For Bigge, it was important to prevent contact between the female convicts and the male inhabitants of the town. To this end, it was crucial to provide accommodation for them. Even Governor Darling, who devised many schemes for the reformation of women, was pessimistic of the chance for reform. During the late 1820s, he contemplated introducing a ticket of leave system to women after a period of probation,

> as a means of affording them an opportunity of marrying or settling in some line of Business. That it will fail in most instances, I have little doubt from the general character and depraved disposition of these Women; But if it succeeds in a few instances, it will justify the experiment . . .[69]

The penal authorities were restricted in how they could punish convict women. They were not allowed to be flogged, were not subjected to other physical punishment and were rarely sent to places of secondary punishment. They could not be hanged, or work on road gangs.[70]

The view that women were 'harder' to manage emerges in most writings related to convict women, especially before the establishment of the female factories. This is because the authorities did not know how to control or manage these women, whose sexual desire, autonomy and lack of shame perplexed them. As early as 1799, Governor Hunter was complaining that the

> continual complaints which are made . . . of the refractory and disobedient conduct of the convict women call aloud for the most rigid and determined discipline amongst the troublesome characters, who, to the disgrace of their sex, are far worse than the men, and are generally found at the bottom of every infamous transaction committed in this colony.[71]

Other commentators concurred. In 1826, Darling claimed that the 'Women in general are so thoroughly abandoned that their disposal is

attended with much difficulty'.[72] Peter Murdoch observed that 'to reform the unfortunate females . . . is impossible', because they 'contaminated all around them; and that they were the most complete nuisance
that we had in the colony'. Sir Roger Therry recalled, during his time as
attorney-general and a judge in New South Wales, that the 'female
convicts were a far worse infliction on the free portion of the community
than the male convicts', and although he was tempted to put 'manacles
on the ankles of these bold Amazons', instead he kept them on bread
and water for three days. It was acknowledged that although men were
transported for slight offences, females were 'seldom sent out whilst any
reasonable hope remained of reforming them at home'.[73] Ullathorne
concurred, claiming that female convicts were 'acknowledged to be
worse, and far more difficult of reformation than man', because of their
'immodesty, drunkedness and the most horrible language'.[74] For John
Henderson, writing in 1832, because there was no corporal punishment
allowed for women, 'females feel, and act far more independently than
men, they are more difficultly controlled, and complaints against them
are more numerous than against others'.[75]

It is this perception that convict women had the potential to dislocate
the social order that makes them the repository of sexual anxiety for
these commentators. Sexual immodesty, foul language and drunkenness
were accepted as normal male convict behaviour. As we have seen, such
behaviour by women was particularly unsettling in the public space of the
towns. Within the factories, disorder came to assume another dynamic
with a different meaning. The open surveillance in towns like Parramatta, with its long open streets and wide open spaces, encouraged a
particular voyeurism and the women's presence in public spaces evoked
a particular language. The confinement and claustrophobia of the
prison allowed for another type of viewing and raised a fear of collectivity.

The release of women's passions and their rebelliousness within the
factories created uncertainty and frustration in those who supervised
them as to how to contain and discipline them. Even within the closed
space of the factories, there was a concern about what could be done.
This was nowhere more apparent than in the cases of lesbianism in the
female factories. Women were charged with gross disorderly conduct if
such claims could be proven, and hence, there was a need to quarantine
them from other female prisoners. The case of Agnes Kane is instructive.
Kane was a prisoner at the Ross factory in Tasmania, serving a sentence
of fifteen years. In April 1851, she was accused of assaulting the prisoner
Margaret Knaggs. She pleaded not guilty but enough evidence was
apparently presented against her and she was sentenced to eighteen
months hard labour. If the testimonies of prisoners Bridget Grady and
Knaggs are to be believed, Kane was relentless and, at times, ruthless in

her pursuit of her object of desire. Grady claimed to have seen Knaggs in the 'act of letting down her clothes, she was crying, the Prisoner [Kane] told her to hold her tongue, when I entered Kane's hand was under Knaggs' clothes having connexion with her'.[76] Grady also claimed that she heard Knaggs say that Kane had destroyed her, but Kane 'laughed it off and said it would not be anything'. Moreover, Grady claimed, she was crying, and 'was suffering so much in her body'. Knaggs spoke of the way in which Kane followed her, and claimed Kane had asked her on 'several occasions' to do something—Kane would show her—if she would let Kane go to Knaggs' berth at night. Knaggs insisted that she would not let Kane 'destroy her' and that Kane had six or seven girls who liked her. 'I told her I would not have that sin upon me', Knaggs claimed, to which Kane replied, 'it was no sin'.

But it was clear to the authorities that such behaviour was sin, and it was the specific sexual practice that was punished, rather than the harassment and intimidation Kane exercised over Knaggs. Separation was perceived not only as a means of punishment but also as the cure: it would prevent further spreading of what Stuart, the presiding judge, called 'the filthy sexuality so prevalent among the female convicts'. Kane had to be separated, not because of the psychological violence she exercised, but because she was an 'active, mischievous and debasing a character . . . [to] be left under strict separation from her fellows, whom she approaches only to indoctrinate into habits and practices of . . . filthiness'.[77] Stuart was concerned she would spread her 'mischief among many young girls'. Like male convict homosexuals, these women were carriers of another disease and different forms of pollution, but they were a source of disorder not only through quarrelling, but also in unsettling notions of female sexuality and desire—and in being predatory, corrupting, and the disease from within. No doubt the authorities were greatly relieved when both women married. The marriage of Margaret Knaggs to Joseph Pierce was recommended in 1854 and that of Agnes Kane and William Patterson, a free man, was approved in March 1856.[78]

From the 1820s, the female factories inspired a particular discussion in relation to women's collectivity. James Bonwick, a school inspector, journalist, novelist and travel writer,[79] in 1870 described how once women had done their work, they 'were at liberty to go whither they pleased, and entertain whom they pleased', but he agreed with Reid that they were surrounded 'by ruffians more destructive to females . . . than a pack of wolves'. Bonwick described the factory as a 'dirty, foul and miserable place'. He observed that 'its moral surroundings of even profounder filthiness' and the 'state of abandonment and distress' to be found there were 'traversing the streets'. But this aspect of the factory was not its only source of 'pollution' for Bonwick. While his description is of depravity and pollution, it is obvious that it was also the women's collective power that was unsettling:

> the seat of idleness, the resort of the vicious. The atmosphere was polluted with the fumes of tobacco smoked by the women; and the walls echoed with the shrieks of passion, the peals of foolish laughter, and oaths of common converse. The beginners in the walks of vice associated with the abandoned veterans of crime.[80]

'The fact of the [Female] Factory being a source of moral contagion to the colony was recognised by the thoughtful men of the time.' Authorities were 'plagued with a host of these unmanageable, idle women'.[81] The social disorder engendered by these uncontrollable women was pronounced and presented a threat by virtue of their collectivity as a united, coherent force. The image of convict women being huddled together, not only suggested contamination of each other, the completion of 'the education of every female in vice',[82] but also a fear and anxiety of their collective power. This was particularly evident in the descriptions of the presence of the 'Flash Mob' within the female factory at the Cascades, Hobart, who had a particularly 'bad influence' on the others.[83] The belief that convict women preferred the female factory to domestic service horrified officials, who firmly believed that this collectivity must be curbed. The 1837 inquiry into transportation was particularly interested in this and Macarthur confirmed officials' concerns when he admitted to having heard 'women say when they were sentenced to the factory, that they did not care about it, that they would rather go there; and I have understood that to be the case from the medical officer who attended the factory'.[84] The management was considered 'loose' and the punishment not stringent enough to deter women from committing offences, so they returned willingly. Mudie reported that convict women under his employ preferred the prison, and 'made a point of doing what they could in order to be sent to the factory, and said, "Why not send me to the factory? I wish to go to the factory"'.[85]

As the subversion of conventional notions of femininity by convict women's sexuality was more pronounced in the towns, and, during the 1820s to the 1840s, in the female factories, so the perception of disorder was greater there. The fear and fascination with their collective promiscuity aroused sexual anxiety, and revealed the unsettling potential of the 'other'. When we consider how convict women could be figures of erotic desire, these themes are even more explicit.

The Eroticisation of Convict Women

During a visit to the female factory at the Cascades in January 1851, Godfrey Charles Mundy, a highly decorated lieutenant colonel, recorded a series of observations of convict women in his travel diary, which was subsequently published as *Our Antipodes*. A member of the British Army, Mundy's documentary of his tours in New South Wales and Van Diemen's Land was a highly successful commercial account, published to four editions. He was particularly intrigued by the female prison in Hobart.

By the time Mundy had written his observations in the early 1850s, the factory in Van Diemen's Land had transformed from a space which simply housed women in an open plan, to a prison based on a cell model. Surveillance was austere and silence formed a part of the prison's regulatory practice where the women were allowed little contact with each other.[86] For the male observer, sexual tension was heightened within the prison walls by the women's inaccessibility and containment. Mundy noted that the uniform worn by the women was a 'very unbecoming one to the person, however becoming to the station of the wearer', and he was particularly impressed by the dead silence that was observed; 'One would have thought them all deaf and dumb'. While he considered the children 'mostly healthy and pretty', their mothers were, in his judgement, not so. 'As for their mothers', he observed, 'there must . . . be a good deal in dress as an element of beauty—for I scarcely saw a tolerably pretty woman in seven hundred'. After entering a few cells, where 'one woman was carding', another 'combing wool', it was the woman in a third cell who excited his attention. The cell, completely darkened, 'looked like the den of a wolf', and 'I almost started back when from the extreme end of the floor I found a pair of bright, flashing eyes fixed on mine'. His prurient fascination with its owner is apparent: 'a small, slight, and quite young girl—very beautiful in feature and complexion—but it was the fierce beauty of the wild cat!' 'I am a steady married man', he reassured his readers,

> but at no period of my life would I, for a trifle, have shared for half-an-hour the cell of that sleek little savage; for when she purred loudest I should have been most afraid of her claws! . . . the turnkey informed me that this was one of the most refractory and unmanageable characters in the prison. That said beauty is a sad distorter of man's perceptions! Justice ought to be doubly blindfolded when dealing with her . . . the pang of pity that shot across my heart when that pretty prisoner was shut again from the light of day, might have found no place there had she been as ugly as the sins that had brought her into trouble.[87]

The description of a 'wild cat', a 'sleek little savage', and his fear 'of her claws' reduced this convict woman not only to an animal to be (sexually) tamed but also to a wild 'savage', animalistic and beastly. Again, the animal metaphor suggests the ways in which the convict body was perceived as caught at the boundary that separated the human from the animal. The distinction between the civilised and the savage framed Mundy's interpretation of convict women's behaviour in such a way that at once expressed both a fear and fascination with the forbidden forces of danger and darkness the convict woman represented.

The voyeurism evident in Mundy's account characterised male travel accounts of early nineteenth-century New South Wales and Van Diemen's Land. Most of the accounts written by men who travelled to the colonies include at least some commentary on convict women. These accounts are written with the inquisitiveness and curiosity of any traveller observing an unfamiliar environment. But for many of these writers, the appearance and activities of convict women had a particular allure and enchantment. The men were tantalised and enticed by their 'difference', and their voyeurism embodied a sexual component. The male gaze, as E. A. Kaplan argues, 'carries with it the power of action and of possession'.[88] Looking is never neutral, as sexualisation and objectification of a woman takes place not simply for the purpose of eroticism, but also to annihilate the threat the woman poses. Sexual fear, therefore, is derived from the challenge of convict women's activity because convict women too could activate the gaze. The sexual promiscuity of assigned convict servants was a complaint of many masters who found it difficult to punish and discipline them. While they should have been performing domestic duties, they were often found to be with men either as prostitutes or as their sexual companions.[89]

As a source of danger, convict women were the focus of intense fascination for ruling-class men. Unlike other working-class women, they represented a milieu which has been described as the 'carnival of the night, a landscape of darkness, drunkedness, noise and obscenity'.[90] Within this sexualised encounter, the men's responses were varied, and some wanted to touch, to kiss, or even to save these women. But it was the fear of women's sexual power and autonomy, and the need to control and contain this 'disorder', that 'disturbs the public/private division of space, so essential to the male spectator's mental mapping of civic order'.[91]

Convict courtship, where male convicts came to select a bride from within the female factories, provided such a fascination. In the same way that the arrival of a convict ship (especially one with women) excited interest and became a form of popular entertainment—crowds gathered to ogle and catcall—so too did the event of convict courtship.[92] James O'Connell, a doctor, described in detail the process of selecting a convict bride. The procedure was a spectacle. 'We visited them from curiosity', he asserted. He rightly observed that this display was not unlike the ways in which slaves were selected. The girls, he claimed, were 'all agog for a husband', and they adopted different flirtatous poses. Some, all sheepish smiles and blushes, would look as foolish as all young ladies are supposed to, when a third person happens in upon an interview at which the question has just been popped. Others would avert their faces in a sort of indifference; as though a refusal is seldom met by an applicant, still these seekers for help mates are not all of such an appearance as to tempt a woman half way. A third set would most prudishly frown upon a proceeding which pays so little respect to prescriptive rights of the ladies; while, as if purposely set in contrast to these fastidious ones, others would make attempts, not always successful, or with the best grace, to appear as amiable and pretty as possible . . .[93]

O'Connell was not disappointed with the spectacle, which contrasted with the patterns of etiquette and sexual mores to which he was accustomed. James Mudie also described the procedure with a mixture of fascination and disgust. They are 'turned out, and they all stand up as you would place so many soldiers, or so many cattle, in fact in a fair; they are all ranked up'. The convict

goes up and looks at the women, and if he sees a lady that takes his fancy, he makes a motion to her, and she steps on one side; some of them will not, but stand still, and have no wish to be married, but this is very rare.[94]

Convict courtship became engrained within folklore, and a song was even written, called 'Australian Courtship', which revealed the author's attraction to women in the female factory:

The Currency Lads may fill their glasses,
And drink to the health of the Currency Lasses,
But the lass I adore, the lass for me,
Is a lass in the Female Factory.[95]

The combination of fear, disgust and fascination that formed the responses to convict women also drew on understandings of colonial anthropology. The derogatory terms used to describe convict women were similar to those used to describe Aboriginal women: they were 'savage' and uncivilised. But unlike their indigenous counterparts, who were perceived to be somehow naturally in this state, convict women had been dehumanised by being reduced to this condition of 'savagery'. The anxiety aroused by convict women was particularly potent because, unlike Aboriginal women, who could be dismissed as totally alien, convict women challenged the distinction between the 'civilised' and the 'savage'; they represented the capacity within all of us for disintegration.

The unknown and the forbidden world of these women with unruly passions is complemented by the similarly fascinating world of the Aborigines, for convict women were not only eroticised, but in being depicted as 'savage' and 'vicious', male commentators were also drawing on images of the 'uncivilised savage'. Racial and ethnic differences played a part in this. Building a new vibrant colony with these women was a problem, because their behaviour was, as Marsden noted, 'incompatible with the character and wish of the British nation'.[96] 'Britishness' meant Englishness in this context and such national references were consistent with the national stereotypes of the day. But while these ethnicities were discussed, the common characterisation of convict women was as unruly, a 'race apart', not properly civilised or properly British. The polarities of cleanliness and filth, virgin and whore were also understood by the metaphor of the civilised and the savage.

The observations of travellers were shaped by particular racial and ethnic understandings which reinforced a particular national identity. The ways in which such an identity is sustained are always precarious. The consolidation of national identity, Mary Poovey notes, is dependent on difference—on an awareness of 'the national "us" from aliens within and without'.[97] Catherine Hall suggests that during the 1830s and 1840s English identity was formed 'through the active silencing of the disruptive relations of ethnicity, of gender and of class'. The meanings of Englishness and Britishness were not given or assumed but shaped and reshaped.[98] More centrally, it is in the issues seemingly unrelated to national identity where this is most telling. As Poovey notes, national identities are often 'marked at every moment by competing currents whose energy derives from . . . interests only incidentally related to the nation or national issues'.[99]

Convict women provided a pivot around which such national identities were defined and redefined. James Bonwick records his disgust with the behaviour towards convict women in national terms, when he claims that the 'licentiousness and vice' and the style of convict marriages 'took place in the nineteenth century, in a portion of the British dominions, and in the presence of Christian Englishmen, and was exercised upon no heathen or savage, but upon a country woman and fellow Christian!'[100]

Such an attitude identifies convict women as 'worse' than savages, because they were from a 'civilised' country and threatened the morality of the Empire. Sir Roger Therry concurred. Drawing on the collectivity motif, he argued that convict women 'the most abandoned women of the Empire were huddled together'.[101] In a theme articulated throughout the nineteenth century, those considered immoral, abandoned and depraved not only threatened class and gender relations, but also undermined national and imperial strength by 'contaminating' the Empire.[102]

Yet others insisted on a more benevolent view. George Hammersley drew on colonial and imperial discourses to argue for a more paternal attitude towards the prisoners. 'The liberal benevolent and Christian spirit of the British nation', he claimed, 'is always alive even to the Distresses of the enemies; and is anxious to impart the inestimable Blessings of Liberty, Morality and Religion to the oppressed African; and to the south Sea Islander'. He asserts that such notions of benevolence extend to the treatment of British criminals; 'If the miseries and crimes of her own children in N South Wales were known to her; would she not be equally or more anxious to relieve them from the one, and reclaim them from the other!'[103]

These issues of race and empire were inextricably linked to descriptions of convict women. John Henderson didn't save his disdain for the Scottish, but condemned the English women as well:

> The Scotch women are reckoned the most abandoned, but from my observation, I should conceive that the Scotch and English women might honestly and fairly divide the palm between them. The British female, when once she passes a certain line, knows no further bounds, but becomes depraved in proportion to the nature of the temptation. In this respect, she differs, in some degree, from her sex in other European countries; and there is a wide difference betwixt her and the male of her own country, whose progress to crimes is slow, but determined.[104]

The assumption that the Irish were a 'savage and barbarous people' had certainly been prevalent in the Victorian imagination. Without reservation, the British authorities treated the Irish convicts as a 'different class of people'.[105] When asked about such objections to the Irish, John Macarthur claimed that 'it is imagined the Irish would be less disposed to good conduct and industrious habits than English and Scottish emigrants'.[106] Generally, however, there seems to have been little distinction made between racial identities of convict women. Convict women were considered 'collectively', a 'race' apart. 'In point of vice', observed Josiah Spode, the superintendent of convicts in Van Diemen's Land in 1840, 'the English, Scottish and Irish are much upon a par'.[107] They were the 'poor outcasts of our race', notes James Backhouse, a Quaker missionary. Lieutenant Breton referred to these women as 'a rare unruly race they are', a separate entity, apart, 'the other':

> As to the females, it is a melancholy fact, but not the less true, that far the greater proportion are utterly irreclaimable, being the most worthless and abandoned of human beings! No kindness can conciliate them, nor any indulgence render them grateful; and it is admitted by everyone, that they are, taken as a body, infinitely worse than males!

Certainly, male convicts were considered 'savage' also, and Breton alludes to this when he refers to a bushranger/convict, transported in

1812 for seven years, as 'this gloomy savage'.[108] But it was women's 'savagery' that was characteristically associated with disorder.

These descriptions resonate with the images used to describe Aborigines at this time: in terms of their 'savagery', 'uncivilised' behaviour and 'pollution'. The Reverend Daniel Tyerman and George Bennett, members of the London Missionary Society who passed through the colonies on their way to establish missions in the Pacific islands, observed in 1825:

> we have, this day, seen a party of natives, and surely, there never trod on the face of this earth more abject creatures. Both men and women were in a state of absolute and shameless nudity, and several of them were stupidly intoxicated. One woman had an infant at her back, swung in a bag of kangaroo-skin. They were all of low stature, with meagre limits; their hair black, but not curly; in their complexions as dark almost as Guinea Negroes and their persons loathsome with filth.[109]

Like their fascination with convict women, this obsession with the body is common in travellers' observations. G. Bond recorded that the 'natives' were 'entirely black', their limbs 'strong and robust', 'capable of bearing the most severe weather'; their hair was of 'curly nature' and they had the 'teeth of fish'. Several years later, Robert Cartwright wrote to Governor Macquarie stressing the need for 'the moral and spiritual improvement of these savage youths'. For Governor Darling, their habits were 'extremely disgusting' and represented the habits of 'mankind in a savage state'. By the 1840s, such attitudes were well entrenched. Lord John Russell reported to Sir George Gipps in August 1840 that the Aborigines were 'half civilized', little raised 'above brutes', who were 'weakened by intoxicating liquors'. He identified a need to imbue them with Christian teachings, as they were a 'race of suspicious, ignorant and indolent savages'.[110]

But generally, for most travellers, Aboriginal women were not considered to be socially threatening, however uncivilised they may have appeared. The perception of the indigenous population had of course changed over time. Ryan notes that the few books published about Van Diemen's Land by the 1820s either made no mention of the Aboriginal population or considered them 'timid, gentle people' who would not resist settlement. However, as resistance by the occupants of the land intensified, alarm, fear and brutality characterised the response by the European invaders.[111] By the end of the 1920s, notes Henry Reynolds, there was an escalation of warfare between white settlers and Aborigines in what became known as the Black War.[112]

Public support for the extermination of the indigenous population increased as their resistance became more fierce and determined. But for many of those who travelled to the colonies, especially to New South Wales, the Aborigines were still perceived as on the periphery, outside their experience. Not only did they 'show a degree of timidity and bashfulness', and a 'pleasingly soft and feminine' disposition, as Marines Captain Watkin Tench recorded in 1789, but he could observe them with 'distance and reserve'.[113] Responses such as these were not only expressed by those like Tench, who was a keen observer and watched Aborigines with a 'sympathetic tolerance'.[114] Even Mudie, who had close contact with Aborigines on his estate, claimed that 'by kind treatment towards them, I was safe; in fact they said that they would 'not touch me, or allow me to be touched'.[115] Aboriginal women, too, were eroticised, but in different ways to the convicts, often in terms of the innocent and the exotic.[116]

It is important to stress the notion of convict women as the disease from within the centre. Bigge concluded in his 1822 report of inquiry that while the female factory was 'some distance', it was 'not an inconvenient one, from the town of Parramatta'.[117] In Hobart, they were 'an evil that the free people of the community [are] obliged to accept'.[118] Although convicts considered themselves 'different' to the Aborigines and somehow 'above' them,[119] in the eyes of the military, government officials and the judiciary, both were loathsome. The two states that aroused disgust were venereal disease and alcoholism, abhorred in the convict women, and attracting scorn for the Aborigines. James Mudie observed that venereal disease was 'extremely common' amongst the Aborigines and it was because of this that 'the class of the better sort steer very clear of them, for . . . they break out in blotches, and are horrid figures'.[120] The 'maudlin native of New Holland', wrote Breton, 'becomes intoxicated by a vulgar beverage made in the most simple manner possible'.[121] There was less likelihood that white men would be 'contaminated' by Aboriginal women, than there was by convict women, whose promiscuity was a constant source of infection and pestilence within the colonial society. It was in this way that convict women blurred the distinction between the civilised and the savage. As a figure of conscious and unconscious representation, the convict woman coalesced anxieties about disintegration and possibly abandonment, potent fears for those living so far from home.

Travel writers during the nineteenth century used particular understandings of imperialism to reinforce a national identity. Journalism of this kind colonises, categorises and regulates certain groups, makes particular groups visible, and opens them up to classification and judgement. Within this genre, categories are formed which become the measure by which all else is defined. Many of these texts contained a 'colonial voice' and presented the colonised country as a natural part of the British Empire. But we can also see the way a masculine British identity was shaped in these texts. Within the understandings of masculinity and femininity, pollution and cleanliness and uncivilised and civilised, all defined within class terms, these writers moulded an identity and a sense of self which was formed in relation to their fascination and fear of the 'other', embodied in convict women.

This was expressed through a conflation of sexual deviance, disorder, pollution and savagery, which can be gleaned through these two particularly striking aspects of the early nineteenth century in Australia: that of the towns being 'polluted' by convict women; and the fascination of the male gaze in the genre of travel writing. Stallybrass and White's argument that 'what is socially peripheral may be symbolically central'.[122] In the context of the early nineteenth century, writings by ruling-class men on convict women reveal, first, how many of these commentators formed their own identities as 'white, male and middle class' through their understanding of the 'Other', and, second, how convict women induced sexual anxiety by unsettling the masculinity of those who so vocally condemned them.

Convict women not only destabilised masculine control in this way but, as we shall see in the next chapter, also challenged and provoked the power of the authorities through a range of overt, subversive acts.

CHAPTER 3

Disrupting the Boundaries
Resistance and Convict Women

In 1838, Sir John and Lady Franklin visited and inspected the Cascades Factory in Hobart and attended a service in the factory chapel. At the time, services were being conducted by the Reverend William Bedford, a Church of England clergyman whom convicts knew well because of the sermons and prayers he delivered at the prison and its barracks. Bedford was the butt of convict ridicule—they called him 'Hollie Willie'—and was, on more than one occasion, the target of female convicts' jests and pranks.[1] In one incident,

> as he was crossing the courtyard of the Female House of Correction, some dozen or twenty women seized upon him, took off his trousers and deliberately endeavoured to deprive him of his manhood. They were, however, unable to effect their purpose in consequence of the opportune arrival of a few constables who seized the fair ladies and placed them in durance vile.

This same refractory spirit was illustrated by another occasion when convict women violated the boundaries that confined them. In defiance of their subordinate relationship to the Franklins and to the penal authorities, while standing in front of the vice regal party who addressed them from an elevated dais, all of a sudden,

> the three hundred women turned right around and at one impulse pulled up their clothes shewing their naked posteriors which they simultaneously smacked with their hands making a loud and not very musical noise. This was the work of a moment, and although constables, warders, etc. were there in plenty, yet 300 women could not well be all arrested and tried for such an offence and when all did the same act the ringleaders could not be picked out.

This cheeky behaviour had the desired impact. Although the witnesses to this event claimed that their 'indecencies and insults had not the effect of creating either irritation or annoyance', clearly the governor and his party had been 'horrified and astounded' and were determined 'that this visit would be their last'.[2] However, the ladies in the governor's party, it was said, in a rare moment of collusion with the convict women, 'could not control their laughter'.[3]

In the female prisons, the expression of laughter, jest and the indulgence of 'play' was a punishable offence. Although on the one hand the penal system treated convict women like children, with a system of reward and punishment, on the other, it recoiled at the expression of childlike pleasures.

Another incident further illustrates this power dynamic. In March 1842, when Hobart factory superintendent John Hutchinson heard a noise at about eight o'clock, he took his keys and went to investigate. He looked in at the window of the ward, and allowed himself some time to identify the five prisoners, Ellen Arnold, Elisabeth Armstrong, Frances Hutchinson, Eliza Smith and Mary Deverena, who were

> dancing perfectly naked, and making obscene attitudes towards each other, they were also singing and shouting and making use of most disgusting language. There was a sixth woman but I could not positively swear to her, the disgusting attitudes towards each other were in imitation of men and women together.

Although this was obviously sexual play, the women claimed they were washing themselves. But Hutchinson was clear as to their purpose. When he went into the room he discovered that there were no tubs, and 'the language they used and the attitudes they made use of corresponded in obscenity so that no mistake could be made by me as the nature of both'. One of the convicts, Eliza Smith, claimed that their behaviour arose 'from a mere joke' but Hutchinson was not moved, claiming he saw only a 'dirty, beastly action'. Although Frances Hutchinson was found to be 'only dancing and not making any indecent attitudes', she was given a six-month sentence, while the others received twelve months hard labour. All the women involved in this act of merriment were placed in separate confinements.[4]

A few months later, in a similar spirit of animation and frolic, women in the prison in Hobart were reported to be 'singing and dancing and making a noise'. They refused to cease despite several requests for them to do so. When Mrs Hutchinson, the matron, entered the room, the women squatted down and refused to give the names of the ringleaders. The women 'shouted and clapped their hands, stamped and made noise with their feet and this took place to such an extent that I conscientiously say it was a riot'. The superintendent attempted to persuade them to name the leaders, but did so with little effect. The women, insisted Mrs Hutchinson, had plenty of opportunity to declare themselves 'not belonging to the Mob'. The tumult continued each time the superintendent left the room. The police were called in to contain the calamity and the 'hurrahing', as District Constable Brice referred to it. The women 'kept up a tremendous clatter with their tongues', he reported, despite continued efforts to encourage the women to distance themselves from agitators in the group. In a display of solidarity, the women said they were unwilling to divide their own ranks in this way. 'We are all alike, we are all alike', they chanted. When Brice entered the room he was impressed with how 'such a body of women could have placed themselves in such a regular manner in so short a time'. The disturbance lasted for four or five hours, and eventually the stalemate ended when the prisoner Ann Maloney pointed out the ringleaders. Six prisoners were reprimanded; two had their sentence of transportation extended by one year, while nine women were sentenced to six months hard labour following solitary confinement for twenty-one days.[5]

Singing and dancing in the wards at night was an effective means of challenging authority. The women's songs were loud and strong, explicitly violating those measures in place which aimed to restrain their pleasures and amusements. Mrs Hutchinson reported to the inquiry into convict discipline that

> their songs are sometimes very disgusting. They leave off when they know I am coming. When they do not (which is sometimes the case in a wet night when they do not hear my foot on the pavement) I turn out the whole ward till I get at the woman whom I send to a cell.[6]

John Price, the police magistrate, who, through his long dealings with criminals, knew of the 'cant language' of convicts, observed that the women convicts were in the habit of 'composing songs ridiculing the authorities'.[7] In the context of the prisons, this laughter and play was a potent way of subverting a system which was so emphatically designed to deny the expression of such intemperance. The *True Colonist* reported in 1837 that while the 'horrors of the crime class' had shocked inhabitants of Van Diemen's Land, what was more disagreeable to moral evangelical sensibilities was the fact that

> many women prefer this class to the others, because it is *more lively!* There is more *fun* there than in the others; and we have been informed, that some of the most sprightly of the ladies divert their companions by acting plays![8]

In a penal society based on prohibition, any moments of spontaneous pleasure amongst criminals were subversive. Women in particular were subject to restrictions, limitations and expectations based on their sex and because there were firm assumptions about how women should behave, they were perceived to be somehow worse behaved.[9] In terms of daily contact, sexual behaviour and in the use of language theirs was a more restricted world than that of male convicts. Transgressing gender boundaries was in itself disruptive. For women, laughter became an important part of this transgression. Mary Douglas notes that 'the idea of loud vociferous laughter may be unseemly in polite company. But what counts as loud and vociferous may vary greatly'.[10] These moments tested the authorities. These women were indulging in acts deemed vulgar, as their exuberance was deemed 'unfeminine'. To laugh loudly and vociferously in a prison, which aimed to regulate and order the very being of its inmates, was an act of impetuousness that represented an important transgressive moment. More crucially, it was the expression of desire and pleasure—those aspects of convict women deemed uncontrollable and volatile—which was perceived as reckless but also dangerous. Many of these punishable offences were efforts by the women to indulge themselves in pleasure and entertainment: they were punished in their efforts to claim self-expression.

It is to the actions and behaviour of convict women that we must turn, for the existing records are hopelessly deficient in recording their voices, the range of their emotions and their motivations. The various forms of subversion are a key to understanding their actions, which also need to be more broadly understood within the context of the exercise of power within the colonies.

Power and Resistance

In colonial society, 'power' was despotic and autocratic, where governors kept both convicts and ex-convicts under 'direct and intimate surveillance'. Movement and travel were circumscribed through a range of regulations and constraints.[11] The exercise of colonial power changed considerably during the period of transportation. Under the naval officers Hunter, King and Bligh, there was a belief in the reforming capacity of convicts, which was challenged under the brief but harsh governorship of the New South Wales Corps. The organisation of a colony along more efficient, ordered and structured lines came with Macquarie's term as governor and was reinforced under the rule of Darling, Brisbane and Arthur. During their commands in the 1820s and 1830s, the penal systems in New South Wales and Van Diemen's Land were refined and became more efficient.[12] This move towards a rational and scientific model of punishment coincided with broader developments in Britain during the nineteenth century, which elevated rationality and order in science, medicine and the law.[13] Autocratic powers in the colonies at this time were also being diffused, with the appointment of legislative and executive councils in 1824.[14] Prison reform was also affected by these profound changes. In Britain, prison discipline tightened after 1820, followed by a centralisation and rationalisation of prison administration. Labour discipline within prisons assumed a particular form, which resembled a factory model. Similar developments took place in Australia with the establishment of the female factory, which was designed with a sharper discipline, more rigid management and classification.[15] As Alastair Davidson has shown, concomitant with this was an elaborate system of passes for both the bonded and the free.[16] The work of convicts was constantly regulated, with men on the road gangs and women in the female factories subject to weekly and monthy reports, as well as a timetable of discipline, silence and the treadmill, and later, silence.

A penal settlement based on this power structure produced its own form of resistance.[17] The challenge to such structures, however, did not always derive from a single act of rebellion. Convict 'protest', recalcitrance or resistance took place in a range of actions and practices. Historians have not taken account of sexual difference when they have conceptualised understandings of 'resistance'. Alan Atkinson has identified four patterns of convict protest, which he conflates with male convicts: attack, physical or verbal, 'showing a fundamental rejection of authority'; appeal to authority; withdrawal of labour; and compensatory retribution, all premised on the belief that they had 'some rights either as servants, on the English pattern, or as prisoners'.[18] Female convicts were certainly noncompliant in some of these ways. Attack and a withdrawal of labour were crucial methods of resistance by convict women who worked as domestic servants. But the avenues of protest available to women were not synonymous with those of male convicts. The punishment and conditions of labour also differed, but resistance was bound by gender. W. Nichol's compelling argument about how 'malingering' provided convicts with an 'effective method of resistance' is a case in point. Complaining of illness may well have been utilised by women as well as male convicts but, too often, illness was a euphemism for pregnancy.[19]

Applying the category of 'protest' in the way that Atkinson uses it is also limiting when referring to women, for it exclusively delineates acts 'inspired by general principles'. Such a definition cannot readily take into account the multiplicity of convict women's resistance. Many acts that transgressed boundaries were not inspired by 'general principles', but were no less effective in unsettling power relationships. When the refractory women of the female factory exposed their bottoms, they were confronting the disciplinary gaze by challenging the boundaries of the sexual, of femininity, the body and spaces of power. 'Protest' or resistance considered exclusively in relation to 'principle' raises the importance of particular forms of activism and narrows our understanding of 'subversive' acts.

For instance, Atkinson dismisses the murder of Charles Waldron by two convict women, commenting that such an action cannot be understood as resistance because it was not driven by a 'principle'. To be sure there was no broadly public 'political' agenda behind this act, but the case is interesting because of the behaviour of the two women, who were determined to remain together. Waldron had warned Mary Moloney that he would go to the police office and report her insolence and improper language. Sarah McGregor was determined to go with her. 'If Mary goes, I'll go', she insisted, 'we came together and we will go together'. Waldron said that she had done nothing that would send her there, at which point it was claimed she struck him, and 'gave him several violent blows on the neck and head'. According to Waldron's wife, the prisoner 'pulled up her petticoats and exposed her person to the view of the whole family . . . the language of the prisoners during this time, was of the most disgraceful description'. In both the murder and the display, the women challenged the expected behaviour of domestic servants and feminine decorum. But their subversive behaviour was also evident in resisting a most probably violent master and in acting together. Clearly there was a solidarity between the two women and they were prepared to flout regulations in order to remain together and return to the factory. The desire to return to the factory in itself was a defiant act, for it undermined efforts to separate the women, and suggested the ineffectiveness of the factory as a form of punishment. Whether or not they were responsible for his death is a contentious issue, for there were witnesses who testified they had not seen the prisoners strike him. Nonetheless, the women were found guilty and hanged.[20] It is the silences in this episode that are telling, for the expressed desire and direct action by the convict women to remain together and be returned to prison undermined government efforts to separate and punish them. With no voice in the existing records, it is only through the actions of the convict women that we can interpolate meaning.

Other historians have similarly displayed little awareness of the distinction between male and female convicts. 'There was remarkably little organised convict resistance to the system', note Buckley and Wheelwright. There was no 'revolutionary focus for opposition to the status quo' largely because 'most felons were not bereft of hope for the future'. The legal system, they rightly observe, did not 'strip a convict of all rights'.[21] In their discussion, Buckley and Wheelwright do not allow for a broader understanding of acts which may be considered subversive because they understand protest to mean organised, premeditated resistance driven by a political consciousness.

Some writers have passed judgements on the behaviour of women convicts and believed such behaviour to be misguided, foolish, or irresponsible if these women hoped to improve their station and take advantage of the opportunities to become 'respectable' citizens. There were those, writes Babette Smith, who 'were hot tempered and fought back when it would have been more prudent to remain meek'. Others have argued that the women's lack of respect for the law has been exaggerated, while some claim the need to defend the behaviour of some convict women. John Williams insists that Irish women were no more recalcitrant than others and that, on the contrary, they were relatively well-behaved and law-abiding. They were not so 'inured to crime as other female convicts' he claims. The emphasis on recalcitrant behaviour, writes Portia Robinson, has given convict women an 'undeserved reputation'.[22] Within the respectable/unrespectable debate, which has informed their discussions, there appears to be no room for those women who were at some stage in their lives 'unrespectable', riotous or 'disobedient' and then became 'respectable', or vice versa. Just as these views have restrained the ways in which we conceive of convict women's behaviour beyond moral judgements, so too has resistance been conceived in limited terms.

It is important, too, to consider how challenging power took place not from one source, or from a single point, but through a range of actions within a number of contexts that unsettled the power relationships. Opposition came from a range of sites and actions, rather than exclusively from one sustained oppositional force.[23] We could explore, as Michel Foucault does, the way in which there was a 'plurality of resistances . . . resistances that are possible, necessary, improbable; others that are spontaneous, savage, solitary, concerted, rampant, or violent'. Resistances are not simply a reaction but are 'present everywhere in the power network'; they are 'distributed in irregular fashion', and spread over time and space at varying degrees of intensity. There are 'radical ruptures' but more commonly, points of resistance are 'mobile and transitory'. This view, that resistance is not somehow outside of 'power' but always within it, relates to Foucault's argument that power is productive; that repression and resistance are not distinct but that repression produces its own resistance.[24]

For convict women, resistance took place within three broad categories, all of which were shaped by gender considerations but defined by pleasure and desire. The first was female sexuality as a form of disturbance. Convict women's promiscuity, whether heterosexual or homoerotic, undermined the authorities' efforts to discipline, contain and mould these women in ways which male sexuality could not. The second category was what could be referred to as overstepping spatial boundaries: domestic servants' stealing, staying out all night, drunkenness, and use of insolent and abusive language had gendered and sexual meanings. The female convict body, wandering within an uncontrolled space, was understood in different ways to that of a male convict body. The third category was collective action. Women did act collectively and riot, although these acts of defiance were conceived differently to those by men. Women's mutiny was often presented as a spectacle, bizarre and ludicrous, a 'frolic'. In the press, their activities were eroticised, the constables and other male officials presented as 'taming' the wild emotions unleashed by these recalcitrant women

Sexual Transgressions

Convict women often openly defied the boundaries of sexuality, morality and femininity prescribed by the authorities. The assertion of female sexuality was itself a form of resistance, evidenced by the way it was punished with severe retribution. This took place most explicitly in three forms: as prostitutes; as assigned servants engaged in sexual acts; and as lesbians. With the exception of homosexual acts, such sexualised disruptions to established boundaries did not characterise male forms of resistance because of the different moral standards for men and women. In these instances, the power nexus of the master–servant relationship was challenged and, thus, one of the major forms of reform and punishment for women was undermined.

The Assignment System

The assignment system provided a particular forum for convict women's recalcitrance. It was considered to be a means of regulation and reform, with settlers obtaining labour through their local district magistrates.[25] Convicts had been assigned as servants since the early beginnings of the colony. It was a cheap source of labour for settlers and alleviated the financial burden of the government. The Select Committee on Transportation found in 1812 that during the earlier part of transportation, women were 'indiscriminately given to such of the inhabitants as degraded them, and were in general received rather as prostitutes than as servants',[26] although from about 1818, when a more systematic set of regulations stipulating the obligations of master–servant were introduced, this practice ceased and they were assigned to 'respectable' households.[27] During the 1820s and 1830s, the assignment system came to be considered the cornerstone of reform. Servants were allocated according to the number of acres held by masters and mistresses.[28] It was hoped that female convicts would be 'reformed' through the model presented by the bourgeois respectability of their mistresses.[29] It was a lottery, but a less arbitrary form of punishment than previous forms of an open prison. Convicts were given a set of clothes, bedding, and lodgings; in Van Diemen's Land female convicts were paid £7 and male convicts £10.[30] However unpredictable the treatment from masters and mistresses may have been, it was misguided to believe that convict women would feel inclined to model themselves on their mistresses. Indeed, as domestic servants during the 1820s and 1830s, women were considered 'worse' behaved than men. Hirst notes that more was expected of women and they were subject to closer confinement and surveillance under the sharp eye of the master or mistress, whose direction and instruction they were bound by, and had little time or space to themselves.[31] This characterised the punishment of convict women during this period, as the movement and assignment of convict women was closely monitored. But the master–servant relationships had become so disruptive that a 'great inconvenience' in the 'uncritical manner' in which female convicts were assigned was noted. The 'frequent change of service', which became a pattern amongst convict servants, warranted closer regulation. By 1840 no woman, it was stipulated, would be reassigned in the same town within six months, and if returned to the factory a second time from the same town, would never again be assigned in it.[32] If women misbehaved they were punished by going to the second or third class of the factory for punishment. Convicts did have a form of redress through their local magistrates, but fewer women than men used this avenue, and it must be remembered that magistrates were themselves masters.[33]

In terms of their sexual promiscuity as assigned servants, to what extent women were pressured, and how far they were willingly promiscuous is impossible to know. Obviously, many of them were prostitutes. The chief police magistrate and principal superintendent of convicts in Van Diemen's Land, Josiah Spode, reported to the Committee of Inquiry into Female Convict Prison Discipline in 1841 that it was difficult finding the haunts of convict women when they had absconded and gone out all night, but 'the Constables frequently take them out of common brothels'. Promiscuity challenged the existing expectations of women in ways that did not apply to men. It is important to note that contemporaries themselves recognised this double standard. As the Committee of Inquiry noted, 'society had fixed the standard of the average moral excellence required of women much higher than that which it had erected for men'.[34]

That women were in the company of men was a common complaint and one source of anger and nuisance for employers of female servants.

John Buckland was one employer who, in July 1832, complained to the Bench of Magistrates about the behaviour of his two assigned convicts, Ann Shannon and Henry Lewis. He reported that he had 'observed a man go into the rooms of the female prisoner . . . tried the door of the female servant's room and found it fast'. Buckland got the key and opened the door, and 'on entering found the male prisoner in the woman's bed—but she had left the room'. Formerly, he had 'found the female prisoner on the berth of the male prisoner but overlooked that offence'. Buckland concluded that the female servant's 'conduct is altogether so bad that [he] cannot keep her'. Much to his relief, she was sentenced to serve six months in the third class of the factory.[35]

In April 1833, Mary Ann Mildenhall, also in Buckland's employ, was discovered to be absent at about ten o'clock. She was subsequently found by four of her master's men, 'in one of the paddocks some distance from the house, in company with one of Mr. Macarthur's shepherds named Marmont'. The bundle she clutched suggested that she had intended a permanent departure. She too was sentenced to the third class of the female factory, although for a shorter period—two months—and was not to return to her previous master.

This was not the last of Buckland's wayward servants. In September 1833, Ann White and Ann Fogarty were accused of 'gross disorderly conduct'. On the previous Saturday evening Buckland had found the prisoners 'in bed with two of the men away from their room'. The following day, as he sent them to court, they abused him 'of grossly indelicate and shocking language', within hearing 'of persons in the house'. They, too, at the request of their master, were returned to the government.[36]

Buckland was not the only master who found it difficult to exercise discipline over convict women who were promiscuous. Margaret Keating had left the premises of her master without permission and was found the next morning with a man. Ellen Colville was found to be missing by her master George Harper when he was about to lock up the house. Constable James Stewart went in pursuit of her and at about ten o'clock saw the prisoner with two men in the bush near Myrtle Creek. After some time, he saw the prisoner come out of the bush into the road with the two men, who ran away. He was unable to catch them, although he apprehended the prisoner. On this occasion, at the request of her master, she was reprimanded, discharged and returned to her station. Sarah Johnson had continued an 'illicit intercourse' with a person named Brown although she had already been 'charged with a similar offence' and 'warned to give up the acquaintance'. The police were sometimes known to be complicit in such behaviour. Constable Sorrell was a frequent visitor to the hut of Matilda Bell. When her mistress claimed she would no longer allow it, Bell 'asked for a pass, picked up her things; would no longer do any work that day . . . When asked to do anything, she looked black and would not attend to any instructions'. A similarly defiant mood characterised Elisabeth Phillips' response when told that 'she should not frequent the men's huts'. She told her master, 'if I prevented her I might get another woman tomorrow for she would not stop. She then went into the house got her bundle of clothing and went off towards the Bush'. Mary Ann Sullivan was similarly 'absenting herself', noted her master, 'for several hours from the house going to the men's hut . . . contrary to the order of her mistress'. Both Eleanor Langunge and Amelia Jones were convicted of disorderly conduct for admitting 'strange men' into their bedrooms. Janet Alexander was also accused of allowing a man in her room and allowing him to escape through her window, 'in the morning before daylight'. Such efforts of concealment were common: Hannah Wilson was charged by her master for 'concealing Miles Flinn under her bed', and Mary Watson had been similarly caught. Captain Dumas rose sometime between six and seven o'clock: 'hearing one of the men servants in the kitchen I got up to look—passing to the kitchen I saw a man jump out of the kitchen window and run off. At the same time he was buttoning up his trousers'.[37]

While these sexual practices, and the retaliation when attempts were made to make these women comply, defied imposed order and undermined the master–servant relationship, women's bodies were seen to be the focus for further disorder. Pregnancy rendered a convict woman redundant. In 1828, the police report of prisoners described Maryanne Robinson and Eliza Green as useless, 'in having a child'. Mary Keevey was so far advanced in pregnancy that she was incapable of working as had been Elizabeth Smith. Being in the 'family way' meant Sally Hall, Marg Callaghan and Mary Munay were all returned to the second class of the female factory and rendered 'useless' servants. Sarah Hanberry was similarly 'unable to work' because of her pregnant state.[38] Governor Arthur expressed his frustration with the regularity of women being returned to the prisons for this reason. As domestic servants, he told the Select Committee on Transportation in 1837, they are 'liable to the strong temptation continually to which they are exposed; and in that respect they are too often returned on the hands of the government in the family way'.[39]

Lesbianism

Within the factories, it was lesbianism that similarly transgressed boundaries and created disturbances. During the 1840s, the committee inquiring into female convict discipline found that lesbianism was rife, and cited the case of two women who had recently been 'detected in the very act of exciting each others passions—on the Lord's Day in the house of God—and at the very time divine service was performing'.[40] Both the practice itself and the disputes and tensions between sexual partners were perceived as unsettling the harmony within the factories. Sexual violence within the factories negated the smooth running of the prison. In January 1843, Catherine O'Brien and Caroline Justin were charged with the 'indecent assault' of Mary Newell, who had been sent to the factory for six months hard labour for misconduct. O'Brien was Newell's bedfellow, but was in the practice of not going to bed 'for an hour and a half after me as she sat on the side of the Hammock talking to Caroline Justin'. During the course of the particular evening, O'Brien put her knee across Newell's stomach and Newell, as she reported it,

> felt her pass her hand to my private parts and from my not being able to move my legs I believe someone had hold of them . . . I felt her pass her hand down she forcibly thrust her hand opened with the fingers projecting up my privates with great violence, apparently as far as she was able she gave me great pain. She kept her hand there for sometime moving it about and trying to find out . . . if I had any money or tobacco concealed there . . .

Newell did not report the incident immediately, not out of 'fear but shame', and her attempts to gain sympathy and support from other women were met with resistance. Many of the women 'spoke against me about telling it' although nothing of the sort 'could have happened without them knowing about it'. O'Brien and Justin were each sentenced to hard labour for twelve months, to be served apart.[41]

Lesbianism was the source of another disturbance, reported by Ann Fisher, the wardswoman of the ward in which prisoners Jane Owen and Eliza Taylor slept. Fisher maintained that Taylor and Owen had 'nailed' each other—'indecently using their hands with each other's person'— and that she had threatened to report it. Janet Fraser and Ellen Boyle, two other convict women, denied having heard any movements. 'I am sure no woman would have gone into Owen's hammock', Fraser insisted, 'without my being aware of it . . . because when a woman gets out for anything the whole row of hammocks [is] disturbed'.[42] The case was dismissed for want of sufficient evidence, but as there was 'such strong suspicion existing', it was recommended that the women serve their sentences seperately.

The view of lesbianism as disorder and disturbance emerges in the complaints voiced by W. J. Irvine, superintendent of the remote Ross Factory in Van Diemen's Land. In December 1848, he reported an incident where a quarrel arose from some of the women 'deserting the beds of those to whom they acted in the capacity of men, and betaking themselves elsewhere, there are some of the women who by . . . artificial means . . . are enabled to fill the vile part above mentioned . . .' He named three prisoners—Sarah Clark, Elizabeth Henry and Margaret Kelly—who 'acted the male part'. There was an urgent imperative to establish separate cells, 'in finishing, or . . . preventing the course above alluded to'. The women were eventually removed to Hobart and placed under strict supervision in separate cells at the factory.[43] In another lengthy report, Irvine was emphatic of the need to curtail these 'abominable habits'. Sexual masquerade and performance also unsettled the authorities. It was the habits of what he termed the 'pseudo-male' that he found particularly disconcerting, and the ways the 'artificial substance, mechanically secured to the person form the substitute . . . male organ'. But he found the others equally disconcerting, especially those young girls in 'the habit of decorating themselves, cleaning themselves scrupulously, and making themselves as attractive as they can, before resorting to the "man-woman", if I was to style her, on whom they have bestowed their affections'. Many of the disputes within the factory, claimed Irvine, were from the jealous feeling and quarrels of these women. Such practices 'ruin' the women and hence the need to separate them. He singled out one such prisoner, Margaret Elliot, 'a large size masculine looking woman', who 'was in the habit of acting as a "pseudo-male"', of approaching

the very young and inexperienced and of seducing them and it appears the scenes that take place from the depraved habits of such creatures as this woman are to the last degree disgusting and offensive to the better disposed . . . [because of the] nocturnal orgies and offending their sense of common decency by their licentious and unnatural practices.[44]

The 'mannish lesbian' was a forerunner of the twentieth-century 'butch'. By the early years of the nineteenth century two changes had occurred in same-sex relations: male commentary about women's sexuality had become more widespread and middle-class women had begun to wear masculine clothing, asserting their rights to enter predominantly male areas.[45] This figure later became the 'deviant invert' in the work of the sexologists in the late nineteenth and early twentieth centuries. Male commentators made sense of lesbianism by constructing it in terms of heterosexual relationships, with women adopting male and female roles. While this was certainly the case, this was not the only model adopted by convict women. Although the expression of lesbianism may have been diverse, the 'solution' was universal: to isolate these women in separate cells in the Hobart factory, in order to contain and regulate their sexuality.

Lesbianism was ignored in the criminal codes in Britain during this period, although it was assimilated into prostitution towards the end of the nineteenth century, when 'studies' showed that a quarter of prostitutes had lesbian tendencies. As Jeffrey Weeks observes, it was as if 'lesbians had to be explained and justified always in terms of a male phenomenon'.[46] While commentators in Australia certainly conceptualised lesbian relations in terms of heterosexuality, there is little evidence of a link with prostitution, although both were conflated with criminality.[47] However lesbianism was conceived, it undermined efforts to discipline and punish women. These women were carriers of yet another disease and different forms of pollution, as well as being a force of disorder through their quarrelling and sexual practice.

Crossing Spatial Boundaries

In 1815, Bridget Connell, a servant to Edward Eager, a well-known merchant and later prominent politician in the colony, left his house without permission or request. Her sleeping quarters were the kitchen and attic, 'but he has lately been informed that she was in the habit of opening the window . . . going out and spending the night with a soldier—that on last Sunday night she absented herself all night Monday night and did not return till this morning'. Such wanderings were common amongst female convict servants, although some, like Ellen Clarke, were less forthcoming when interrogated. In 1822, she too was charged with absence from her master's premises at night without leave, and ordered to be confined in a cell on bread and water until she said where she was. Catherine Gough, on the other hand, was far more vocal. In February 1833, she left the home of her mistress, Nancy Siscombe, and did not return again until the next morning. She insisted that 'she would go away when she liked without permission', especially that of the mistress. She stated her grievances as being that she had been employed for eleven months, during which time she had been overworked and received a short allowance, saying she was barefooted. In an equally defiant mood, Mary Keevey and Margaret Robinson approached their master, George Harper, on Christmas Day 1831, and asked if they could 'go to the Gaol and . . . take some dinner to a Woman who was in gaol. [He] said he could not on any account allow it particularly as it was Christmas Day'. But they went anyway, at about eleven or twelve o'clock, and were eventually apprehended late in the afternoon. Prisoner Robinson was very abusive, and 'used language . . . too gross to be repeated in court', and that both used 'very unbecoming language to [their] Master'. Although both 'the women were in a passion . . . neither of them appear to have been drinking'.[48] Absence from service and being at large at night provoked a firm rebuke from the authorities.

As we have seen, the view of the female convict body in colonial Australia drew on the themes of order and disorder, pollution and purity. What it meant to cross boundaries differed for men and women. The idea of 'acceptable behaviour' for men and women came into play, but as Paula Byrne has suggested, the male and female bodies were understood in different ways so defiance took different forms. In both movement of the 'body' and expressions of language convict women challenged and resisted many of the established assumptions about femininity and undermined the power relationships between master and servant.

Good behaviour was recognised through the paternalistic granting of rewards. The freedom to roam at liberty was only permissible for convict women who had been granted a ticket of leave or conditional pardon. In 1821, tickets of leave were given to convicts who had served three years with good conduct and had received the endorsement of their employer and magistrate to this effect. A ticket of leave exempted the holder from assigned labour and allowed her to work for herself and obtain her own lodgings. When a conditional pardon was given, the woman was given freedom, but with restrictions on her movement.[49]

Absconding was a most common form of resistance.[50] Mary Williams was charged with absconding and stealing two caps from her mistress. But her more severe crime was being found at the ferry sometime between four and five o'clock in the morning, 'out courting a young man'. But loitering was a problem even for free women. Margaret McMeanor discovered this when she was charged in October 1836 with 'being in an unoccupied building at two o'clock' and 'not giving a good account of herself'. In 1833, Constable Alexander Henderson claimed that he found Ann Smith, also a free woman, 'round the town about 11 o'clock', for no other reason than 'she did not like her station'.[51]

Absence was often related to drunkenness and women were reported to be intoxicated on the road or the street. For some women, being sent on errands gave them the opportunity to make their own time. In April 1816, Margaret Yates was given instructions by her mistress to buy a pound of sugar, 'with which she did not return till nine when she was drunk'. Margaret Coffey also used the time her master had allowed her to go out for a few hours to indulge herself. After failing to return by nine o'clock he sought her out, and found her in a public house in a state of intoxication. She refused to go home.[52] Other women were less surreptitious and did not bother to go to such lengths to enjoy their excesses. Mary Strange was charged with 'continual drunkedness' in the service of Charles Walker, while Mary Anderson was charged simply with drunken conduct in her service.[53] The result was often disturbance and mayhem at the home of the mistress. In March 1833, Mary Turner was said to be tipsy as she 'took her apron and in a great rage tore it to pieces'. Others tried to pacify her and it soon transpired that she and the cook had stolen a bottle of rum; when ordered to go to gaol, she 'would not go [so] she was obliged to be carried off the farm'. Eleanor Brown was taken away in a wheelbarrow because she resisted efforts to take her peacefully. This was obviously a common strategy for Brown, who had 'kept the house in a continual uproar' because she had been regularly intoxicated.[54] Others were much more excitable. After a bout of drinking with a male prisoner, Ann Curley was evidently 'worse for liquor'. When Constable Patrick Lannigan took both prisoners, the female 'tore his shirt and waistcoat'.[55]

Such disorder and disturbance could often only be contained through force. In 1840, William North had no choice but to take Ann Walsh, his prisoner, to the watch-house against her will. She was 'in [such] a state of intoxication', that he could not get her there 'without tying her hands behind her', and it was 'not the first time that she has behaved in this same manner'. Rose Daly was in a similar condition. She insisted she 'would not mind the children anymore' and had beaten them.[56] When Lieutenant Banow 'returned from the races', he found Caroline Smith in such a 'beastly state of drunkedness that she could neither walk nor stand'.[57] Being 'in liquor' probably gave many women the courage to defy authority and challenge those who exercised control over them.

Other convict women, however, did not need the help of liquor to refuse to work, or to confront their superiors. Elizabeth Turpin, who, in March 1831, was assigned to George and Margaret Harper as a housemaid and washerwoman, claimed that she 'had not been accustomed to washing or work, and as the place did not suit her, she would not take it in hand'. She also refused to clean her room and nurse the child. Sarah Jones adopted a similarly defiant stance. In May 1832, Mrs Antill found that after the prisoner had been washing about a month, she was 'only spoiling the Clothes, and that she could not get through the work at all'. She had reprimanded her for being idle and dirty, and when she again refused to work in the nursery, decided it was time to go to the factory for another woman. Mr Antill reported that Jones would not get out of bed, even 'after she had been called by other servants'. The Antills had the same problem with Sarah Hall, another laundress to the family, who was 'very backward in getting her work done'.[58]

It was clear that some convict women used these strategies to return to the factory and were unashamedly direct about their desire to do so. Eleanor Brown, who later would be taken off in a wheelbarrow, had, 'for some time past', been particularly insolent and grumbled about everything she had to do. She was 'continually asking to be returned to the Factory', and was keen, it seems, to make her way back there. 'In consequence of making a great noise' in the house, her mistress ordered her to be quiet. She replied that 'she would not, that she would speak her mind'. Then began a torrent of abuse, as she insisted she was entitled to a pass. Although she later apologised for her behaviour, she absconded that evening. Mary Newland also refused to follow orders, saying that she 'would neither work nor stay', because she 'had lost more things there than she has gained'. The servant Mary Mallen was more forthright about her intentions. John Buckland 'saw her seated in the kitchen with her arms folded and called to her to go about her work immediately which she refused to do'. If he didn't send her to gaol, 'she would go herself'. Margaret McGar had also made a complaint 'for the purpose of being turned into the factory'. Catherine Carmody had, according to her master, 'firmly wanted to be returned to government'. Mary Coran was able to intimidate and harass her master, John Buckland, as he claimed 'she has frequently told me she would do as little work as possible in fact her conduct has on very many occasions been most insolent and irritating . . . that for some past I have been afraid to speak to her and have allowed her to act as she pleased'. In 1834, Hannah Maria declared that she had absented herself from her employer because 'the work was too hard for her'.[59]

The explicit desire expressed by convict women to return to the factory was used by critics of the factory system as proof that it had failed as a place of reform and punishment. Only rarely was it found to be the case that the mistress could be to blame for these altercations, thus forcing the women back to the prison. In one such rare case, the courts found that, in the case of Michael and Mary Carr, their place was 'not an eligible place for a female servant' because 'Mrs. Carr was in the habit of getting drunk'.[60]

Abusive and insolent language often ensured a sentence to the female factory. Women also used particular language to resist authority.[61] This was the case with male convicts as well, but, again, the offence carried different connotations for women.[62] It was not always clear what constituted offensive language, but for women it appeared it was the use of masculine language, which not only undermined the decorum expected of women, but, more subversively, suggested transgressive knowledge, usually of sexual behaviour.[63] An example of such language was that used by Mary Hamilton (a free woman) in September 1836, when she was charged with using 'obscene language' in the street. Constable John Galloway claimed that the 'prisoner was in Harrington Street last night. There were several women in the street. The pr was following and calling them bloody whores and tells them to go and f . . . k themselves'.[64]

Language also became an issue when Mary Ann Coran, who had been 'repeatedly checked . . . for such misconduct', was 'coaching a child of . . . about two years old to repeat most horrible expressions'. Another government servant had overheard her making use of language 'too gross to be repeated', and teaching the child to 'repeat the expressions after her'. For Caroline Batkin, it was by breaking the boundaries of silence, obedience and subservience that she continued to press her desire to be returned to government employ. She then proceeded to make a 'great noise for about two hours', saying what she would do, and despite efforts to move her, 'she would go where she pleased'. She continued swearing, would not remain quiet, and 'made use of most gross, and outrageous language too indecent to be inserted'.[65]

It was not only insolence, but this 'gross language' that unsettled relations between convict women and their masters. 'Gross abuse' did not only refer to swearing, but also to insolence. At the dinner table of George Simpson, the convict servant Ann Anderson brought in a quart of beer, which was taken away from her, although she argued, with 'gross abuse', saying that 'whenever she could get either spirit or beer she would have it'. Abusive language in front of children was deemed particularly offensive. Catherine Watson was alarmed that her children were making use of 'horrid language', which they had learnt from the servant.[66] Others attempted to deny they had used or to excuse their use of such language. Jane Campbell claimed that 'I speak very fast and when I am in a passion I say things I do not mean'.[67] When analysing these cases in the police records of this period, it should be noted that the proliferation of cases of women being 'drunk and disorderly' was in the interests of the police, as were the charges of indecent exposure and obscene language, because before 1850 the police received a portion of the fines.[68] The police were accused at the time of paying too much attention to such relatively minor offences as drunkenness and disorderly behaviour.[69] Nonetheless, apprehension of female servants in the streets certainly carried with it moral overtones and particular notions of disorder in the towns.

Stealing was another effective way in which convict women disrupted master–servant relations, and convict servants regularly robbed their mistresses and masters.[70] They stole clothes, money, pieces of furniture, food and alcohol. This is perhaps not surprising, given that most women were transported in the first place because of theft.[71] In Britain, most of these goods would have been resold rather than used directly.[72] Stealing clothing and material in the colonies was especially common, not only for resale value, but also quite possibly because women did not have adequate material for menstruation. Women stole not only fine cotton print, which they could sell, but also calico, which was often used by women for menstruation, and items of clothing that could have been torn up for the same purpose. Another possible reason for the proliferation of clothes stealing was that a trade in second-hand clothing may have begun in Australia as had operated in Britain since the seventeenth century. Supplies of clothing were often in short supply and shipments were erratic.[73] The *True Colonist* was fully aware of the problem. Although it was the responsibility of the master and mistress to supply adequate clothing (as well as food and shelter),[74] there was evidently a deficiency in how much they were prepared to provide their servants. In an article documenting the 'problem' of female convict discipline, it was demanded that an 'advantageous rule' be passed that

> no servant should be sent out of the Factory without a proper quantity of clothing, and that this clothing should be preserved . . . The alteration and inconvenience which the absence of some such rule as this, gives rise to are unlimited, and we verily believe that one half of the female servants in Hobart Town are supplied with clothing, as well as money, by the most disreputable and abominable means.[75]

The *True Colonist* was right to be so alarmist. Mary Carroll, for instance, had devised an elaborate plan to steal a shirt and other articles of clothing from her master, John Wild. Wild had discovered some towels and pillow cases pinned inside her gown. Further investigation revealed articles 'wrapped up inside other things'. With 'nothing else to say in her defence', Carroll was sent to twelve months in the third class of the female factory. Similarly, Maria Clarke was accused in 1834 of stealing three pieces of cotton print: two pieces containing eight yards of cotton print; and another containing fourteen yards. The police seized them from her box after her mistress had identified a 'very small piece hanging out of the corner'. The prisoner denied the charge and claimed that somebody else must have put them there, but such a plea was dismissed and her sentence was extended by three years. Susan Doane was equally shrewd in her attempts to procure several materials from the nearby store owned by one Joseph Hall. She ordered several pieces of cloth ostensibly for her mistress, Helena Midwood, but intended to keep them for herself. Doane was found guilty of stealing two pieces of printed calico (the value of which was twenty shillings) and another piece of calico (valued at thirty-seven shillings). Her assigned term was extended by three years. As well as stealing substantial quantities of beef and pork, Mary Whitehead and Mary Little also stole one yard of printed cotton and one pinafore (both valued at two pence) from William Lindsay and were sentenced to twelve months in the factory.[76]

Certainly, some convict women complained about the lack of provisions given to them by their masters. In 1834, Jane McDonald protested that in the three months she had been assigned to Thomas Toole, she had only received one shirt, one handkerchief, one pair of shoes and one pair of stockings. Toole insisted that he had given her an additional jacket, petticoat and cap, but McDonald refused to return to her master. Elizabeth Burkinshaw suffered a harsh sentence. She was punished with hard labour for two years for stealing money from her master, John Anderson Brown, which was meant to go to the purchase of green peas and a jug. Mary O'Neil had collected a range of items from the house of William and Catherine Kearney, most of which was clothing. She had stolen two yards of printed cotton, seven white cotton stockings, four caps, one shirt, one silk handkerchief and three gloves. Despite her pleas of not guilty, she was sentenced to six months hard labour. After Mary Keegan had absconded from her master in Launceston in 1834, it was found that she had taken away a shawl and cap, the property of her master. The possession of clothes also seemed to be at the centre of a dispute between Maria McLean and her master. McLean informed him that she would not wear any of her clothes in his house and would rather go naked. He insisted he had supplied her with adequate clothing and intended to give her more, but she had 'stolen about three yards of lace'. McLean claimed she was in need of a gown, and her master claimed that 'I told her that as she had stolen the lace I would not give it to her she then tore the lace off the cap before my face and threw it in the fire'. She earned three months hard labour in the wash tub in the female factory. Francis Clifton and Ann Saunders were apprehended in the bush by a constable after they had absconded from their master. Amongst other things, they had 'bundles with them . . . containing weaving apparel and also a piece of calico about three yards, and a pair of new black worsted stockings'.[77]

It was not only from their master that convicts would steal. Margaret Byrne was convicted for removing four silk handkerchiefs 'at an early hour' from the shop of Mr Pritchett. When the shop assistant had turned his back,

> the prisoner made off and said she would call again when Mr. Prichett was at home; but in consequence of some alarm having been given, the prisoner came in a few minutes afterwards, and [put] four black handkerchiefs on the counter.[78]

There were also countless instances of free people stealing. The *Sydney Gazette* reported that Eliza Patfield and James Connor, 'both free', were 'fully committed to take their trial at the Quarter sessions for owning certain pieces or remnants of blue-cloth', which 'they know to have been . . . stolen from the stores of MRC Pritchett . . . when his house was . . . broken and entered on the morning of the 23rd December last'. Similarly, John Smith and James Wright were 'indicted for stealing several pieces of cloth' from 'the premises of Mr. Robert Cooper'.[79]

Some prisoners apologised for their criminal behaviour in the hope that they would receive a more lenient sentence. In some cases, this revealed a paternalistic relationship between the master, mistress and their servants. Sarah Emery, 'in her defence', said she was 'very sorry' for her 'insolence and neglect of duty'. Some mistresses were particularly patronising to their servants, treating them like petulant children. Catherine Watson said of Emery that she was 'sorry to say she is a very bad girl'. Mrs Francis Hall promised her servant, Sarah Marsh, who had been insolent, that if she said 'she was sorry for what she said I would forgive her and not send for a Constable'. Such apologies often did earn a more lenient sentence. Mary Anthony, charged with 'gross contempt', stated she was 'very sorry for what she has done', which earned her a reduced sentence. After Mary Miller had given the cook a black eye and 'threatened to hit him with a spade', she expressed her regret at her conduct and 'promised to behave better for the future'.[80] Surreptitious behaviour like stealing was not always a sufficient form of noncompliance. Convict women were also violent towards their masters, mistresses and fellow servants. Laura Whitaker attempted to 'strike her mistress' and throw a 'bucket of water over her'. Mrs Wilkinson claimed her servant, Sussanah Stone, 'pushed her fist to my face . . . I told her to hold her tongue. She burst into a laugh and said to me, you are a pretty dolly for a lady'. Mary Brown struck a fellow servant, Mary Wilkinson, with 'teacups at her head, which was severely cut in consequence'.[81]

Absconding, theft, drunkenness, language and stealing were actions of defiance that assumed particular meanings within the assignment system. The women's desire to return to the factory can be included within this rubric of insubordination. Invariably, these were individual acts of defiance. Within the prisons, the response was more collective although, ironically, often considered less threatening.

Voyeurism and Collective Resistance

One Saturday in October 1827 the town of Parramatta was a scene of bustle and rioting. The cause of the uproar was the actions by convict women who were protesting about the lack of provisions. Removing 'most unmercifully the hinges and panels of one of the gates', they rushed, and dispersed through the town, proceeding 'to beat up the bakers' and butchers' quarters'. Many of the bakers, rather than be troubled by such customers, 'threw into the street whatever loaves the women required, they devoured with "avidity"'. Another group of women shouted out 'starvation' and proceeded to dislodge beef from the stall of the butcher. Parramatta had never before witnessed such a scene. The bugles sounded to call in the assistance of the scattered soldiery. The

women had their aprons loaded with provisions, the 'spoils of van-
quished bakers'. About a hundred went into the town; nineteen women
managed to escape and the remainder returned to the factory.

The women's protest was perceived with a mixture of fear and frolic, as
a 'tragic-comical scene', in the words of the *Australian*.[82] While this was a
'scene of clamour', a 'storm' that 'raged too violently', the scene was
nonetheless a rather 'whimsical' example of 'factory frolics'. In the press
it was represented as an incident to be met with 'astonishment, strongly
mixed up with the ludicrous'. Such an episode was both disturbing and
disruptive, yet it was trivialised and reduced to frivolity. The actions of
women in the public realm appeared fanciful, while the female convict
roaming in a free space unsupervised was, according to contemporary
accounts, a source of bemusement. Three years later, in 1830, John Piper
Junior wrote with glee that about '50 women broke loose from the
Factory, and came on the course to the amusement of all the people, the
mounted policemen and constables pursued them in every direction'.[83]

The pursuit of convict women by the police was a spectacle of
much delight. All of Parramatta, reported the *Sydney Monitor* in February
1831, were 'in glee' to 'see the sport' of the police chasing convict
women. The sexual implication of this was not lost on the reporter who
noted that the soldiers' greatest dread was that 'the Amazons would not
effect their escape to the bush where the heroes hoped to have a choice
as well as a chase'.[84] The newspaper report expressed some voyeuristic
delight in watching women cross the boundaries imposed on them:
of being free and bonded, of public and private, of masculine and
feminine behaviour.

In another incident, in May 1839, female convicts 'broke out in open
rebellion' because their bread had been leavened with barley meal. Two
hundred women were in possession of the building, which was soon
occupied by a dispatch of constables, although there was at one stage fear
that the buildings would be set alight and 'engines were accordingly, sent
for from town'. This incident was not considered threatening. The ring-
leader of the 'Anti-Barley insurrection' (as the *Colonial Times* coined it)
was a 'strapping damsel' named Haig, or Faig. The paper suggested
punishment equivalent to her offence, namely, 'a week at the wash-tub'.
The discussion of the incident shifted to the impact such a riot had on
bourgeois society, rather than on the plight of the women themselves. By
'their misconduct', observed the editor of the *Colonial Times*, many
families are 'inconvenienced', for 'the want of servants'.[85]

Interestingly, these women were masculinised in these descriptions of
their mutiny. The *Sydney Gazette* commented on the way the women were
armed with

pick-axes, axes, iron crows . . . the united force of which, wielded as they were by a determined and furious mob . . . the inmates of the factory were quickly poured forth, thick as bees from a hive, over Parramatta and the adjoining neighbourhood.

These 'Amazonian bandetti' were violent, but soon subdued, clutching their aprons with bread and meat. Although most had been captured, some remained at large, and the women resisted any attempts to punish ringleaders, for 'if one suffered, all should suffer'.[86] Colonel Godfrey Charles Mundy wrote of the 'Amazonian inmates . . . headed by a ferocious giantess', and their 'unladylike ebullition', which had created 'the most formidable outbreak that ever occurred in the colony, not even excepting that of Castle Hill'.[87] Such outbreaks shocked those in the town. Three years later, when female prisoners failed in their attempt to escape, but 'destroyed all the spinning-jennies and spinning wheels, together with everything which appertained thereunto', the memories of the earlier riot were revived as the *Sydney Gazette* commented that experience, ' "makes fools wise". The Parramatta bakers, on hearing of the probable descent of the Amazons, took such prompt measures that in an instant not a loaf was to be seen in the town'.[88]

Both male and female convicts organised acts of riot and protest. The most notorious of these was the uprising at the government farm at Castle Hill in 1804, when several hundred convicts attempted to seize power and take over the colony.[89] In 1834 on Norfolk Island, there was another attempted mutiny, which failed because of poor planning and co-ordination.[90] Disturbances by women have received considerably less attention by historians. These have been explained mainly in terms of the nature of the women's demands and the ways in which their protest resembled the British 'food riot'.[91] This sparse attention did not characterise the coverage by contemporary writers as a riotous outbreak by convict women excited intense curiosity and interest. Women's protest was, however, perceived in different ways to that of men's rebellion. Their 'riot' was constructed by the press on the one hand, with a mixture of 'fear' of the unruly mob, with the language of invasion being evoked, and on the other, as a 'frolic', a sport and a spectacle. Their actions were not seen to be as threatening as those of male convicts.[92] The discussion of women in rebellion carried sexual overtones in two ways. First, they were defeminised in engaging in such acts, as the press evoked the image of the masculinised woman, the female warrior of the 'Amazon'. Second, there was an eroticisation of the female riot, where women were 'tamed' by the male authorities.

While the press may have considered such disturbances the source of amusement, the authorities took these rebellious acts seriously. In

February 1831, the 'riotous conduct and outrageous behaviour of the Women in the third class of the factory' created particular concerns for the authorities. The ringleaders were gathered, separated and punished.[93] In February 1843, the police officer in Parramatta wrote to Governor Gipps: 'Sorry to report that the spirit of insubordination among the women at the factory has not yet subsided'. His concerns were correct and they did riot.[94] Tyhe, the visiting justice of the factory, called for twelve more constables, 'steady men', and stronger hinges were applied to the doors.[95] In addition, applications were made for twenty pairs of handcuffs, but 'care must be taken to have them selected of the smallest size; as the women are able to get their hands through the ordinary ones'.[96] The women were clearly determined as later that year it was reported that women confined in the cells had been able to break a number of the padlocks that secured the inner doors.[97]

Disturbances did not always end so peacefully. The disruption which erupted at the Launceston factory, when almost two hundred women united to free Catherine Owen ('an extremely bad character . . . ranked as a leader upon all occasions'), indicates a remarkable degree of unity and solidarity amongst the women. Owen had been sentenced to almost two months solidary confinement, but when the matron went to visit her cell, she was 'seized and held . . . whilst others conveyed Owen from the cells to the Mess Room . . . One and all stating they would not allow her to serve the remainder of her sentence in the cells'. At this point, the whole class resisted and 185 women barricaded themselves. The women had beaten off police with the spindles from the spinning wheels, bricks taken from the floors and walls of the buildings, knives and forks. The women were left to themselves for a while. Finally, in the evening, they claimed that if they were given their rations, and a promise not to punish the ringleaders, or put Owen in the cells once again, they would submit. The police refused. The next morning, the prisoners became 'very outrageous, breaking the furniture and windows and attempting to burn the building'. Fifty 'special' constables were ordered into the building, furnished with 'sledge hammers and crowbars'. The Crime Class ward was forced, and 'the most refractory and violent of the female prisoners were captured and removed'.[98] The seventeen women who had abstained from participation were granted tickets of leave, while the ringleaders were brought to trial and sentenced to hard labour, exhibiting 'the most outrageous conduct abusing and threatening the magistrates to their face'.

Not all disturbances took place in the form of a concerted, organised campaign, either. During the 1820s and 1830s, within the factory, as outside it, language was a common form of transgressing the boundaries of punishment. Using 'infamous language' earned Elizabeth Wilson, Ellen

Dunn and Margaret Kelly, all second class prisoners, ten hours solitary confinement. It seemed third class prisoners were more harshly punished for this offence. Margaret Grayson and Ellen Murphy, both from the third class, each received twenty-four hours confinement for using 'bad language' and Mary Griffin was given a seven-year sentence for 'teaching a child beastly expression'.[99]

'Indecency' was expressed in actions as well as words. Ann McIson behaved in a 'very improper manner to the constable who brought her', while Margaret Wesson was handed a day-long sentence for 'indecently exposing her person'. Perhaps more directly disturbing were fighting and quarrelling. Mary Conners, Catherine Carey and Mary Farrett, all of the third class, were caught 'fighting with each other' and punished by being confined for twenty-four hours.[100] Being complicit in such behaviour also earned women punishment; Margaret Kelly and Ann McConnell were charged with aiding in a fight between Margaret Fawkes and Margaret Clark, and all four earned twenty-four hour confinements, later extended to forty-eight hours. 'Quarrelling in the bedroom' may have been a euphemism for sexual jealousies or disputes, but whatever the nature of such disagreements, this was a source of disruption and earned the women severe punishment. Elizabeth Johnson, Ellen Wihilar and Julia Burke were all accused of 'quarrelling in the bedroom'. The bedroom (or at least the sleeping quarters) was the scene of many disputes. Penelope Burke was charged with 'cruelly treating a woman in the bedroom'; Caroline Williams was accused of using 'shameful language in the bedroom', while Alice Leonard and Elizabeth Livingstone were punished for 'quarrelling about their beds, in the sleeping room'. 'Irregular conduct in the sleeping room' earned Abigail McJouran a twenty-four hour confinement and Mary Campbell thirty-six hours.[101]

More conventional forms of resistance, such as refusing to work and stealing, abound in the records of punishment. This punishment varied according to the class of women. Catherine Keefe of the third class received a hefty four-day punishment for refusing to work, while Catherine Hoare, Bridget Fahey, Margaret Keogh, Alice Leonard, Margaret Reynolds and Ellen Connors, all of the first class, received thirteen hours and were degraded to the second class. On the other hand, Beth Byrne of the first class received forty-two hours, while Margaret McKenna of the third class received twenty-four hours.[102] Whatever the punishment, it is clear that women did often refuse to work collectively. Catherine Hoare and nine others were accused of 'neglect of work', and Margaret McKenna and two others 'refused to work'. In 1827, Julia Burke and fourteen other women were punished for 'neglect of work'. Clearly, refusing to work and neglecting to work had different meanings and were ascribed different punishments. 'Disobedience of orders' was similarly a common offence, and, again, women were often charged together. In 1827, Margaret Boyle and three other women from the first class were charged with this offence, as were Ann Gorman and Margaret Sullivan of the second class. In 1828, Charlotte Leopard and Ann McCoy were also charged with disobeying orders. These pockets of collective action did not translate into a unified front against the authorities, but were nonetheless instances of collective resistance by convict women within the female factories.

More individual and less regular behaviour occurred in the offences of stealing, sleeping at the wrong times and violence. The stealing of food and clothing was less common than refusal to work or using offensive language. In 1828, Alice Leonard and Ann Dillon broke into the matron's garden and stole a number of peaches, as did Rose McCarty and Sarah Wright on another occasion. Amelia Peacock was accused of 'stealing Constable Braggs' dinner',[103] while Elizabeth Smith was accused of 'giving a man a petticoat to take out of the factory'.[104] Other seemingly inoffensive behaviour was punished: Margaret Hayes was accused of 'knitting on the Sabbath', which earned her a twenty-four hour sentence; Elizabeth McMahon and Mary Keefe were discovered to be 'sleeping during divine service'; and Hannah Wallace and Anne Donahoe were accused of 'playing cards'.[105] Acts of breaking machinery were rare and isolated: Ann McConnell broke a flax wheel, while Elizabeth Kinday a spinning wheel. Both received twenty-hour confinements.[106]

These examples provide a tantalising glimpse of the ways in which convict women exercised their resistance to the power relations within the female factories. It has been argued that most of these and other acts were conducted by a small group of women.[107] The issue is not necessarily the size of the sample, but the avenues that women used to shape some autonomy and agency for themselves. Within the power structures of a colonial settlement, the expressions of such resistance took place in many and varied ways. These were not all well-organised, systematic actions, but were exercised through a range of different and varied responses—in large part defined by the expression of desire and pleasure that ruptured existing relations.

CHAPTER 4

Defeminising Convict Women
Headshaving as Punishment in the Female Factories

The systematic practice of convict women having their hair cut short was introduced by Governor Ralph Darling in 1826. This was to be applied as a form of punishment to women in the third penitentiary class in the female prisons and to 'incorrigibles'.

The question of women and punishment was a constant source of frustration for the authorities because of the limited means they had to punish relcalcitrant women. Following the riot in the female factory at Parramatta in 1839, the *Colonial Times* lamented the fact that the factory had yet again proved to be an inadequate form of discipline, punishment and reform of convict women. 'What punishment', despaired the editor, 'will be sufficient for these rebellious hussies?'[1] It was generally agreed, as the committee inquiring into the state of female discipline concluded, that 'a more refined system of discipline than is required for male prisoners should be enforced in the case of females'.[2] In 1817, flogging of women had been outlawed in Britain.[3] After this time, incarceration became a major form of punishment for women in colonial society. This was particularly the case in Van Diemen's Land, where the factories were the only places of punishment for convict women. In New South Wales, women could also be sent to prisons of secondary punishment like Port Macquarie or Moreton Bay.[4] The prisons that were established in Australia were not, however, exclusively asylums of penal servitude, but served a range of purposes. The larger factories, established in Parramatta (1821) and Hobart (1821), and the smaller ones in Bathurst (1817), Newcastle (1820), Port Macquarie (1821), Moreton Bay (1824), George Town (1824), Launceston (1834), and Ross (1848) also operated as workhouses and marriage bureaux.

Within these institutions, headshaving was considered to be a most effective means of imposing discipline. The need to contain lice and uphold a standard of cleanliness within the factory may have been a consideration for Governor Darling, although there were few recorded incidents of lice. In one case, recorded in 1837, the prisoner was 'covered with vermin' and in such a 'filthy state' because of a 'neglect of cleanliness of Person' that her head was shaved and a 'change of clothes provided'.[5] In Britain, it was usual practice for male prisoners' heads to be shaved for hygienic reasons.[6]

But Darling explicitly stipulated the purpose of the exercise was punishment for women 'in their second commitment to the Penitentiary', who were to have their hair close cut and 'kept so during the period of their confinement'.[7] Headshaving as punishment was not unique to convict women at this time and African American female slaves also had their heads shaved as a punitive act.[8]

While the authorities attempted to feminise convict women through domestic service, headshaving was a process of defeminisation, a fact that was not lost on contemporary commentators. James O'Connell readily made the association between this and the masculine nature of other punishments, as 'when convicts are degraded from the second to the third class, employment suited to their sex ceases; their heads are shaved, and they are set to breaking stone, wheeling earth, and cultivating the grounds about the factory'.[9] Women were made more mannish by the punishment process itself. Interestingly, such a punishment did not disrupt women's effectiveness as workers within the prison: they may have been removed to be shorn, but they could readily be returned to their workplace. The devout Quaker missionary and prison reformer, James Backhouse, especially noted the severe impact of the punishment.[10] On 'being sent hither for misconduct', he observed, 'the women are dressed in a prison garb and have their hair cut off, which they esteem a great punishment'.[11]

As a bodily inscription, headshaving was a lasting sign of punishment and an outward sign of moral corruption and weak character. In a practical way, it meant the prisoners' success as prostitutes may have been diminished, as would have been their ability to secure a husband, success at one of which was crucial for a woman's economic survival in the colony. For a woman 'to look mannish', Yvonne Knibiehler has argued, 'was to look freakish'.[12] Those who ventured within the prison walls were not the only observers who were struck by the custom. It repulsed other observers. In May 1828, the *Blossom* reported the incidence of headshaving, commenting in no uncertain terms that those at the paper 'abhor that practice'.[13] Crucially, headshaving also denoted feminine shame as those so punished were desexed and defeminised with their vanity undermined.

Elizabeth Fry made it clear that these effects were intentional when she began her work in the reform of prisoners in Britain. Feminine adornment was prohibited and earrings, dresses and finery were confiscated from female prisoners. To further engender the 'humiliation of spirit' the women's hair was cut close and they were issued with white uniforms. In an effort to have them mirror the appearance of their reformers, who aimed to set a moral example, these dresses were modelled on the plain dresses worn by the Quaker women.[14]

Fry's efforts reflected the general perception during the nineteenth century of how to punish and reform female prisoners. She advocated a system of routine, order and regulation with an emphasis on useful labour and self-reflection. Unlike those who had gone before her, Fry believed that 'fallen' women could be reformed and she stressed women's responsibility to 'save' their fallen sisters. As a committed Quaker, religious instruction and teaching were the basis of reform for Fry, who insisted that women should be exposed daily to reading the scripture. She was a part of the religious revival and social reform movements of the 1820s and 1830s which proselytised the view of individual and social salvation.[15] Through women's committees, Fry envisaged that middle-class women could inculcate virtues of respectability and deference and remedy the bad habits of their 'immoral' sisters.[16]

Despite this faith in redemption, by the 1830s Fry had developed more exact methods of punishment and surveillance and her proposals for reform had become more punitive. She advocated rigid methods of classification and a hierarchy within prisons based on a system of rewards and privileges; she devised a more thorough model of regimentation and 'moral accounting' through a system of numbered badges and uniforms. Fry also favoured headshaving as an effective means of punishment for women. These markers—uniforms, badges, classifications and headshaving—were designed to inculcate regular and constant forms of humiliation within the prison.[17]

Contemporary commentators such as Fry noted the effectiveness of the punishment. For her, short hair was a 'certain, yet harmless punishment' and promoted 'that humiliation of spirit which . . . is an indispensable step to improvement and reformation'.[18] She was acutely aware of the impact of headshaving on convict women. When asked by the Select Committee on Transportation in 1832 whether 'cutting the hair short would be punishment', she encapsulated the dilemma of punishing women: 'Undoubtedly it would. One thing is very clear . . . there is still great difficulty in knowing how to inflict punishment on women'.[19] James Mudie shared the opinion that headshaving in particular distressed these women. He told the Molesworth Committee on Transportation that 'I believe that there is nothing that mortifies a convict woman, if she is a young woman and has good hair, more than shaving her head; I think that annoys them more than any mode of punishment'.[20] In 1841, Josiah

Spode in Van Diemen's Land lamented that the practice of headshaving had been abandoned. It was, he reported to the Committee of Inquiry into Female Convict Prison Discipline, 'adopted in cases of disorderly conduct in the House of Correction and . . . was found to be very effective'. It was abandoned as a punishment 'about five years since', but he was of the 'opinion that it would be advisable to resume that custom'.[21] The custom was identified as an appropriate form of punishment for all women, irrespective of age. Inmates at the Female Orphan School were punished in this way. In 1821, Sarah Patfield had her head shaved for selling garments to her sister outside the school. In order that some 'proper example . . . be made of her before the other children', the committee of the school deemed it appropriate that

> a suit of Factory clothing be provided for her—a collar of wood marked Thief to be worn day and night—that her head be shaved in the presence of the other Girls—and that solitary confinement and bread and water be continued 'till the next meeting—and that she be brought down to prayers in that disgraceful manner night and morning.[22]

Headshaving elicited a violent response and was often a catalyst for rebellion, as it had been on board the convict ships. In 1827, the superintendent of the Hobart factory met with the following reception when she told the assigned convict Ann Bruin that she was to be shorn for absconding:

> She screamed most violently, and swore that no one should cut off her hair . . . She then entered my Sitting Room screaming, swearing, and jumping about the Room as if bereft of her sense. She had a pair of Scissors in her hand and commenced cutting off her own hair . . . Coming before the window of my Sitting Room [she] thrust her clenched fist through three panes of glass in succession . . . With a Bucket broke some more panes of glass and the Bottom Sash of the window Frame.

Robert Hughes, who recounts this story, is right to suggest that this was the 'protest of a woman whose physical rights were brutally transgressed'.[23] Bruin's seizure of the scissors was a particularly potent act of empowerment.

Headshaving could also precipitate riot. In March 1833, at the female factory, the monitoress from the first class refused to cut the other women's hair. Samuel Marsden reported that they were 'very determined not to submit' to their hair being cut

> The women had collected large heaps of stones, and as soon as we entered the third class they threw a shower of stones as fast as they possibly could at the whole of us—at last they were overcome . . . and at length their hair was cut . . . All the three classes were under great excitement. It will never do to show

them any Clemency—they must be kept under . . . but they must not do as they please . . . all the officers who saw their riotous conduct will be convinced of the necessity of keeping them under by the hand of power . . .[24]

Headshaving was also often used as a symbol of resistance. In February 1831, when women of the third class attempted to escape from the prison, they seized the superintendent, Mrs Gordon, and had her 'hair either shaved or closely cropped'. The 'chief of the insurgents were heard to say that if they got to Sydney, they would shave the heads of the Governor and his mob'.[25] This performance disrupted the distinction between 'public' and 'private' spaces. In this theatrical resistance, which Judith Butler would call 'theatrical rage', the women mimicked their oppressors.[26]

Why were women so resistant to such punishments? Headshaving became a way in which women could be shamed, and women's feminine dignity could be undermined. Humiliation and disgrace was the aim of this punishment, as the judge David Collins observed when a convict woman had been shorn in the 1790s:

one of the [women was] made a public example of, to deter others from offending in the like manner. The convicts being all assembled for muster, she was directed to stand forward, and, her head having been previously deprived of its natural covering, she was clothed with a canvas frock, on which was painted, in large characters, R.S.G. [receiver of stolen goods] . . . This was done in the hope that shame might operate, at least with the female part of the prisoners, to the prevention of crimes . . .[27]

Through this practice, colonial authorities attempted to instil shame in women they believed were immune to such humiliation. Their sexual licence and drunkenness, as well as their resistance to authority convinced the authorities that these women were shameless, lacking any sense of decency and virtue, qualities required to feel a natural sense of shame. This view legitimised repressing and containing women's wild, disorderly and uncontrollable passions and determined that their punishment would be different to that of men, who were emasculated through the lash—although this could be a source of masculine pride—and that effecting punishment would be more difficult because many of these women were perceived to be depraved beyond redemption.[28] For convict women who absconded from their masters, or attempted to escape the factory, headshaving was intended to taint and stigmatise them. Catherine Reily was charged, in January 1822, with 'making her escape from the . . . Factory and when being apprehended by a constable attempted to stab him with a knife'. She was ordered to live on bread and water for a month and 'to have her head shaved, to wear a Log and Cap

of Disgrace being incorrigible'.[29] When the convict woman entered the
factory it was her vanity which was to be attacked when her head was
shaved, as a visitor to the colony, John Henderson, noted: 'When the
convict receives sentence of solitary confinement, the depriving her of
her hair, is ever considered, by the new comer, as the most severe portion
of the punishment, for vanity is still her ruling passion'.[30]

The response by convict women to such treatment needs to be con-
textualised within contemporary understandings of femininity. Within
the prisons and amongst groups of women, 'femininity' assumed a
particular meaning. Women's networks and subculture saw an exchange
of women's knowledge and skills for survival in the colony, as well as an
opportunity for women to reject the passivity and modesty of ideal
femininity.[31] The testimonies of two convict women reveal these dynamics
and the construction of gender within them.

Mary Haigh, formerly of Wakefield Gaol, was transported on the
Arab, having been sentenced to seven years. Her description of the prison
can by no means be considered an unproblematic account because it
was mediated, but it does convey the remarkable movement between
inside and outside the prisons and how this interaction shaped the
culture within the prisons. On arrival in the colony, she was sent to the
factory, along with other women convicts from the ship, to await
assignment and remained there a week. Trafficking of goods took place,
'in exchange for our clothes, tea, meat, sugar, tobacco' and they were
told the 'ways' of the colony; how to manage if they got into bad places.
Haigh had mixed fortunes with the various households to which she was
assigned and the fluctuating fortunes of domestic servants are well
illustrated by her various experiences. First, she was assigned as a nursery
maid to a 'gentleman's' family, in which she remained for four or five
months, but was returned to government service for refusing to obey
instructions. The factory did not provide harsh punishment. She had
little work to do and amused herself as she wished: she confessed that the
turnkey's favourites 'had nothing to do'. Her second assignment was to
look after a child, where she remained for six months until charged with
insolence because she quarrelled with her mistress. Once again in the
factory, she was searched, but 'could have passed in anything I liked', and
placed in the Crime Class where food, money and information were
exchanged.

The time was passed in singing, dancing, playing cards and talking
about the different services in the colony. 'The women named the bad
services and advised each other not to go to them.' 'Bad' services were
those where women were well kept and clothed, but 'coerced', while
'good' ones were where women were 'allowed to do as they pleased'.
Women also exchanged information about where they could obtain

liquor on the sly, and those houses where they might be sheltered if they absconded. Smoking and the consumption of rum were both common within the factory—Matron Mrs Hutchinson's servant was apparently 'allowed out and can pass any part of the building'. The well conducted were certainly berated within this milieu, and were 'sworn at and struck if they found fault with the other women'. The 'Flash Mob' in particular influenced the young girls, wearing handkerchiefs, earrings and rings, the 'greatest blackguards in the buildings'. Even in the cells punishment was not so severe: 'I could obtain whatever I wanted through the turnkey', although Haigh considered that to be there all the time would be 'severe punishment'.

Another position found Haigh in Devonport, where she remained for eight months, in comfort, although she was strictly kept, until she again had a quarrel with the mistress. In a common occurrence, the constable, who escorted her back to the prison, wanted to 'take liberties' on the road and 'assaulted me', but Haigh found 'it was of no use to prosecute him as the other women who were with him . . . wanted to have connection with him'. There are many places, she concluded, where 'servants ought not to be assigned such as those where women are allowed to be on the town'.[32] Assignment was indeed a lottery. John Price, the police magistrate in Van Diemen's Land, confessed that many masters were 'totally unfit to be entrusted' with servants 'from a perfect disregard to the morality of their female servants'.[33] Despite these vagaries and fluctuating fortunes, Haigh eventually married in 1847.[34]

The experiences of Grace Heinbury reveal the arbitrary and fickle nature of the convict woman's predicament and the interchange be-tween the inside and outside of the prisons. On her arrival in the colony, a 'woman came from the second yard . . . to traffick with the newly arrived prisoners'. Her assignments were marred by illness. Those with money in the prison 'can always get enough to eat whilst the others are hungry'. One assignment provided her with very few amenities: 'There wore all my clothes out and could not obtain soap to wash myself with— No money was given to me'. She ran away from this service. In another assignment she was asked to prostitute herself: 'he was a married man and his wife selected me herself from the Factory'. Back in the factory: 'I saw plenty of fried meat and tea passed in by the turnkeys from the cookhouse . . . I could smell spirits but never saw any . . . I learned that women who had money could get it'. In her next assignment she was assaulted by the men servants. When she left her situation she was sentenced to six months labour. There was minimal labour to perform, however, and smoking was common, the language which was used was bad and the women quarrelled regularly. Women would also 'act plays and dress themselves up'. In the dark cells, she could get 'anything that

[she] required'. The influence on some prisoners, she believed, was detrimental: 'some of the women are very bad there by whom the young girls are led away'. She, too, stressed the laxity within the prison. 'The work is nothing in the factory except in the Workhouse Yard, but there the overseer is not very strict. She allows the women to smoke there and does not take away their pipes . . . All the disorderly houses that will receive absconded women are well known in the Factory, and women are directed to them when in the factory'. Clothes could be procured from the stores. Women with money could obtain goods and anything could be passed.[35]

The striking aspect of these narratives is the way in which the movement between the two carceral worlds—being factory and assignment—influenced the nature of the women's experience in and out of the factory. The movement of goods and information shaped the behaviour of the women. This frustrated the authorities for such indulgences undermined effective forms of punishment. The turnkeys of the prison in Van Diemen's Land, Julia Leach and John Clapham, both expressed frustration at attempting to reform the women while they had access to such goods.[36]

The prevalence of lesbianism, the use of abusive, 'masculine' language, fighting amongst themselves, and the refusal to be submissive and passive displayed by the refusal to work also suggested ways in which the factory allowed women a space to challenge society's ideals. But responses to headshaving indicated that convict women's feminine identity was shaped by movement in and out of these public and private spaces.

While the punishment took place within the factory, the true shame and humiliation occurred when these women entered the male-dominated space beyond the factory walls. The gaze of men outside the prisons (unlike the predominantly female gaze within its walls) engendered a particular anxiety. Some women experienced this as a moment of anxiety about their femininity. It was no wonder that women attempted to retrieve the remnants of their hair when they ventured outside the factory. After having their heads shaved, wigs could be worn when the women left the factory'.[37] Convict women could make a wig from their shorn locks, thus giving the impression that they had not been punished, saving them humiliation and disgrace. The *Sydney Gazette* noted that:

> We have always remarked that on the return of a female from the Factory after having served her time of incarceration . . . that she invariably appears as if her hair had *grown* considerably longer in front, while the back part of the head being carefully covered with a cap, conceals the wiry appearance that would otherwise be exposed to the vulgar gaze.

As the *Gazette* continued, in disgust, some women managed to retrieve their locks, and when they were released from the factory, these locks made 'a nice litle plait for the front, which gives her all the fascinating appearance of having long hair, and of course of not having been punished'. The paper expressed its protest that this was allowed to happen. 'This is not quite correct', it said, 'for as the present punishment for the women principally consists in "close shaving", they should not be allowed to make themselves appear as if they had not been relieved of the exuberance of this "female ornament"'. It was such practices that led the paper to condemn the punishment of convict women as 'mere farce'.[38] Some women made a concerted effort to conceal this bodily inscription, while other women seemed to become immune to its taint. Mary Orange, transported for seven years and an assigned servant to John Wild, was accused of 'insolence and repeated neglect of duty' by her master. When threatened with punishment because of her 'grossly insolent' behaviour, she

> commenced a torrent of abuse . . . and said she had been treated worse than a dog in the place and that she wished to be sent to the factory, that her head had been shaved too often for her to mind it now, and made use of many impertinent expressions . . .[39]

Her 'torrent of abuse' had the desired effect, as she was sentenced to the third class in the female factory for two months. For Orange, the very form of punishment—headshaving—became the basis for opposition. But it appeared that few women exercised their agency in this way by reinscribing its meaning. The inquest into the factory in 1839 concluded that

> the loss of the hair is, we believe, the only thing, which inspires a disgust of the crime class, and even the bad effects of this is obviated, by the substitution of false hair, when the women leave the factory.[40]

The movement between the male-dominated space of the public arena and the female space of the factory helped to define this response.

The act of hair cutting was not only a violation of convict women's femininity, but also defined their identity. It has been argued that a middle-class woman's identity was shaped by her beauty, and many nineteenth-century publications assigned beauty to women as a way of controlling their bodies.[41] Equally, for working-class women, the violation of their bodies engendered an anxiety about their feminine identity. For both classes of women, 'abundant and lustrous hair connoted beauty'.[42]

Although there are very few sketches of convict women, we can gain some idea about their appearance from remaining records, especially from absconding notices in the colonial press. Many were 'pockpitted' or marked with scars on their arms and faces. Some had rings on their fingers. A few had their ears pierced and it was common for the women to have lost a number of teeth, either through poor diet or dental neglect. Tardif has estimated that on the *Harmony*, the grin of every fifth woman was marred by at least one missing tooth.[43] This condition would not have been improved in the colony, given the excessive amount of sugar that was consumed by the population.[44]

Other bodily markings included tattoos, a defining feature of both convict men's and women's bodies. Some women had names inscribed on their bodies, or a series of initials or symbols, or all of these. Ann Harding was a 24-year-old plain cook and nursemaid from London sentenced to fourteen years, who had dark brown hair and eyes. She had absconded in 1836 from her master, William Miller, in Launceston. The *Hobart Town Gazette* recorded that tattooed on her body was an 'anchor, heart, darts, TRHCDAWTS on her right arm, JJ heart and dart, I love John Johnson, JBWH on her left arm'.[45] The extent of her tattoos was exceptional, for women were seemingly less inclined to imprint elaborate designs. Mary Smith was another convict who had enthusiastically marked her body. A 20-year-old house servant from Middlesex, she too had been sentenced to fourteen years. She had imprinted 1011 EHECNHJL heart and star inside her left arm, and John Roach JL heart on the inside of her right arm. Ann Thompson, a cook and housemaid, who had been sentenced to life in 1832, was also moved to etch the names of men who had been or were her lovers. Her array was comprised of five dots between the finger and thumb on the right hand, Thomas Jones, star and anchor SB on the right arm and Joshua Chamberlain on the same arm. Rosina Sullivan carried two names on her person: Mary Glover (inside her right arm) and William J.B. (inside her left arm) as well as 13 stars and an anchor (on her right arm). Tattooing was more common amongst men who were more likely to have decorated their bodies with elaborate artistry. A preliminary survey suggests that men were less likely to have the names of women or men imprinted on their bodies. John Jones, who had been tried at Cornwell in 1832 and sentenced for seven years, had a particular eye for detail in his choice of tattoos. He had a king's coat of arms imprinted above the elbow on his left arm, G.W. Tomb, star, Hope and Anchor, SA on the same arm, crucifix, sun, half moon, star, unicorn and lion and ship on right arm star between finger and thumb left hand, anchor, compass, moon, three stars and several dots on the back of his right hand, and a cross on his chest.[46]

Absconding notices provided a glimpse into other aspects of the appearance of some women. Some were identified by their disabilities and their scars. Ellen Boyd, a housemaid from Manchester, had a 'scar

on right thumb . . . left hand crippled'. It was been reported that
Elizabeth Lefebrve's 'left eye turns to nose'. Ann Davis, a nursemaid
sentenced for life, had a scar on the 'tip of [her] nose', and another over
her right elbow. The authorities focused on a range of distinguishing
features. Sarah Beasley, aged 24 and sentenced for life, had a 'dimple in
the centre of her chin', while it was noted that Hannah Kite had a 'very
frowning countenance, eyes sunken'.[47]

Convict women's complexions were universally 'pockpitted'. Margaret
McKee, a 44-year-old servant who escaped from the factory, was five feet
two and a half inches, with grey eyes, dark brown hair and a pale freckled
complexion. Ellen Sheehan, a 20-year-old laundry maid, with hazel eyes,
brown hair and a fresh pockpitted complexion, had run away for the
third time in October 1827 and remained at large. Similarly, Sarah
Gardener, a house servant with grey eyes, brown hair, sallow and pockpitted complexion was in 1826 last sighted on her way to Bathurst. The
sallow, pockpitted complexion seemed to have characterised convict
women of all ages: women as young as 15-year-old servant Ann Ross, who
was said to have had a sallow freckled complexion, to Eliza Hargraves,
over double her age at 31 years, who had a ruddy pockpitted complexion. In these notices, more detail was provided for men, like Michael
Condron, a labourer, who had 'only three fingers and thumb on each
hand'.[48] While these women's complexions may have been sallow and
pockpitted, so too, in general, were the complexions of middle-class
women. A clear, 'pearly white flesh tone' was an important aspect of
bourgeois beauty at this time. The difference between these women was
that bourgeois women had access to facial adornment, which concealed
such imperfections, as well as being able to retain their hair, a woman's
crowning glory.

The iconography and symbolism associated with cutting hair were
related to controlling and disciplining women by undermining their femininity. This was also a way of containing 'wild animal passions and
impulses', which was the source of disorder, which unsettled the state,
society and nature. In response to women's uncontrollable sexuality, the
authorities sought to defeminise and masculinise them. The scars and
markings differed on the male body. This form of punishment was
vehemently despised and resisted by women convicts whose vanity and self-
esteem were undermined by the act. Women's 'punishment' was defined
by forces 'outside'. Within the prison, humiliation and degradation took
on a particular form and definitions of 'femininity' took on particular
meanings. Convict women's response was determined by the way in which
their feminine identity was defined by the two worlds they inhabited.

Although there may have been a subculture within the factory
that may have challenged ideas about femininity, notions of feminine

appearance were at the same time not immune from the standards imposed by society at large. The theatre of headshaving stripped women of their feminine attributes, defeminised and desexed them, and for this reason appeared, as surgeon Robert Espie noted in 1822, 'to be the only [punishment] they regard'.[49]

Inside and Outside the Female Prisons

The practice of headshaving is an illustration of the inside/out nature of women's prisons. While shaving took place within the confines of the factory—where femininity could assume a different expression than it could outside—it was nonetheless one of the most effective means of inflicting punishment on women's bodies and instilling 'feminine' shame and humiliation. Those women who did go outside the factory with shaved heads wore wigs. The subculture within the factory was shaped and influenced by women coming back and forth. There was an exchange of knowledge and information of the outside world but, more importantly, the availability of goods like tobacco and alcohol allowed the women to indulge themselves in ways that challenged conventional feminine virtues. While the prison certainly operated along the lines of a more conventional prison during this period, this movement of women meant that these factories, nevertheless, did not resemble contemporary women's prisons in Britain and the United States.

To some extent, the confinement of male prisoners operated in similar ways. After the establishment of the Hyde Park Barracks in 1819, male convicts were placed under constant surveillance for the first time, working for the government the whole day and then spending the evenings in the barracks.[50] They were also employed in private service. But the movement between these worlds for men acquired a different meaning. For women, what was at stake in punishment was the process of defining the feminine in the intersection between the internal and external worlds.

Historians have not analysed punishments of women within the female factories in this way. The discussions of female factories have been led by the questions of whether or not the factories provided adequate or inadequate opportunity for the reform of convict women, or whether women preferred what has been characterised as the camaraderie of the factory to the violence and abuse of the colony outside the factory. What is implied in some of these writings is that the two penal societies were separate and distinct. To argue this, however, is to deny the variety of convict women's experience—exemplified in the testimonies of Haigh and Heinbury—as they moved between the inside and outside worlds of the prisons.

According to these arguments, prisons were either a harsh form of punishment or they were refuges for women. Hilary Weatherburn considers the prison an institution that enforced 'moral and social standards upon women', but failed to achieve its desired aim of reforming women. Under Gipps, she claims, some women 'found conditions in the factory intolerable'. Crimes of 'insubordination' were severely punished; the food and clothing of the third class were inferior; 'they suffered excessive overcrowding and their punishments were degrading'.[51] Laurel Heath suggests that 'a significant number' of convict women did not hold the view that prisoners preferred life in the factories because it provided a refuge. She cites several cases of women attempting to escape from the female factories.[52] Anne Summers, on the other hand, claims that the prisons were a refuge for women, for many of them 'at least regarded a spell in the female factory as a welcome rest from the restless exploitation which the assignment system produced'. She asserts that 'many of the women looked upon the factories as their hope and did their best to remain in them'.[53] The companionship and protection afforded in the factory, she claims, were much more desirable than the isolation of domestic service. Both of these interpretations are valid in that some women expressed a desire to return to the factories, while others experienced violence and assault there.

The assumption that underlies many of these arguments is that there was only one convict women's experience within the prisons. Such an assumption does not take account of the range of women's encounters. If we consider women's encounters within the factory beyond either a complete hell or haven, we will broaden our understanding of that experience.

Related to this broader perspective is the view that the female factories were not separate from the wider society. Our understanding of convict women's experience becomes more varied when we consider the interaction process between their inside and outside worlds. While convict women certainly defined the consciousness of the outside world, so too did the world outside inform the world within the prison. The female factory was a society within a society but not one which was totally isolated from the outside.

The model of inside/outside is useful in understanding how the factory, like all prisons, was a society within a society. But it is limiting, particularly when analysing the space women occupied, moved between and transgressed. The nature of punishment of convict women meant that they were constantly moving between the inside and the outside worlds—that is, between societies and spaces which defined their identities, behaviour and actions—and this forces us to reconceptualise the way in which the prison operated. Rather than the factories resembling the model of the inside/outside, they were institutions that functioned along the model of inside/out: they both defined and were dependent on the outside, as colonial society defined itself in relation to its carceral centre, despite the vast distance in some cases between these factories and colonial society.

Within the female factories femininity was defined in constant reference to the outside. Those who entered it in turn shaped ideas of femininity by what they saw from within. The factories became a space where women could challenge the expectations of the outside world, but without being immune to these expectations imposed on them.

Punishment and Women

Both before and during the nineteenth century in Britain, male and female prisoners experienced incarceration in different ways. Women were considered morally depraved and corrupt as they had perverted one of the values of Victorian society: that of the pure, chaste, and moral ideal of bourgeois femininity. Assumptions about the characteristics and traits of femininity meant that institutions were designed to inculcate particular values and train women in them.[54] In the United States at this time, women's 'crimes' were in large part related to their sexuality. Crimes against the 'public order' and 'decency', like prostitution, comprised a significant number of the crimes committed by women.[55]

The punishment of women was a central part of the debates during the eighteenth and nineteenth centuries, when previous forms of punishment, which relied on public ritual, were being superseded by more systematic and continuous forms of regulation based on confinement. The penitentiaries of the nineteenth century saw the rise of a more efficient, rational and organised form of surveillance. Jeremy Bentham's panopticon encapsulated the model prison for many reformers who argued for a more efficient form of punishment. Rather than inflict punishment on the body, this system aimed to punish the mind.[56] Based on a model of regulation and self-surveillance, Bentham's panopticon was a circular building with a supervisor in the centre who could monitor each prisoner. Continuous surveillance was a central part of the new disciplinary process, but so too was self-regulation, where each prisoner, alone in a cell and isolated from other inmates, would it was hoped achieve a heightened sense of moral consciousness and reform. Labour was a central part of this model, where conscientious, obedient and docile workers would be produced.[57] In Britain, the management principles of this system were abandoned largely because of cost although Bentham's ideas inspired and influenced the structure of several penitentiaries, such as Millbank, where the circular model was adopted.[58] Bentham argued strongly against transportation, maintaining that it was an illogical, arbitrary and inefficient form of punishment.[59]

In Australia, the design, purpose and outlay of female factories had been informed by these developments.[60] It was in the interests of the British authorities that women did reform, given their aims for the colony to become self-sufficient and to promote marriage, despite the fact that transportation created a society where, throughout the 1820s and 1830s, men outnumbered women by 4 to 1, excluding the indigenous population.[61]

In many respects, the female factory was an experiment for it it did not conform to the model prisons in Britain and America.[62] It could never entirely fulfil the aims of its visionary designers because the prisons were constantly overcrowded. Governor King wrote confidently to Lord Hobart in 1804 of the prison in Parramatta that he had 'the pleasure of informing your Lordship of the completion of the upper floor of that building . . . for all female convicts who came by the experiment'. But by 1818, the prison was in urgent need of attention because of the overcrowded conditions. Macquarie established a larger factory but overcrowding remained a perennial problem. The female factory above the gaol comprised two rooms which served as space for accommodation and employment of women convicts. With a lack of bedding, ventilation, and light, it was difficult to maintain the level and standard of cleanliness, order and discipline, and solitary confinement was impossible. Under Governor Darling the factory was extended, but from the late 1820s to the early 1840s overcrowding remained a feature. While it was designed to accommodate 300 women, it always housed larger numbers. By 1829 it had 537 inmates and 61 children living under cramped conditions.[63] Overcrowding was also commonplace at the Cascades female factory. In 1832 it housed about 300, but less than ten years later, 500 women had been admitted.[64]

In other respects, however, the architects of female penitentiaries did implement contemporary ideas about reform. Labour was perceived to be a key element of factory discipline as well as providing economic return, although the production of linen cloth on a widespread scale was never as successful as the authorities had anticipated. Work, it has been argued, was 'the religion of the prisons'.[65] It proved to be important in regulating and ordering women as well as utilising their skills, which played a crucial part in the economic development of the colony.[66] Work 'taken in' was perceived to be an important way of reforming the women and imbuing them with feminine qualities. They were employed in washing for the government, for the orphan schools and penitentiary, or in carding and spinning wool. In 1841 Gipps instructed that washing be taken at the female factory. 'The charge', it was announced from the Colonial Secretary's Office, 'will be two shillings per dozen for the ordinary washing of families and in proportion for articles which may not come under that denomination'.[67] Articles were to be paid for in advance and where they were to require 'more than ordinary care or trouble, the charge will be increased accordingly'. Needlework 'of all sorts' was also available in 'the best possible manner and at very moderate charges'.[68] Such work, noted the Matron Mrs Hutchinson of the Hobart prison, teaches 'industrious, useful habits'.[69] Another contemporary aspect of these reforms was that punishment became seen as a systematic, rational, and scientific enterprise.

Convict Women and Scientific Surveillance

During the 1820s, both Governors Arthur and Darling were committed to transforming their respective colonies to a system of punishment modelled on 'scientific management'.[70] After Bigge's visit and his subsequent report, which proposed a more systematic and effective mode of punishment, efforts were made to refine the system of classification. By 1821 Macquarie had already adopted a hierarchical model based on reward, good conduct and privileges. The General Class was comprised of the aged, married and young women; the Merit Class was comprised of those who, for six months after their admission, had exhibited 'general orderly good conduct, sobriety, industry, cleanliness and humble deportment'. From this class, women were permitted to go to service or, after twelve months, to get married. Women in the Crime Class were distinguished by a badge, to differentiate them from those in the Merit Class.[71] The outcome of Bigge's report was the establishment of a board of management and with it, a detailed system of classification. A new division of three classes was devised.[72]

Darling's classes fixed women in their respective positions and interaction was forbidden between the three classes. The first comprised the recently arrived and the destitute, and assigned labour was drawn from this class. The second class comprised women who had returned to the factory because of improper conduct after being assigned, and those who had advanced from the third class. The third class was the penitentiary class, referred to as the Crime Class. These women were subject to hard labour each morning by stone-breaking.[73] Classification was a central component of the revisions introduced by Darling. Like Macquarie's, this system established a hierarchy of worth and value, where privileges could be given for good behaviour, and punitive measures were exercised for breaking the rules.

Uniforms reinforced humiliation. Headshaving began this process and, as we have seen, Fry in particular was an enthusiastic exponent of this form of punishment to reinforce humiliation.[74] The concept of 'ranking' developed in the eighteenth century and by the nineteenth century had become a part of surveillance and punishment. 'Discipline is the art of rank', reflects Foucault, 'it individualises bodies . . . distributes them . . . in a network of relations'.[75]

These divisions stressed differences in clothing and work although the hours of work and portion of food, mostly bread and soup, were the same for all classes. The regulation of hours ensured a routine was imposed on the women that changed at various times throughout the year. The clothes of all the women were made of the same coarse and cheap material and consisted of a cotton gown, a petticoat, a jacket and apron, and a straw bonnet. Similar regulations were implemented in Hobart towards the end of the 1820s. Before the women were assigned they would be examined by a surgeon, 'bathed, washed, and dressed in the clothing of the establishment; and, if incarcerated for any offence, she shall have her hair cut short'.[76] As if to extinguish any connection with the outside world, the prisoners' clothes were burnt if they were foul or unfit, but otherwise, they were washed and kept for the benefit of the prisoner when she left the factory.

As the women in the first class were considered of 'good character', they were permitted freedoms and indulgences. These women's dress had no distinguishing mark; they were cooks, task-women and hospital attendants. Women in the second class, being those who had committed minor offences, or who had improved in their conduct and had risen from the third class, wore a large yellow C on the left sleeve of their jackets and were employed in making clothes, or 'getting up linen'. Women in the third class, or penitentiary class, had either been sentenced for crime in the colony, or found guilty of offences within the factory. They were distinguished by a large yellow C in the centre of the backs of their jackets, one on the right sleeves, and another on the back part of their petticoats. Uniforms of this kind were issued to adult convicts in New South Wales and Van Diemen's Land from the mid-1820s. These developments signified a move towards a more rigid classification. Yellow was the traditional 'colour of disgrace' in Europe and was worn as a form of punishment in the eighteenth century. It became associated with convicts during the 1820s and 1830s.[77]

Like those of other penitentiaries, this routine was based on an infantile system of punishment and reward and reduced the prisoners to the dependent status of children.[78] Such rigid and stark classification and identification reinforced the prisoners' humiliation and degradation within the factory and fixed their position within the factory's hierarchy. It meant that female prisoners were subject to a regime of scrutiny and surveillance not experienced by their male counterparts.[79] Women in each class were formed into messes of twelve: the best-behaved woman was the overseer of her mess and was responsible for the conduct of the other eleven. Each mess slept in the same room, and their hammocks were put together. It was hoped that with the 'utmost cleanliness—the greatest quietness—perfect regularity—and entire submission . . . patient industry will appear, and reformation of character must be the result'. Women were expected to follow a rigid daily pattern. In the summer months, from 5.30 to 6 a.m. they mustered, then began work until 8 a.m., at which point they breakfasted and had prayers until half past eight. They had dinner at twelve, laboured until sunset, had their evening meal at 7.30 p.m. and prayers at 8 p.m. This timetable was altered marginally for the winter months.[80]

In Van Diemen's Land, the superintendent of convicts sent regular returns and reports to the lieutenant governor on the increase or decrease of crime amongst the female convicts, the quantity of work performed and the general state of the prison. The superintendent was directly in charge of the daily running of the prison. Reading scripture and prayer before breakfast and after supper every evening was an important part of his duties. Inspection of rooms and classes was part of his daily routine. He was empowered to confine women in a cell for disobedience of orders, neglect of duty or other improper conduct and was to record offences, note the expenditure of all articles furnished, and documented daily occurrences.

The matron was responsible for 'the employment of the Women as falls within the province of a Female', and she inspected the separate wards and sleeping rooms daily, and ensured the women were properly dressed and clean. Her task was to ensure that everything was done with 'extreme cleanliness, and order, and industry, and economy'. The overseer and the task-women of the criminal class were to particularly inspect women in the cells, to issue them bread and water, and 'even the slightest deviation is on no account to be allowed or passed' without punishment.[81] The porter monitored movements of individuals into and out of the prison, and kept an account of all articles, while the constables acted as messengers. They were not to be permitted to 'converse with any Female confined within the walls of the Establishment'. A task-woman was appointed to superintend the women of each class. They checked that the women rose at the proper hour in the morning; that they were washed, their bedding was properly made up and that they were in readiness for inspection from the superintendent and matron.

Over ten years after the institution of these regulations it was discovered that they were generally ignored. In 1841, an inquiry into prison discipline in Van Diemen's Land concluded that, although it found 'order and regularity' and an attention to cleanliness highly creditable to the superintendent and matron, it recommended the introduction of the separate cell system for more efficient surveillance. Gipps adopted the recommendations of the inquiry, aiming to make the factory more efficient, and introduced reforms through the cell system.[82]

While, like many other prisons of the nineteenth century, the female factories from the 1820s classified women, kept them under surveillance, ordered and structured their time and space and imposed a discipline of isolation, work and silence, in other respects, they differed. Foucault considers how such disciplinary practices and methods of punishment produced the 'docile bodies' of modernity. But his discussion of the prisoner's body[83] cannot fully take into account the differences between men and women. Male and female prisoners assumed a particular relationship to the institutions of discipline and punishment, and bodily inscriptions such as headshaving had different meanings. Rather than producing a 'docile' body, headshaving became for women fuel for resistance and mobilisation. These distinctions between men's and women's experience need to be understood within the framework of the peculiar nature of female incarceration.

Femininity: Inside/out

In January 1829, J. D'Arcy, the magistrate of George Town, wrote to the Colonial Secretary that it was reported to him by Robert Graves—the superintendent in charge of the local female factory—that 'some persons supposed to belong to vessels laying in this harbour . . . had endeavoured to have access to the women in the factory and so far succeeded'. Evidently, the sailors were able to 'convey spirits to them by getting the Women to hand down a cord by which some liquor was hauled up by them and which was discovered the following morning'. The women, it was observed, were 'much affected by drink' and a tin vessel was found which 'had a strong smell of liquor'. The sailors had 'thrown a stone at the window boards' at which point the women got up and received the spirits'. D'Arcy took the precaution 'of placing some men in ambush to endeavour to seize the persons in question', should they attempt to gain further access to the factory. As a consequence, the constable on duty, Constable King, was dismissed for, had he performed his duty, 'it is quite impossible that the circumstances would have occurred'.[84] Others observed that provisions such as 'tobacco, tea, sugar, chocolate, coffee, snuff, rum and various other articles' were bought and sold amongst the prisoners, with the turnkeys and officers being complicit.[85]

The female factories were peculiar in that inmates came and went and there was continual contact with outside society. This made a mockery of the prisons as places of reform or of punishment. The *True Colonist* noted with disgust that the inadequate management of the factory meant that the prisoners 'had no dread of the factory', and that 'the system of discipline . . . has been so careless, that instead of being useful, our women servants, are, in nine cases out of ten, positively nuisances'.[86] The *Colonial Times*, in 1827, had foreseen these problems when it had resisted the suggestion that the female prison in Hobart be located at the distillery. 'If they can scale the high walls', the paper noted, 'which surround the playground of their present seminary . . . these pretty misses will very easily elude the vigilance [at] . . . the distillery at Cascade'. As for the potential for sexual activity, 'five or six daring fellows could set the whole "sisterhood" at liberty any night'.[87] Despite the refined system of classification and surveillance introduced by Governors Arthur, Darling and Gipps between 1820 and the 1840s, the female factories retained this peculiar characteristic. In the remote prisons, like those in Ross, George Town and Launceston, there was possibly less security surrounding the prison walls. Arthur noted in 1829 that the factory at George Town had been 'ill adopted either for the punishment or reformation of female convicts' because of the remoteness of the situation, and 'the insecurity of the prisoners'. It was recommended that the prison be moved to Launceston, where employment could 'conveniently be provided for the women, and a more effective system of discipline introduced'.[88]

The system of assignment and domestic service formalised the interaction between the inside and outside worlds. Further intrusions into female prisons were made by the women's organisations that entered its walls. Unlike male prisoners, women were also under surveillance from the bourgeois gaze of female charitable organisations. Like their counterparts in Britain and the United States, where 'Lady Visitors' posited themselves as pillars of feminine virtue, women reformers in Australia attempted to avert female prisoners from their wayward path through example.[89] In New South Wales, a Ladies' Committee for the 'Charitable Superintendence' of female convicts was formed to visit prisons, with the aim of imparting 'persuasions to good conduct' and rewarding women of good character with 'pecuniary rewards or presents of clothes'. Women were also to be visited on the ship so the ladies might 'encourage the most deserving by small presents which will be provided for that purpose'.[90] Eliza Darling, the governor's wife, conducted moral instruction classes as well as classes in reading, writing and 'domestic' skills.[91] Like Fry, on whom she modelled herself, Darling envisaged that her committee would promote 'morality and honesty' among women in the female factory. The committee offered monetary reward to any woman from the factory who completed one year as a satisfactorily assigned servant.[92] As others have noted, philanthropic work and visiting prisons was one way in which white middle-class women could enter into public life and this was certainly the case in Australia.[93] The Board of

Management of the Parramatta Female Factory reported the formation of the committee with enthusiasm:

> the Board have much pleasure in adverting to the circumstance of the formation and introduction into the Establishment of a Ladies' Committee . . . the object of which is . . . to inculcate moral instruction, and excite and raise into being a better feeling for their condition and a desire to improve (by becoming good Servants) their stations in Society.[94]

Evidently they had some success as the Board reported a year later that 'The Ladies who have with so much humanity formed themselves into a Committee of Inspection . . . have been productive, in some instances, of improvement in their attainments and conduct'.[95]

But in 1840, Governor Gipps argued against the continuation of such a committee. Although not 'unmindful of the desire . . . that a Committee of Ladies should be established to superintend [the factory] gratuitously', he claimed it would clash with the authority of the visiting magistrate, 'in whom the principal authority over the whole Establishment is now vested'.[96] This observation was made, despite the fact that the Committee Inquiring into Female Convict Prison Discipline was informed in 1841 that convict women were more likely to respond to female rather than male reformers. In her testimony Mrs Hutchinson added that 'I think they would pay more attention to the ladies'.[97]

Another group that took an interest in the deliverance of convict women was the order of Catholic nuns, the Sisters of Charity. In 1839 these Catholic sisters visited the factory to inculcate religious teachings and values. In April they were met with 'obstacles' but this provided a 'stimulus to persevere in the good work'.[98] By Christmas they had recorded that 'great indeed has been the change in the female prisoners of the Factory . . . Religion has gradually effected what could never be done by human means or coercive measures . . . [there is a] visible reformation in the conduct of the women'.[99]

Whether or not they were successful, both women's groups were intruders from the outside who entered the factory, attempting to reaffirm particular values and norms of feminine behaviour. While these groups may have had some influence, convict women shaped a femininity that was distinctive and defined by their own subculture. Their 'rough culture' assumed a particular expression within the factory walls and through their smoking, singing and recalcitrant behaviour, convict women certainly challenged conventional models of femininity, which the Ladies' Committee and Sisters of Charity were attempting to make the norm.[100]

But it was 'contamination' amongst themselves which most alarmed the authorities. 'Pollution' became associated with the contaminating

influence the convict women had on each other. Mrs Hutchinson had
also testified to the inquiry that 'it would be advisable that they should
have separate sleeping places. They would be less liable to contamination'.[101] Hutchinson empathised with those women who attempted to
'escape from the cursing and swearing and obscenity'. 'It must be a miserable thing', she observed, 'for a woman having any sense of propriety
left to be in one of these yards'.[102] This 'rough culture' suited some
women and not others; some wanted to return after assigned service
while others, perhaps previously subjected to violence or sexual assaults,
dreaded it.

Femininity became a controversial issue, for in the movement between
the prison and the wider penal society, the prisons were perceived as
places of contamination of women's femininity, rather than places of
reform. Superintendent Robert Person at Launceston expressed such a
concern. In 1841 he claimed that he did not think the 'women consider
it a punishment'. He could not prevent things being thrown over the
wall, which adjoined the public street, nor prevent the submatron obtaining objects for the women. Overcrowding produced contamination, and
the conduct was generally 'most depraved and disquieting'. What was of
most concern to him was that women's femininity was being debased and
corrupted. He claimed the depravity of women was evident:

> a girl coming into the factory however virtuous or modest she may be on
> entering, must inevitably become corrupted in a short time. I have known
> numerous instances of girls and women, whom I have considered of a better
> description at first but who have come in a second time nearly or quite as bad
> as the worst.[103]

By the late 1830s, the question of women, prisons and reform had
reached a heightened level of anxiety within the press, which bordered
on hysteria. The *Colonial Times* concluded that the female factory in Van
Diemen's Land

> is totally unfit for the purpose to which it is at present appropriated. As a place
> of punishment it is worse than useless—it is mischievous and utterly in-
> efficacious . . . calculated to demoralise and deteriorate, certainly not to
> amend and reform.[104]

In British penal history, the 1840s were characterised by efforts to
introduce the separate cell system into prisons. The women were not in
total solitude, being visited by staff, but they were quarantined from
friends and relatives.[105] The separate cell system was advocated as an
effective means of punishment. In the Parramatta factory there were
three levels of cells. The first was comprised of thirty-six dark cells, each

cell 8 feet by 5 feet, which had no windows. The second and third levels each had eighteen cells and were 12 feet by 8 feet in size. These had small windows. The dark cells were intended to house those convict women who had committed serious crimes in the colonies.[106] The introduction of such cells would certainly have limited the movement of goods. Women would also no longer have been in close proximity to each other, which would have affected the dynamics of their own subculture. It was during this time that convict discipline shifted from assignment to probation, where prisoners were segregated rather than dispersed throughout the free population.[107] The women's prisons drew the attention of prison reformers interested in experimenting with different forms of surveillance, confinement and cell development. The 'double cells', which combined both the inner or sleeping cell and the outer or working cell, were designed for the Cascades female factory in the early 1830s.[108] The 1841 report concluded that the separate system was 'likely to be more lasting than those with which the female, after the shock of conviction, and expatriation, enters upon her existence in the new world'. It was hoped that the power of the separate system, 'expelling bad feeling and . . . filling the mind with ideas of an opposite tendency', would benefit convict women, but more particularly operate as an effective mode of reform. It was the separate system that the report 'unhesitatingly' recommended as the means 'above all others the best suited to the exigencies of the moral state of the wretched inmates'.

There was an optimism and a hope placed in the effectiveness of the separate cells proposal. In 1848, the Comptroller-General advised that the separate compartments were of crucial importance. There was accommodation for 100 women in separate cells by the end of 1848, and the authorities were convinced that the 'internal discipline and general efficiency' of the prison would be 'greatly improved by the arrangements now in progress'. The solitary cells as they existed were ineffective. They were 'so defective' he observed, 'that refractory, noisy women confined in them, disturb the whole establishment, keeping other, vicious, troublesome prisoners in the yards in a state of excitement and remaining unsubdued themselves'. It was hoped that such evils would be averted and the separate apartments would 'preserve the general tranquillity of the prison, and be greatly dreaded by even the most turbulent and otherwise unmanageable women'.[109]

But the dark cells, supported by Gipps, were condemned by progressive reformers as 'most fearful dungeons' where there was 'no pure air'. In 1841, the *Austral Asiatic Review* argued that the plight of the female factory had to be addressed. The *Review* expressed alarm at the seemingly ineffective form of punishment exercised in the factory. 'Pollution' and 'contamination' again assumed a particular significance,

for the factory was perceived not as a reformatory or punishing institution, but one which further contaminated. 'Such close immediate evil
contact', the paper noted, 'would corrupt an angel'.[110]

In a society that aimed to be both reformatory and scientific, some
circles considered the dark cells inappropriate for the punishment of
women. Other reformers declared these cells 'horribly offensive', and
claimed 'we would not incarcerate a human being, much less a female, in
a dark and filthy hole, into which we would not put a hog'. It was within
the prison walls that contamination and disorder took place, rather than
outside, where there was real chance of reform. The dark cells were
terrifying and awesome. The combination of lack of natural light and
solitary confinement within a small, claustrophobic space was surely an
especially severe form of punishment. The impact of such confinement
during the nineteenth century can never be fully known or understood.
But it was the case that women in British and American prisons who were
placed under these conditions recorded a high rate of mental disorder.
Although these cells were an efficient means of surveillance, it was
realised by the governments of the day that the particular form of brutality they introduced into the prison system was not the most effective
way of reforming prisoners. Gipps's reforms lasted a mere two years and
in 1840 he was given the directive to allow light into the dark cells.[111]

Assignment continued to be considered the most desirable method of
reform for women, who could then draw on the positive models of
behaviour of their masters and mistresses. The report of inquiry of 1841
found that confinement had produced 'the worst and most revolting
consequences' and recommended the 'continuance of assignment
because the evidence before us proves it with equal certainty to be
beneficial in its operation'. In the factory, intercourse was restricted to
the 'degraded of the sex'; in assignment, female convicts were
'influenced by the examples and benefited by the advice of the virtuous'.
The testimonies to the inquiry reinforced this view. Mrs Hutchinson
claimed that 'a continuance in one of the wards . . . finishes a woman's
education in vice and takes away her sense of shame. The feeling seems
to abate with every return to the building but is again somewhat revived
when she is sentenced to the cells'. While she was willing to concede that
some households of domestic service were undesirable, she expressed
confidence that they provided 'good example and regular employment'.
The prison contained 'moral evils' that 'have existed all along though
have increased in proportion as the Buildings have increased and
become crowded'. Van Diemen's Land's superintendent of convicts,
Josiah Spode, concurred, claiming that 'the oftener a woman is sent into
the factory, the more reckless she becomes particularly if placed in the
yards among the other women'. He argued that assignment would

provide better examples for convict women, 'both in a moral point of view and in teaching them those useful habits of domestic life'. The police magistrate, John Price, perhaps best summarised the view of the prison by administrators and the police:

> To the ill behaved it is not a place of punishment: the labour is not sufficient; they have not the means of enforcing regularity or keeping up a degree of discipline which makes confinement irksome; I believe it to be a punishment to the well conducted on their first entering the House of correction, from the conduct and conversation of women with whom they are compelled to associate.[112]

Within and outside the factories, femininity continued to be a source of concern as authorities became alarmed at the ways in which the prisons corrupted women. For some, it provided a space to go beyond expectations of them, while for others, it could have been oppressive. The opportunities within the prison for convict women to redefine their femininity were limited; the punishment of headshaving effectively stripped them of any feminine attributes, and all women considered it abhorrent and a violation. This form of punishment challenged their feminine identity and threw into relief the tensions between the inside and outside worlds they inhabited. Convict women represented the tensions of one sort of femininity within the colonies. Convict children and, by definition, convict mothering, represented another repository for colonial anxieties.

PART TWO

Family Life and the Convict System

In Part Two, the shaping of gendered, sexual and racial identities is further explored. As in Part One, these identities are examined in the context of punishment and resistance. But in this section we also consider how women's incarceration made all aspects of family life problematic, especially motherhood, marriage, and the treatment of children.

The theme of motherhood begins this section, with particular reference to the contradictory place of convict maternity in colonial society. While on the one hand colonial authorities wished to feminise convict women and populate the state, on the other, they denied them the essence of nineteenth-century femininity: maternity. The practice of removing children from their convict mothers recalls the treatment of Aboriginal mothers. 'Motherhood' pointed to concerns about the civilised and uncivilised; the pure and the polluted.

These themes are further explored in Chapter Six, in an analysis of the male and female orphan schools. Convict orphans were both punished and protected; they were the source of social and political anxiety. Racial purity and virility—the cornerstones of British imperialism—defined understandings of the 'orphan', largely as a reaction to fear of contamination from Aboriginal children. Both sanitary and racial cleanliness defined British identity.

Finally, the meanings attached to understandings of motherhood, fatherhood, and in the identities of being free or bound come into focus in the final chapter. The motifs of the abandoning, wandering and absent mother and the flight of the father are examined for cultural meaning. The central theme of Part Two is the various familial identities that are shaped in colonial society: of father and mother; of child; of free and bound. Interwoven with this is the theme of the complex relationship between the oppressed and the oppressor. Convicts resisted by flight and forms of defiance, like sulkiness and gossip in the case of children. But the response by the state to such behaviour was never unified as others have suggested. The concern for the plight of children, expressed by surgeons in Chapter Five, and the ambiguous response to the situation of orphans by authorities in Chapter Six suggest that the expression of power relations was more complex.

These chapters highlight the difficulties in setting up new forms of family life, and the enormous problems authorities faced in attempting to establish institutions that would replace convict family life.

CHAPTER 5

Convict Mothering

In 1838, the *Colonial Times* publicised the deaths of two infants who died in separate incidents in the female factory in Hobart. The first case involved the prisoner Mary Vowles. The paper warned that the death of her baby had been the result of some 'gross, most culpable, unpardonable neglect somewhere'. Vowles had been sentenced to the factory in early February. Her child had been permitted to go with her, in order that she might continue to suckle the infant, who was about twelve months old and teething. On arrival at the factory, however, he was taken from her by the overseer of the weaning ward. Vowles was then dressed in the customary prison dress 'sent to her yard, and separated from her infant'. She pleaded not to be parted from him. But mother and child were separated, despite a special order obtained by the overseer from Josiah Spode, the superintendent, which allowed Vowles access to her child. The child had arrived in good health, 'well looking and strong', but after five days, his health had deteriorated to such an extent that Vowles could not recognise her baby. He looked 'sickly', had 'altered so much for the worse', and 'neither did the child recognise its mother till she had it in her arms for some time'. Vowles, who had only seen the infant once since her incarceration, begged permission to see her dying child. Her desperate response challenged the claim so often made that because of the high mortality rate in the prisons, poor women watched with indifference when their children died. Vowles was refused permission, but contacted her husband who subsequently obtained a remission of his wife's sentence, after she had been there just over a month. But it was too late: the child died five weeks after its admission into the factory.

The *Colonial Times* reported this incident with anger and disgust. 'Where is the medical man', demanded the editor, 'who understood the principles of his profession, and possessed one grain of humanity . . .?

where was . . . Mrs. Hutchinson'—'herself a mother'? There was never a 'more pitiable and heart-rending spectacle' than the 'remains of this poor infant'.

At the inquest, Elizabeth Cato, the assistant matron and midwife at the factory, claimed it was customary for mothers to see their children once a month, but if the children were very young, they were permitted to have their children with them. The other women who were interviewed at the inquest appeared not to notice that anything had gone amiss with the child. Anne Spruce, the overseer of the weaning ward, who took 'charge of certain children', did not see anything the matter with the child when she took charge of it. The child, she could see, was ill, but not very ill. Elizabeth Bennett, another prisoner, observed that the child looked 'very thin' and she 'did not think there was any milk in his mother's breast'. But she was too preoccupied with her own baby to attend to another child.

Louisa Fuller, also a prisoner, recalled that Mary Vowles was crying because her baby had been put into the nursery. She had seen her feed her child once, when they both went to visit their children, and had reassured her that she should not despair at the bruises on his body, because 'children will fall about'. The doctor admitted that the mother should have been allowed to suckle the child, and it would have been 'more judicious' to have permitted her to do so. The jury of fifteen found that the confined state of the nurseries and the want of proper precaution at the time of receiving the child induced the death.[1]

The ease with which the child died was not in itself unusual given the high rate of mortality in the prisons. The female factory was intended to house children but it certainly endangered their health. In the factory at Hobart, over an eight-year period between 1830 and 1838, Josiah Spode reported the deaths of 208 children out of a total of 794.[2] Although there were limitations as to how mothers could be accompanied by children, contemporary accounts note the large numbers of children from both convict and destitute mothers who were housed in the female factories. The factories served as nurseries where women could provide for their children until they were about three years old.[3] It was also a place where mothers did not have to breastfeed their children in seclusion, an important aspect of nineteenth-century understandings of maternity.[4] From 1833, babies in the factory were removed from their mothers at nine months to make the women available for assignment.[5] The authorities expressed a concern that the children's health would be affected if they continued to associate with criminals, but the women complained that it was the conditions of the prisons and diet they were given that did not allow them to adequately feed their babies.

The authorities' claims seem difficult to reconcile with the fact that the colonial authorities were insistent that the population be boosted. The poor facilities within the factories for adequate mothering, facilities that were offered by the state, came under increased scrutiny, not only by the colonial press but also by doctors and officials who were disturbed by the alarming number of deaths that were taking place within the walls of confinement.

A few months after the incident involving Mary Vowles, the *Colonial Times* reported that the nursery had been removed from the factory to a separate building, but that the move had been attended to with 'a degree of mismanagement'. The press considered it their duty to make public the 'disastrous evils' to which the poor children were now exposed since their removal from the factory. The children, it was reported, were subject to great and shameful neglect, and the women in the nursery were openly disgraceful, drunk and promiscuous. The danger to their well-being, then, was not simply a matter of having a poor diet, but also that 'the moral condition of these poor children is bad and deplorable enough, without any physical suffering thereto'. These children were under the charge and protection of the government, 'in so much as they are deprived of the care of their parents', and thus it was the duty of the government to pay attention to their health and comfort. The children were 'greatly and shamefully neglected'. Earlier, in April 1838, the *Colonial Times* had stated that 'it is a mystery to us how they at all survive their miserable incarceration. Some of them are in good and robust health, but by far the greater number are puny and pale'. The nursery lacked pure air and exercise, which were 'essential to the health and growth of children'.[6]

In May 1838, when the second death occurred in the factory, the paper called 'immediately and promptly' for the removal of Mrs Hutchinson. The *Colonial Times* insisted that Governor Sir John Franklin order the 'immediate removal of the children', and that they be sent away where they may enjoy 'the benefit of pure air and bright sunshine'. The paper reported the case and published the coroner's report into the death of William Spry, an infant of one and a half years old, who had been born in the female factory. Mary Spry, the mother and prisoner, was permitted to nurse her child for eleven or twelve months and after it was weaned, to keep him under her own care and nurse him for fourteen weeks, when she was removed from the nursing ward to the second yard. Spry was permitted to see her child every month and, although she had left the prison on assignment was allowed to see her child whenever she called at the factory, sometimes twice, sometimes three times a week. She applied to obtain her child, but when the head nurse brought him to her, she claimed the child was very ill, was emaciated from being starved and would not live. Jane Dutton, the nurse in the weaning ward, claimed that the child had an abundance of food, and insisted that she 'gave that child the same attention that I would my own'. Dutton could not say what occasioned the child to waste away. Other nurses who were examined supported the testimony. The jury found that the child had the disease 'marasmus', and had died in a 'natural' way rather than from want of food or because of neglect.[7]

In the same year, two further inquests were held into prison deaths which exposed the inadequate conditions within the nurseries. An inquiry followed the death in the factory of Elisabeth Lush. Elizabeth Flint, a prisoner, who was an overseer of the children in the nursery, had been in the nursery three or four weeks when she observed that the child was 'very bad in the bowels'. The mother of the child was absent during the course of the child's illness as she was at the time assigned as a servant. Flint thought the child had died of 'a fever attending the complaint it has in its bowels'.

The child's environment would not have alleviated these ailments. Flint pointed to the overcrowded conditions, which made the nurseries unsanitary. No less than thirteen women and twenty-six children were housed in two rooms of 47 feet long and $11^1/_2$ feet wide. The yard was so small, and confined by high walls, that there was no 'necessary circulation of air'. The children were, however, being fed adequately. Those who had been weaned were given 'porridge and new milk for their breakfast; white bread and tea for their luncheon, fresh meat and soup for their dinner; and tea and bread in the afternoon, half a pint of milk, 3 quarters of a pound of bread per day for each child'. Flint pointed out that overcrowding was the major problem. 'Within the last 7 months', she testified, 'I had as many as 42 children and 14 women in those rooms at one time'. She believed that the health of the children would improve with 'some playground' and that the children do receive 'the full portion of food as far as they can take it'. The women, Flint asserted, could not be blamed for the deaths of children. 'The women in my opinion', she claimed 'take as much care of the children as free women might'. Although there had been a change of nurses, they too had been exemplary in performing their duties. 'The children fret as much after the nurses', she stressed, 'as they do after their mothers'.

The surgeon, Edward Bedford, agreed, saying that the 'weaned children should not be kept in the present nursery, & that an enlarged & more commodious place is absolutely necessary'. He observed that Elisabeth Lush had come into the factory 'in a weak state', and that the conditions had thwarted her recovery. But Lush 'came to her death in a natural way, and not through neglect or injury from any other person'.

The second inquest also disclosed the unhealthy conditions that were an everyday part of incarceration for both mother and child. The high incidence of death within the prisons and understandings in regard to convict 'mothering' seemed difficult to reconcile with preoccupations of the Crown to sustain the birth-rate. In March 1838 it was ascertained that Barbara Hemming had died from the effects of 'diarrhoea and fever'. The lack of space and light was identified as the problem. In this inquest also, the insufficient space for the exercise of the women and children was commented on. 'The limited space . . . and high surrounding walls of the nursery yards might be injurious to the health of women suckling children therein', noted the doctor, John Learmouth. A sudden transition from heat to cold was the reason for the prevalence of diarrhoea. Inquests were not held for all those who had died in the factories; the cause of death of others would remain unknown. William Cato, assistant superintendent of the female factory, admitted that there had been 'no register of deaths kept in this establishment exclusively for that purpose'. He claimed that it was not standard practice to interrogate the cause of each death. 'Two children have died within the last ten days', he admitted, 'without inquests being held on them'. He identified the lack of sunlight as a problem. In the prison, the 'sun shines a very little into the yard at noon day'. For about 'four months in the year, the sun does not shine on the flags of the nursery yard at all'. He agreed that these circumstances were 'injurious to the health of the inmates of that yard, especially the children'. This, he claimed, equally applied to the hospital yard. He had noticed that the 'air of the room in which the women and their children occupy as nurses is very offensive and pernicious in my judgement'. The close proximity of so many bodies produced a lingering odour. Cato described the odour in the nursery room two or three hours after the inmates had been locked up as 'very offensive . . . from the heat . . . arising from their evacuations'. The same stench was present in the weaning ward.[8]

Betsy Inchbald, a prisoner and nursery foreman, claimed that when there had been sixteen women and sixteen children in the nursery, the air had become 'very bad'. She was more direct about the impact of such conditions. Inchbald believed that such an environment had induced sickness in the lower room. The yard, she asserted, 'was very damp during winter. There was no sunshine in the yard in the winter, and little in the summer'. The lack of space and light was poorly compensated by the food given to mothers and their children, which was deficient in both quality and quantity. 'I find the want of more food and a change of diet' and admitted,

> I do not find that the food allowance is sufficient to produce milk sufficient for the nourishment of a child without other food . . . The other women confined in the room of which I have charge complain equally with me of the insufficiency of the quantity of the food allowed—When I speak of the

insufficiency of the food I speak more of its quality than its quantity—The women in my room complain of head aches and the damp weather now and then—we find the place very unhealthy the first thing in the morning from the confined state of the room—we are obliged to throw open the windows— The milk has been very bad—we all complain of it—we have had better meal than this.[9]

Mary Owen made similar complaints when asked to relate her experiences. She was the overseer of the big nursery, where the children were already weaned. Twenty-five children and ten women inhabited the crowded nursery. Their diet was poor and prisoners lacked exercise. She reported that women 'perform the operations of nature in the room'. With thirty-five bodies sleeping in such a room, Owen claimed, 'we are of course much annoyed every night by the smell consequent thereon— The doors are opened now at six o'clock—When the doors are opened it is exceedingly offensive'.[10]

These deaths of children in the female factories were coming to the attention of the inhabitants of Van Diemen's Land through a number of reports in the colonial press. This reportage needs to be placed in context, for the *Colonial Times* had launched a sustained attack on the authorities for their lack of concern and incompetence in relation to the care of the children. The newspaper began a campaign against the administration of Governor Franklin and what it perceived to be the incompetence, inhumanity and inadequate function of the female factory.

In the 1830s criticisms of the female prisons were also being voiced elsewhere. Shortly before these attacks, the Molesworth Committee had begun its investigations into the convict system. It was critical of transportation, the arbitrary system of assignment and the inadequate punishment of women. Franklin was not only having to defend the transportation system from this chorus of complaint, but was also caught in the mounting pressure for a free and self-governing colony. It was within these currents that the *Colonial Times* insisted on scrutinising the workings of the factory. In March 1838, it reported that the female factory was of a 'frightful and most disgusting nature', and argued that 'great alteration' was required in the 'moral and physical' management of the factory and that, from 'every possible point of view, it is worse than useless, because it is pernicious, and ruinous to what little morality, or character its inmates might occasionally possess'. Successive governors, the paper argued, had only paid gratuitous attention to the factory. Arthur 'occasionally paid . . . a formal visit, in order to note the same in his official journal', while Franklin had visited it once, 'merely out of curiosity, and not for any purpose of investigation or enquiry'. The administration of the factory was not conducted 'with that attention to impartiality and fairness, which ought to characterise it'. In terms of the management of the women, it was observed that 'the strictness of discipline is not very abundant', because additional food and luxuries, like tea, sugar and tobacco, could be purchased. Theatricals—like 'singing, telling funny stories, and, of course, recounting former adventures'—also took place to 'pass away the dull and lagging hours. Many declare that they would rather be in the factory than elsewhere'.[11] The paper continued a relentless campaign to expose what it believed were the inadequacies of the factory system. It was during this coverage that the deaths in the factory of the two children were reported, thereby confirming complaints.

Why did the government authorities continue to allow these conditions to prevail in Van Diemen's Land when it was in their interests to promote an increase in the birth-rate? Convict motherhood and mothering occupied an ambiguous and contradictory place in colonial society. While ideas about maternity and sexuality—the civilised and uncivilised, the polluted and the clean body—came together in discussions on maternity, unlike in many other historical contexts, in this case maternity did not allow for the expression of female virtue. Convict motherhood was not valued, romanticised or idealised; procreation was valued, but convict mothering carried negative connotations. 'Mothers', writes Jane Flax, 'represent the impossible borders, the confounding of the dualities of western culture'. They are at once nature and culture, subject and other. The nursing mother's breast, she argues, defies the border between sexuality and maternity, between woman as the man's object of desire and as the mother of his children.[12]

What is important to explore in the paradox of convict mothers is that while the colonial authorities attempted to 'feminise' convict women through their productive and reproductive labour, in fact, maternity—a crucial part of nineteenth-century femininity—was denied to them. To deny convict women maternity was to negate the expression of a range of emotions and an identity through which to express these emotions. It worked as an effective form of disciplinary action for it punished women not only by the torture of the mind or an inscription on the body, but through the power of emotional yearning created by absence. The force of this deprivation would become apparent years later when, once free, some former female prisoners would apply—with desperation and hope —to retrieve their children from the orphan schools where they had been placed at a tender age.

Most historians, while discussing colonial motherhood, have focused on practices within families or discussed the issue in regard to the insistence by government authorities to procreate. The particular paradoxes of notions of 'motherhood' during the early part of the nineteenth century, however, have not been examined. As we will see later the motifs of the abandoning mother and the wandering mother—both of which resonate with references to Aboriginal women—are writ large as symbols of cultural anxiety. What is implicit in these representations is the tension between the good and the bad mother: convict women were by definition bad mothers, who were polluted and diseased and had the capacity to contaminate their children. There was a clearly marked tension between the conception of a good mother, defined in terms of nurturing the child and being involved with it, and the elaborate boundaries and restrictions that were established by the authorities to prevent this amongst convict women. On the one hand, understandings of maternity stipulated that it was in the interests of the state for women to embrace their mothering and yet, on the other, motherhood amongst convict women was devalued and their identity as mothers was disavowed.

These attitudes need to be seen within the context of women as reproductive fodder. It is indisputable that the reproductive function of convict women came under the scrutiny of the state. The Select Committee on Transportation of 1812 noted that while the committee was aware that the women who were sent out were of the 'most abandoned description', 'these were the mothers of a great part of the inhabitants now existing in the colony' and from this 'stock only can a reasonable hope be held out of a rapid increase to the population; upon which increase . . . its growing prosperity in great measure depends'.[13] This became an ongoing point of concern and the authorities encouraged procreation. The birth-rate rose rapidly during the first few decades of settlement. The number of children in the colony had increased from thirty-six in 1788 to 862 by the end of the 1790s, when it was said 'there were as many children as women'.[14]

But understandings about motherhood also need to be considered beyond ideas of population increase promoted by the state. The contradictions in state ideology point to an anxiety regarding who should mother, and what proper procedure was involved for adequate mothering. Kociumbas observes that while convict mothers were perceived to be depraved and children to be innocent, this attitude brought them under greater control of the nascent colonial state.[15] In the female factories, where the following discussion is focused, the authorities expressed surprise at the fact that convict women were capable of being good mothers, for to be so was to be nurturing, emotional and loving. Mrs Slea, matron of the nursery in the Hobart factory, observed that 'there are few who do not conduct themselves as good mothers'.[16]

These opinions, however, were given little credence and throughout the period of transportation, convicts were deemed unsuitable mothers. We can glimpse the depth of this opinion by considering the popular view of the need to keep children away from female convict servants: they were not to be given the dignity of motherhood. One observer to the colony noted that 'female convict servants are deeply initiated in all the mysteries of human depravity', and 'in the very inmost recesses of home, vice is inculcated, and taught, until desire and ability produce practice'. For children in the presence of female convicts, the 'book of vice and sin stands open before· them, with all its thoughts, longings and desires revealed'.[17] John Price, the police magistrate of Hobart, testified to the Inquiry into Female Convict Prison Discipline that it would be 'beneficial to the children to cut off the connexion with the mother'. It was girls, he observed, who suffered a 'pernicious effect' when with their parents. The boys are 'taught to disregard truth' while the girls are 'liable to suffer from the ill effects of the connexion with their parents as girls'.[18] Another observer of such events, the master of the orphan school in Van Diemen's Land, the Reverend Thomas Ewing, agreed. In no case, he insisted,

> is it advisable to admit the mothers to associate with their children; in every case I think it is a disadvantage. If the illegitimate children were kept wholly from their parents, there would be much greater chances of their turning out well.[19]

Separation of mother and child was an effective form of punishment because, unlike other punitive acts, it was inflicted on the basis of emotional distress. Slea insisted that the 'only inducement to conduct themselves well in assignment I consider to be the hope of being permitted to see their children'.

It was the authorities themselves, not the mothers, who caused the deaths of hundreds of children in the factories. The alarm expressed by doctors and officials when children died in these institutions suggests that the state's response was not uniform but was characterised by an ambiguity and anxiety about convict mothers and their mothering. In attempting to understand this response, the key points we should keep in mind are, first, that 'mothering' was discussed in terms of who should do it and how, and, second, that the ideology imposed by the state was contradictory. On the one hand, there was potential for empowerment of convict women as mothers, in terms of asserting their status as contributors to the colonial society. But the removal of children from convict women, as it was for Aboriginal women, became a potent symbol of disempowerment and dispossession.

The concerns about mothering were expressed well before the arrival of convict women in the colony. Surgeons on the ships were aware that children were being weaned at too early an age. Surgeon George Fairfowle reported the death of a child because it had been 'injudiciously weaned at the early age of three Weeks', so that the convict mother would be able to embark for the colony. Governor Darling acted swiftly to prevent it from happening again.[20] Following this incident, there were new laws introduced to prevent the embarkation of women who were breastfeeding babies under six months.[21] But it appears that fewer children died on board ship than within the enclosed walls of the female factories.[22]

As the deaths indicated, the history of children within the factories was a tale of neglect and administrative incompetence. In Van Diemen's Land, overcrowding within the prisons and the high mortality rate forced the authorities to transfer a nursery to Dynnyrne House, to which children from the Launceston and Hobart factories were moved in 1842. But this made little difference to the number of deaths within the prison. When Slea was questioned in 1841 about the nature of the nurseries, it was the overcrowded conditions that she, like many others, stressed. 'We require more room', she said, 'the building is not at all adapted to the object; the back very much exposed—the apartments are much too close and crowded especially at night—the attics are very much confined'.[23]

It was no surprise, then, that when a new factory for women was established in Ross, in 1848, the mortality rate declined. In 1851 a new wing was built in the Ross female factory, but an outbreak of disease created further anxieties, with 102 babies dying between 1851 and 1852. It was somewhat predictable that, when an investigation was conducted into the convict department in 1855, it was found that these deaths were due to mismanagement and neglect.[24]

This incompetence extended to hygiene within the prisons, although medical superintendents were instructed to maintain cleanliness and order within the female factories. They were ordered to keep them 'sufficiently clean and thoroughly ventilated' and the nursery was to be in a 'neat, clean and orderly manner and . . . like all such establishments, always ready for public inspection'. It was up to the surgeon to provide guidance by weekly inspection and to instruct the midwife.[25] The nurse or midwife was responsible for the efficient running of the hospital and nursery.[26] Both of them were to follow the instructions of the medical officer. While there were some experienced midwives, most, according to some surgeons, were untrained.[27] 'On no account', stipulated the instructions to nurses and midwives, were they 'to deviate' from the instructions. Midwives were to take charge of the linen and ensure that the patients received the medicines prescribed by the surgeon.

By the nineteenth century, the medicalisation of childbirth had become the norm in Britain. Likewise, in the colonies, the midwife assumed a secondary status to that of the doctor, a development that reflected a trend in Europe and the United States.[28] As doctors assumed control of obstetrical practice, the midwife became redundant. Her skills

were no longer considered viable, as scientific and technological expertise were valued over the knowledge and understanding the midwives
could offer.

The midwife was to attend to the sick, and 'behave kindly and atten-
tively to the patients and see that the nurses under her do the same;
and that the rules for their guidance are fully and strictly carried into
effect'.[29] The overcrowded conditions made it virtually impossible to
carry out these instructions. Surgeons also complained that there was a
shortage of midwifery equipment.[30] In 1829, the overcrowded state of
the factories moved the board of management of the female factory in
Parramatta to deter women from using it as a maternity home, and to
urge the government to 'oblige the Fathers to provide for their illegitimate offspring by the payment of a sum of money, or a weekly rate for
its support'.[31] These circumstances merely exacerbated the extra-
ordinarily difficult conditions for childbirth in the colony. The assistance
that surgeons and midwives could obtain was minimal, and in some cases
women, both convict and free, were forced to work up to the time of
delivery.

Nutrition was another area where authorities were negligent despite
some efforts by the medical authorities to ensure adequate provisions
were available. The stress was on quantity rather than quality. Children
under a year old were served 6 ounces of bread and 8 ounces or half a
pint of milk, while those from one to three years old were served 12
ounces of bread, 16 ounces or a pint of milk, and 4 ounces of beef or
mutton.[32] After it was discovered that the children were given bread and
tea for breakfast and supper, the board recommended that porridge
made of Indian corn or wheaten meal with half a pint of milk would be
healthier.[33] The diet was considered to be 'good' by the doctors, who
concluded it was the children's 'diseased constitutions' that prevented
them from having the 'strength to bear up against the bowel complaints'.
Diarrhoea and convulsion were the most common forms of illness
amongst the children.[34] The children from the female factories were
identified as being 'more subject to disease of the worst kinds than any of
the others'.[35]

Michael Belcher asserts that 'the evidence indicates that nearly two
thirds of children who died did so in the first twelve to fifteen months
and that those who survived this period . . . had a reasonably good
chance of reaching adulthood'. During the 1830s, the authorities kept
children in the factories until they were three years old, when they were
sent to the orphanages. In Hobart, weaning took place between nine and
twelve months. Diarrhoea was common, and exacerbated by suddenly
weaning the child.[36] Many believed during the nineteenth century that
'no woman could love the living proof of her sin' and an 'unwed mother

was not fit to be called a mother at all'.[37] However, the authorities were not indifferent to the rate of mortality in the prisons, and this must be taken into account when considering how convict motherhood was perceived.

The inquiry into Barbara Hemming's death in 1838 concluded that children could not take exercise except in a 'wet flagged yard', where the 'sun's rays never penetrate' and 'it is never otherwise than in a wet state'. The confined space of two small rooms, each about 28 feet by 12 feet, in which there were seventy human beings, was 'most injurious to the infants confined there'. The dark cells were 'extremely offensive' and the amount of food 'extremely limited'. The fact that not all deaths were investigated was deemed inadequate, and the jury noted that 'Twenty deaths have taken place since the first of January (last) and . . . two have taken place within the last fourteen days, and that inquests have not been held'.[38]

This concern for the predicament of children, convict women and the state of nurseries was shared by others within the government bureaucracy. By the 1830s, there was a range of difficulties experienced by the officials and management of the factories. In January 1831, Samuel Sherlock resigned from the female factory in George Town, claiming that the establishment was different 'from what I expected and Mrs Sherlock's large young family being most of them little girls and the establishment being a very improper place for young children, there being no detached apartments for young children . . .'[39]

Josiah Spode, the superintendent of convicts, wrote in July 1832 requesting an improvement in provisions for the factory children. With the number of children having increased, and 'no clothes having been furnished to the establishment for them', he requested they be sent as soon as possible, as 'at present they are very badly off'. More importantly, he requested that 'it would be desirable to send some of them and their mothers to Hobart Town', as accommodation at the factory was insufficient.[40] Children who were confined in a crowded space drew considerable attention, but this was expressed in terms of concern for the health of the children and in terms of their mothering rather than from any concern for their mothers. The authorities were reluctant to provide funds to establish a proper nursery, in spite of the concern amongst medical authorities about the overcrowding, lack of exercise and ventilation.[41] The state proved to be an inadequate provider for the children under its charge.

But not all government authorities were indifferent and this was not a universal response. In a detailed report in April 1834, the acting assistant surgeon recommended that a nursery be built in connexion with the orphan schools so that children could be removed from the factory when they had been weaned. He concluded that from 'bad feeding, bad nursing, confinement to one spot, and want of exercise, the mortality amongst the weaned children is exceedingly great'. He observed that there had been 'dreadful effects' resulting from a particular mode of nursing, where two of the most healthy children in the factory, 'to whom the mothers had been most attentive', had been removed from their mothers for five weeks, after which it had been necessary 'to place the Children in their Mother's charge again to try and save their lives'. It was the case, he observed, that when women weaned their babies and placed them in the charge of the nurses, the 'deaths are very numerous indeed'.[42] These nurses, he observed, had no incentive or inducement for 'constant care'. The diseases that afflicted the children were caused by 'impoverished living and want of exercise' but, it was observed, 'so long as they are not weaned and require their mothers', they do well, 'but as soon as they are in the care of nurses, their deaths are very numerous'.

Another cause for concern was the way in which children had been taken from their mothers. As punishment for becoming pregnant, women had to 'suffer six months imprisonment in the crime class'. This action rendered women useless as pregnant women, but pregnancy was also a public taboo.[43] For these reasons, he recommended that a nursery be established, 'in connexion with the Orphan schools to which the children might be removed from the factory upon their being weaned'.[44]

The acting assistant surgeon in Van Diemen's Land elaborated further on the conditions under which these children were nurtured. Overcrowding appeared to be the central concern, with twenty-seven women and twenty-eight children housed in the same room. He believed that children should be removed from the female house of correction at as 'easy an age as possible', and recommended that as soon as the children were weaned, they should be removed from the prison. Therefore, only rooms for nursing children and those being weaned would be required. A nursery was thus necessary to alleviate the 'crowded state' of the rooms. A hospital, he noted, should also be established for the reception of female convict patients. Furthermore:

> proper rooms should be built for the reception of nursing children, those being weaned, and an infirmary for such as may require separation from the others ... I do not see any reason why the female hospital and the nurseries required in connexion with the female House of Correction may not be in the same yard, and under one roof.

He finished by stating that the wards of the hospital could not be further ventilated, 'there being in each apartment three ventilators as in the other upper rooms of the building'. In June 1834, a committee investigated the plight of children recommending that children should be immediately removed 'from the female House of Correction to the Orphan schools at New Town where proper nurses should be provided, and the necessary arrangements made for their accommodation'.[45]

In October 1834, the coroner found it insidious that the rigid discipline of the third class for pregnant women extended to 'unborn infant privations', which, he said, was evident when the child was born and after its birth. He found the system of management of the hospital and the nursery 'objectionable'. The coroner suggested a range of recommendations: a lying in hospital to be attached; a large playground; that the superintendent of the nursery be selected 'from amongst the deserving of the women without respect to class' and, perhaps more importantly, that those in hospital, lying in, or in nurseries, should not be considered 'as prisoners'.[46] A similar alarm was raised by the deputy superintendent of hospitals, John McClarke, who wrote to the Colonial Secretary in September 1842 after his inspection of the nursery in Liverpool Street with Dr Muir, the principal superintendent of convicts in New South Wales. 'That more disease does not exist among them', he noted, 'is surprising'. With the approach of summer, he cautioned, there was much to be feared, as it 'will bring with it serious malady'. He and Muir both saw 'the condition of the children and women in their present miserable tenement as involving great risk of health and life'.[47] Earlier, McClarke had made similar observations about the overcrowding in the female factory, claiming that it held double the number of women it was intended to house (300). It was only the 'admirable cleanliness and order maintained throughout the establishment' that countered the danger of a 'mass of human creatures congregated and confined within the limits so narrow'.[48]

Five years later, the issue of the overcrowded nursery was still on the agenda of the officials. After visiting the Nursery Hospital in Liverpool Street, the governor noted it was 'extremely crowded' to an 'unwholesome extent'. He formed a committee to investigate 'the necessity of obtaining other premises better adapted for an Hospital, and so situated as to afford the women and children the means of taking air and exercise'. The Committee (consisting of Major Kegall, royal engineer, Dr Officer, colonial surgeon, and W. Gunn, principal superintendent of convicts) concluded that the Nursery Hospital in Liverpool Street, originally a temporary arrangement, 'is unsuitable for the purpose and does not admit of any satisfactory extension or improvement from its construction and situation'. Therefore, it recommended that a new building be erected. It also observed that it was impractical to employ women in a useful way, but in a bigger building 'affording sufficient accommodation', they might be employed in sewing or knitting.[49]

It took many years for these concerns to be addressed. In 1843 in Van Diemen's Land, Josiah Spode noted that it had become impossible to provide for the wants of the children. From the smallness of the accommodation generally, he observed, 'the admission of children and suckling mothers in a place of punishment proved very detrimental to its discipline'.[50] A further five years on, and ten years after the first reports of this issue, it was noted that there was still no separate nursery at Launceston, and the female factory was 'so much crowded by lying in women and young children as to interfere very seriously with both the discipline and health of the inmates'. It was suggested that women and children be removed to Ross, to make it a depot for pregnant women. In 1855, the convict medical department was accused of 'neglect and mismanagement' and therefore causing 'excessive mortality among the infants in the nursery', although these charges were refuted.[51]

This inability on the part of the authorities to apply a uniform approach to the dilemma posed by convict mothering suggests a considerable degree of anxiety amongst them. While on the one hand, convict women were despised as mothers, and it was important that their offspring be saved, on the other, there was concern that the factory created conditions that induced death, which called into question the suitability of the state to assume the mothering role. While the eventual 'solution', the removal of the children from their mothers, did not carry with it the physical scars of other forms of punishment, it inflicted a powerful emotional pain.

For some convict women, this was a long-term punishment. Once children grew beyond their infancy, they were placed in orphan schools and the ensuing years would be spent attempting to retrieve them.

CHAPTER 6

'Wretchedness and Vice'

The 'Orphan' and the Colonial Imagination

The Reverend Samuel Marsden identified the 'problem' of the children in the early years of the colony's settlement. 'The children are very numerous', he wrote in 1799 to William Wilberforce, the evangelical parliamentarian, 'but are brought up at present in all vices of their abandoned parents'. The young girls in particular, he noticed, 'are all likely to be ruined for want of proper persons to superintend their education'.[1] The desire to protect children from their convict parents was a key motivation for the establishment of the orphan schools.

This also became a major campaign for the governor of the day, Philip King. 'Finding the greater part of the children in this colony so much abandoned to every kind of wretchedness and vice', he observed, 'I perceived the absolute necessity of something being attempted to withdraw them from the vicious examples of their abandoned parents'.[2] Like Marsden, he became aware of the 'early abuses the female part suffered', not only from the 'unprotected state they were in' but also from the 'abandoned examples of their parents'.[3] Establishing a refuge became a major priority. It was a 'distressing prospect', that the 'rising generation' could inherit their abandoned parents' 'profligate infamy' just because there was no institution where the children could be sent. In order to remove them from the 'vile examples they hourly witness', King was determined to obtain a building for their 'residence and education, which . . . will produce a great benefit to society at large and this colony in particular'.[4]

Soon after his arrival in the colony in 1800, he witnessed 'numerous children of both sexes going about the streets in the most neglected manner'. As Lieutenant Governor of Norfolk Island during the 1790s, King had established an asylum for the care of female orphans.[5] When he arrived in New South Wales he was inspired to commence a 'similar institution . . . for the purpose of withdrawing those real objects of charity and benevolence from the destructive connexions and examples of their dissolute parents in whom no reform can be expected . . .'.[6] The orphan school served a range of purposes but, primarily, King identified it as the only

> means to rescue the succeeding generation from the great depravity which exists among the present inhabitants of this colony, a sincere hope is formed of its being continued and supported with that earnestness and prospect of success that has marked its commencement.[7]

The first institution to cater for 'orphans' was the Female Orphan School, which was opened in Sydney in 1801. The Male Orphan School was opened almost twenty years later, in 1819. King established a management committee, which was responsible for the supervision and regulation of the schools. Successive Governors Bligh and Macquarie continued a commitment to the maintenance of the schools. Macquarie initiated a series of reforms and introduced rules and regulations that ensured the schools ran more efficiently. Like King, he was committed to promoting the aims of the orphan schools. He looked with confidence to the Female Orphan School as an institution that would 'prove of incalculable benefit to the moral and Religious habits of the Rising Generation, to whom the Colony of New South Wales must chiefly look forward for the formation of a moral and respectable Society'.[8] The objectives and curriculum, the daily timetable and religious instruction were defined more explicitly under Macquarie's direction.[9] The establishment of similar institutions of instruction followed, such as Eliza Darling's School of Industry for Girls, which opened in 1826.[10] Like the orphan schools, it also aimed to train young women as domestic servants, but was designed to educate a better class of young women than that of the orphan schools.[11]

In Van Diemen's Land, male and female orphan schools were established in 1828 with a committee (consisting of Archdeacon Scott, Major Kirkwood, Joseph Hone, Affleck Moodie and the Reverend William Bedford) appointed to 'meet every Saturday morning at 10 o'clock at St. David's vestry and examine and audit the Master's Accounts and Books'. Each of the schools had a master and a matron, who were also responsible for a number of servants. Governor Arthur was especially interested in the progress of the schools and kept a close eye on weekly events. Numbers of children grew steadily, and after five years in operation, the schools in Van Diemen's Land registered a total enrolment of 235 children.[12]

Samuel Marsden had high hopes for these schools, especially those for the young females. 'I cannot but view this institution as the foundation of religion and morality in this colony', and he confidently predicted that it would 'rescue the rising generation from ruin'.[13] The London missionary, the Reverend Rowland Hassall, wrote in delight of the occasion that opened the orphan school.[14] Marsden delivered a sermon, in which he gave a

> true description of the parents of the colony . . . the children's exposedness to ruin on all hands, concluding with an exortion to the children, advice to the teachers, and encouragement to the society . . . urging them to go forward in the work they had engaged against all superstition.

After the service, Marsden 'conducted us to the Orphan House (which is the best house in all Sydney, none excepted)', recorded Hassall:

> we [were] highly delighted with seeing the girls in the greatest order feasting on excilent sort pork and plum puddin [sic], and seemed very happy in their new situation. In short, the whole is much better than I could have expected, and does much credit to those who have the management of the institution.[15]

Marsden was optimistic that the orphan schools' church teachings would have an impact. After his first visit, when he began to instruct them in 'the principles of Christianity', he boldly claimed that New South Wales 'looked more like a Christian country than it had done since I first entered it'.[16]

The conditions for the entry of children into the orphan schools in New South Wales were explicit. No child would be admitted into the institution who had both parents alive or 'even one parent capable of maintaining her' but the Committee was prepared to allow a parent who did 'not possess the means of maintaining his or her child, [to be] considered . . . eligible for admission'.[17] In January 1826, of the 132 convicts in the Female Orphan School, 24 had both parents alive; 88 had one parent alive and 20 had both parents dead. In the year from May 1825 to the end of June 1826, there were 117 boys and 134 girls admitted and 69 boys and 71 girls apprenticed.[18]

In Van Diemen's Land children who could be admitted were those who were entirely destitute; those living in danger of vice from the example of their parents; or those requiring aid from distress or who, being from a large family, could not be supported by their parents.[19] The numbers of children admitted into the schools increased significantly over a short period. Between 1833 and July 1837, the total number of boys and girls at the respective orphan schools rose from 256 to 448.[20]

The orphan schools clearly served the purpose of housing those who had become destitute. There were many 'unhappy children', noted the *Colonial Times*, 'whom are now suffering the very utmost distress, and growing up in all the misery of the most degraded ignorance'.[21] Following admission into the schools, the parents or guardians were to have no contact or control over their children. In the case of girls, they could not 'remove [them] from thence', or from their apprenticeship, until after [their] eighteenth birthdays. The girls were left to the 'entire disposition of the Committee'. At thirteen years of age, they were to become servants or apprentices, for five years, until they married, with the consent of the Committee. The clothing and dress of the girls were to be plain, the diet, 'plentiful, but only plain, wholesome Food', with no waste. The clothing was to be 'suitable to their Condition in life; economical, plain, and uniform', consisting of a blue gown, white apron, white cotton bonnet or straw bonnet. Marriage was rewarded for women with 'a gift of a cow'.[22]

The need to circumscribe these youngsters emanated from a nineteenth-century concern in Britain relating to wayward children and youth. The middle classes were concerned with what was perceived to be 'juvenile delinquents', who posed a threat to private property. This 'delinquency' included drunkenness, gambling, stealing, and roaming the streets.[23] The impact on youth of an increasingly urbanised and industrialised society during this period was cause for considerable alarm. The groups of young criminals who roamed the streets were the target of much moral and social anxiety, a concern that was transported to the colonies.[24]

In Australia, some of this anxiety was reflected in attitudes to boy convicts. The transportation of young convicts has received some attention, although this remains an under-researched area of study.[25] As Kim Humphrey argues, reforming strategies that were adopted towards juvenile offenders related to the shifting definitions of youth. The system of classification and separation that was implemented in the 1820s meant that sharper distinctions were drawn between the adult and the adolescent. This led not only to attempts to reform the young, but also to a redefinition of youth as it applied to young criminals.[26] The boy convicts who were transported were regarded with as much contempt as their adult counterparts. Arthur regarded them as 'entirely useless, and generally so mischievous . . . little rogues . . . the dread of every Family'.[27] The juvenile penitentiary at Point Puer—established by Arthur in 1834 to separate boy convicts—aimed to reform and not just discipline the boys. While there may have been some compassion expressed by Charles O'Hara Booth, who was responsible for the running of the juvenile prison, it was clear that benevolence had to be subsumed to obedience and discipline.[28] Others were not so generous or forgiving. Surgeon-Superintendent Daniel Ritchie, a veteran of several juvenile ships, believed boy convicts were 'not the least dangerous of criminals'.[29]

The prevailing attitude towards those 'orphans' who were the children of criminals but not criminals themselves was more ambiguous. Some historians have assumed that all colonial children were understood in the same way. [30] But during the colonial period, different groups of children were perceived in a number of ways. There was a range of understandings related to boys and girls, Aboriginal and white, free and convict, which needs to be acknowledged if we are to move beyond generalisations about a unified response from state authorities. The orphan schools illustrate the way in which children and youth became a 'key point for social and political anxiety' within the colony. Historically, 'moral panics' have emerged in relation to juvenile crime, public morality and the family.[31] In the context of the nineteenth century, this was evident in two ways. First, efforts to obtain a level of purity and cleanliness revealed an anxiety about social order and stability. During the nineteenth century, the orphan—a term that meant both a child who had lost both parents, or whose parent or parents were deemed unsuitable to care for the child—was another issue around which a number of social anxieties coalesced. These anxieties were expressed in relation to the convict 'stain', and in terms of the body and purity. A belief in the hereditary dimension of the stain motivated authorities to cleanse and save these 'abandoned' children. Children became the symbol of a broader cultural abandonment of transportation within the context of imperialism. As we saw in Chapter Two, British imperial conquest was founded on racial purity: the virility of the race depended on sanitation and cleanliness. The need to rescue these children from abandonment and to cleanse their bodies and habits points to efforts to restore and sustain the social order. These symbols of bodily control took various forms, like cleansing, purifying and establishing boundaries and borders. In regard to racial and cultural contamination, it was assumed that both Aboriginal and convict children would benefit from separation from their parents.[32] The removal of convict children from those deemed unacceptable took place at the same time as Aboriginal children were being taken from their parents. The 'copper coloured' children—as Aboriginal children were called—were for the most part also separated from their white counterparts for fear of racial contamination.

Second, the discussions relating to the orphan schools suggest ways in which these schools were a source of another anxiety. On the one hand, these children were associated with renewal and regeneration. They were the hope of the colony and the innocent victims of their parents' misdemeanours, and were thus deserving of protection. But they were also incarcerated. The state authorities both protected and punished these orphans. In analysing this dichotomy, we can point to the ambiguous place the 'orphan' occupied in the colonial imagination. For while they were innocents, in need of protection and to be separated from their parents, they were also neglected and exposed to another set of dangers.

The recognition of a range of meanings of childhood, and an analysis that moves beyond an exclusive focus on the relations between the oppressed and the oppressor allow us to scrutinise other aspects of children's behaviour. By looking at behaviour characterised as gossip and sulkiness, and attempting to understand its meaning within the nineteenth-century context of the orphan schools, we can challenge the polarities that inform these discussions and come to some understanding of children's actions and their meanings.

Despite efforts to obtain social order and harmony through the containment of the orphan, it was the orphan schools themselves that became centres of social disorder and sexual abuse; dirt and disease; and flight. There was an ambiguous relationship between the state and the orphan and a tension within official understandings, especially in terms of cultural definitions of the child.

Orphan Schools: Institutions of Social Control or Refuges for the Poor?

As others have shown, the very design and purpose of the schools served as institutions of social control. Some writers have focused on the adequacy or otherwise of the schools as educational institutions; or whether they served as free boarding schools or were penal establishments that served the interests of the state.[33] Rather than considering the function and meanings of the schools within these extremes, we might instead explore the way institutions imposed certain controlling values and expectations, and were also refuges for the poor. An examination of the applications to place children into orphan schools serves both these purposes.

In both Sydney and Van Diemen's Land free parents placed their children into the schools. There were applications from parents who were impoverished through misfortune. In 1821, Catherine Sullivan, a widow, submitted a petition to the Sydney Female Orphan School to admit two of her three daughters, and 'in consideration of the particular circumstances', the two eldest children, Mary, aged seven years, and Norah, aged six years, were 'admitted accordingly'. A similar application was lodged by Priscillia Devlin 'for the admission of her two daughters, she being left with six children in circumstances of poverty'. This plea convinced the Committee and her two daughters, aged eight and four, were admitted. Mary Clarkson, aged nine and an orphan, had been under the protection of a guardian for two years. Due to her own circumstances, the guardian was now 'unable to give the child future support'. In February 1822, Mary Stevenson applied on behalf of her daughter Mary Ann. Her father, a sailor, had died on board the *Francis and Eliza*. The Committee concluded that 'considering the helpless state of the applicant, having three other children by another man, who is sick, the child be admitted'.[34]

The King's Orphan School in Van Diemen's Land also served as a refuge for poor children. As in New South Wales, the authorities were concerned with the impact convict parents would have on their children. But the cases brought before the Committee reveal the ways in which the school was perceived by parents as an institution that could at least house and feed their children when they were no longer able to do so. Children who had been left to their own resources also found a home there. In March 1836, Josiah Spode wrote to the Colonial Secretary about 'two little boys [who] were brought in from charitable motives by a man who had witnessed for two or three days their very destitute condition'. The mother had left them and gone to Sydney, while the father was a drunken dissipated character who 'utterly neglects the children'. W. Champ, who had found them, noted that they were 'living by chance; they have no one to support them'. In August 1835, Spode informed the Colonial Secretary of a Mrs Steele, whose husband had been sentenced to Norfolk Island for cattle stealing, and who 'is without the means of supporting her two children', and 'can scarcely maintain herself'. Her two children were five and three years old.[35]

Applications were lodged personally by those in a desperate financial plight. In June 1828, Hannah Matthews applied for admission for her daughters, Sarah and Jane. Their father, Rob Matthews, a mariner, had died at Oyster Bay, 'having no property'. There were three other children (Margaret, thirteen years; Hannah, four years; Elizabeth, seven months). The mother, who obtained her living by washing, was 'wholly unable to support the family'. The three other girls were to be maintained by other families in the island. Under these circumstances, it was agreed that Jane and Sarah be admitted. Jane Hangan also found it difficult to make ends meet. An 'unmarried woman with five children and living in a very immoral manner', she applied to place her son, George, aged twelve in the school. It was recommended that he be admitted, considering 'the fact of the poor lad having not long since lost a brother by the hands of the executioner'.[36]

The orphan schools, then, were refuges for the poor, a point that has been overlooked in many discussions of the social control of schools. Another issue that has been overlooked is that children were never simply pawns within these institutions. The methods available to them for challenging the authorities were different to those of their parents, and they dealt with their predicament in a range of ways. We could turn not only to the obvious actions, like flight and escape, but also to the effectiveness of such behaviour as sulkiness, as well as gossip and rumour, as means by which children asserted some autonomy.

We can also consider the orphan schools in relation to anxiety regarding sexuality and gender, as the schools aimed to shape gender relations. Orphans came to occupy a certain place in the colonial imagination. Unlike boy and girl convicts who had committed crime, the orphan represented helplessness and an innocence. But during the 1830s and 1840s, the orphan also symbolised the threat of unruliness and an anxiety about the future of the colony. Despite efforts to erase the stain from the younger generation, and to save the abandoned children of the colony—concerns that were projected onto the orphan's body—the authorities themselves created an environment that did little to ease their concerns about future generations.

Gender

The aims of the orphan schools were made clear from the outset in terms of the central role gender would play in the training of the next generation. Generally, no child under ten years of age was permitted to enter into service and employers required children to be at least eleven and usually about thirteen or fourteen.[37] The object of the institution was to 'relieve, protect and provide with lodging, clothing, food, and a suitable degree of plain Education and Instruction, poor unprotected Female Orphan Children'. The gender roles for girls were explicit. The rules and regulations of the female orphan institution further stipulated that

> The children of this institution are to be educated only in view to their present condition in life, and future destination; namely, as the wives or servants of common settlers, mechanics, and labouring people . . . they are to be well instructed in common needlework; in making up their own clothes; in washing of clothes and linens; in Spinning and carding; in the Management of a Dairy; in Bakery, Cooking, and all species of Household work; they are also to be worked, occasionally, in the Garden and field, as an useful and wholesome exercise, as well as with the view to fit them for wives of Farmers.[38]

It was 'recommended' by the 'Lady Patroness and the Vice Patroness' that the children be taught with as 'little delay as possible', to knit and spin, and that 'spinning wheels be ordered immediately for this purpose'. It would, furthermore, be 'highly satisfactory' to employ children 'hoeing, weeding and sowing' in the garden. There was also a religious dimension to this daily routine. Each morning and evening, the children were called to attend—in an orderly manner—'the reading of a Portion of the Holy Scriptures and a Short Prayer', and taught the 'Principles of Christianity according to the Doctrines of the Church of England'.[39]

The gender prescription was entirely different for boys. Boys were to be apprenticed out to 'properly qualified, sober, industrious Mechanics, to be instructed in some useful Mechanic art, or as servants to Farmers and Settlers of good respectable character, at the discretion and by appointment of the Committee'. Their future path was similarly determined: they were to be educated only in view to their present condition in life, and future destination; namely as Mechanics and farmers, servants and Labourers; they are 'therefore only to be taught Reading, Writing and Arithmetic, so as to be able to read and understand the Holy Scripture'.

In other respects, independence was encouraged amongst young boys: they were taught 'to make up their clothes, shoes and Hats', and were to be 'Well instructed in Baking, Cooking and all species of Household work belonging to their sex'. Like the girls, the institution maintained complete control over the inmates of the school. It is to be 'clearly understood, as a positive rule of this institution, that when a child is once admitted into it, the Parents or Guardians of such Orphans are to have no control whatever over him, nor be at liberty to remove from thence, nor from his apprenticeship until after he has attained his Twenty-first'.[40]

The punishment of children also reinforced particular gender roles. Headshaving was practised on female orphans, such as Sarah Patfield, with the same result as it had for women convicts—they too were stripped of their feminine qualities. Mary Ann McGrath had 'behaved very ill in the school and in the presence of the Committee having also endeavoured to incriminate one of her school fellows by a gross falsehood'. As a punishment to her, and as a warning to others, it was directed that 'a log be attached to her right leg, as a mark of disgrace, and an impediment to her climbing the trees and other wild conduct'.[41]

Violent physical behaviour characterised the punishment of boys in the male orphan schools. In 1831 a committee was established to investigate the complaints of violence made by David Welsh, one of the boys of the Male Orphan School, against one of the masters, Robert Giblin. It was alleged that Giblin had struck Welsh six times 'right and left with his doubled fists'. He had then taken the boy by the neck and pushed him into the school room, where he was kept all evening and not permitted to sleep with the other children. Welsh, known as a 'respectful lad', also accused Giblin of striking him with his fists on both sides of his face. 'My nose bled and my mouth was cut'. Welsh had also witnessed Giblin's treatment of John Burgess, another victim of such violence. Welsh claimed that he had also seen Giblin strike and knock down his brother, Richard, and 'kicked him while on the Ground'. Richard had been 'obliged to crawl upon his hands and knees under the desk to get away from Giblin. He cried as he got away'. Giblin was subsequently removed. The Colonial Secretary noted that Giblin could not 'remain in that responsible situation for another day'.[42]

While the punishment of the boys was carried out with the intention of imposing particular understandings of gender, it was often not the intention of the authorities for it to be so violent.

Sexuality

The authorities' concern about the sexuality of girls in the orphan schools reflected the general concern in the colony. It was assumed that girls and young women were imbued with a sexual innocence. Children, and especially female children, were assumed to be unaware of 'sexual depravity'. It was believed that sexual knowledge had a destructive impact on young children and that such an awareness was a threat to the moral and social order of the colony. Young girls in the orphan schools were the focus of much attention in order to save their virtue and prevent them from replicating the behaviour of their parents. Young boys and girls were protected by law. However, the law deemed boys under fourteen incapable of sexual practice and it was assumed that girls below the age of ten could not assent to sex.[43] King observed with disgust in his State of the Colony Report of 1801 that, after his arrival,

> the sight of so many girls between the age of eight and twelve, verging on the brink of ruin and prostitution, which several had fallen into, induced me to set about rescuing the elder girls from the snares laid for them, and which the horrible example and treatment of many of their parents hurried them into.[44]

The presence of men in the female orphan schools presented a range of difficulties and there were cases of girls being seduced. Much to his shock, Bigge discovered that Marsden had associated 'with one who had violated the obligations of domestic duty, and had been guilty of seducing one of the girls of the Orphan School in his home'.[45] The Reverend Charles Wilton, the Church of England Chaplain of New South Wales, intervened to prevent further disgrace. Wilton had been appointed Master of the Female Orphan School in April 1827,[46] and had expressed a concern with the potential for sexual disorder within the school. 'As many of the children of this institution', he reported in November 1827, 'are coming up to womanhood, you will I am sure agree with me, that too great care cannot be taken of them at this period'. He therefore recommended that the 'messanger McConville . . . be removed from his present hut' and that the door of his hut should be 'opened in the opposite direction, to that in which it now is', which would prevent communication between 'the children and servants'.[47]

Wilton's concern was not without precedents. In the early years of the orphan schools, a case had been reported in the *Sydney Gazette*, which noted that 'an investigation occurred relative to a scandalous liberty taken with the character and reputation of one of the orphans by H. Simpson, who was brought forward and accused on evidence'. Simpson was sentenced to 100 lashes, but only 'half the punishment was inflicted'. The paper condoned the punishment, claiming that 'doubtless, every friend to virtue, truth, justice and humanity will thoroughly accord in the hope that a single example will be sufficient to shield the subjects of this benevolent institution from wanton and uncharitable slander'.[48] The Reverend William Walker, a Methodist missionary who had been placed in charge of the Female Orphan School in 1825, wrote in the first year of his position that the master who had been in charge before him had 'made several attempts to prostitute the girls and . . . this placed (hd placed) an indelible stain of fitness upon his character, he was not calculated for the office in any respect'.[49] Wilton, who succeeded Walker, agreed, and wrote in frustration in 1828 that it was 'totally impossible for me to prevent immorality in the servants of the Institution, or to protect the morality of the children, many of whom are growing up to be young women'.[50]

The orphan schools shaped sexual difference but it was sexuality that most preoccupied the authorities and was the source of anxiety. The female orphan was vulnerable, but the girls themselves could find ways of unsettling the structures that did not effectively protect them against these dangers.

Sexual Rumour and Subversion

The master of the orphan school in Van Diemen's Land the Reverend Thomas Ewing was not as scrupulous as Wilton in his surveillance of sexual misdemeanours. The case involving Ewing in 1841 highlights the anxiety of authorities in relation to female sexuality. It also points to ways in which talk about sex was used by the young women as a way of undermining power structures. Through the use of rumour, the girls in the orphan schools effectively brought allegations of Ewing's sexual impropriety to the attention of the authorities. Although Ewing was not punished, the girls' private utterances were effective in naming and exposing his behaviour.

The girls were not entirely powerless and were protected by law. By the eighteenth century, the distinction between rape and carnal knowledge had been recognised. Rape and carnal knowledge of a girl under the age of ten was considered a felony and carnal knowledge of a girl between ten and twelve was a misdemeanour. Despite this, the reliability of child witnesses in cases related to sexuality was considered suspect because of the assumptions of childish innocence and of fabrication.[51] It was too easy to dismiss a child witness. In one case, reported in 1837, Charles Collan was 'indicted for assaulting Mary Coleman', a girl of fourteen— about the same age as Ellen Wilson, the young woman at the centre of the Ewing controversy. If it had been taken to the courts, Wilson and some of the other inmates at the school who testified would probably have encountered a response as dismissive as the one Coleman received from Judge Burton, who was presiding over her case. Burton asked 'the prosecutrix if she ever went to Church, if she knew there was a God, if she said any prayers, and other questions of the kind, all of which the unfortunate creature answered in the negative. Under these circumstances his Honour refused to put her on her oath, and there being no case without her, the prisoner was discharged'.[52]

This is not to suggest that such accusations were not taken seriously. The judge presiding over a rape case in 1833 involving three girls was emphatic about the severity of the crime. Hartley Smith was found guilty of 'ravishing' the 'person of Mary Ryan, Harriet Morris and Isabella Smith . . . all about the age of nine years . . .'. In his summation the judge reflected community opinion when he claimed that the offence 'was most dangerous to civilised society', and was 'worse on the child than on a grown woman', because of their 'tender age' and 'their inability to offer resistance'. This behaviour had 'poisoned their mind, it was to be feared forever, and it would be fortunate for them if they ever forgot the vicious lesson he had taught them; if they did not, the fault would be his'. Public morals had to be upheld. The offender was given the severest of penalties: he was sentenced to be hanged.[53]

It was within this context that the Ewing case must be understood. The Reverend Thomas Ewing assumed the position of headmaster of the orphan schools in Van Diemen's Land in 1840. A self-educated man, Ewing had arrived in the colony in 1837 from Scotland.[54] Controversy seems to have followed Ewing throughout his career. By 1873, 'for reasons unclear', Ewing was in the country, and the following year he was embroiled in another controversy, 'one of the larger rows in the Presbyterian Church of Victoria during that period'. Although explanations were 'not offered', 'impropriety [was] hinted at'.[55] According to Joan Brown, a 'good public relations man on his own behalf', he frequently 'wrote to the Colonial Secretary drawing attention to his virtues'.[56] When Ewing was accused, in 1841, of taking 'improper liberties' with Ellen Wilson, a board of inquiry was established to investigate the allegations. While Ewing agreed that Wilson had always been a 'favourite of mine', he denied he had 'connection' with her. Wilson claimed that Ewing had 'untied my frock and put his hands into my bosom'. Ewing replied that it was to warm his hands that he 'put them into her bosom'. Wilson continued: 'He layed me down on the ground. He lay down over me— He did nothing. He pulled up my clothes. I made no noise I did not call out. Mr. Ewing told me to keep a board on my stomach'. She further accused Ewing of 'sitting with his legs across me—He pulled up my clothes and was feeling all about my body'. At another time he 'got me into the bush and tied me down and got upon me'. She did not 'wish to be apprenticed to him'.

Wilson's companions and friends concurred with Wilson's testimony. Another inmate, Elisabeth Long, testified that she and Wilson were 'great friends'. She observed that Ewing was kinder to Wilson than to 'any of the other girls'. Long also reported that Wilson had told Susan Cullyford and Mary Ann Read that he put a newspaper over her face and that 'she did not know what he has done to her'. Sarah Lawson, who had 'raised the alarm' and was another of the girls to testify before the board of inquiry, claimed that all the 'girls say Mr. Ewing takes liberties with Ellen Wilson'. Lawson said that she had seen Wilson 'put her hand into Mr. Ewing's trousers out in the bush'. Wilson's absence was particularly observed by the female attendants of the orphan school. One of the attendants noted that Wilson was one 'of the best girls in the school'. She reported that she could not say 'how Ellen Wilson has conducted herself for these last three or four months after school hours as she has always been at Mr. Ewing's'.

The girls talked about these incidents amongst themselves: in the testimonies there is a suggestion of a close network of gossip amongst them. It was through this rumour that Ewing's honour had been undermined. Rumour circulated about Ewing's practices and connexions with girls and, in particular, with Wilson. Within an enclosed community like the orphan school, rumour, gossip and innuendo were powerful channels through which Ewing's reputation and moral standing could come under scrutiny. The servants, gardeners and teachers within the school had also become aware of his behaviour through the circulation of such talk.

Ewing was alarmed when he heard a report that 'had spread that I had connection with the girl'. In his defence, he claimed that Wilson had 'spread [the] report at school' herself. Mary Ann Read, another inmate, revealed this circulation of knowledge about Ewing when she claimed that the 'girls in the school say Mr. Ewing has done something to Ellen Wilson. It was since talked about in the school for about two months'. She claimed that Sarah Lawson had 'told me that Mr. Ewing had put a newspaper over Ellen Wilson's face. She did not tell me anything else'. Mary Ann Wood noted that 'the girls used to say that Ellen Wilson and

Mr. Ewing went into the bush by themselves—They used to say that Mr. Ewing did something to Ellen Wilson'. The importance of how such knowledge was circulated, in the phrase 'that the girls used to say', cannot be overlooked. The girls also approached Ellen Wilson to ask her 'if she thought Mr. Ewing would deny it if Mrs Gazard [mistress of the orphan school] spoke about it to him. She said he would not for it was true'. But Ewing fiercely denied these allegations and disputed all accusations made against him. The board of inquiry investigating his behaviour decided there was no criminal conduct, but that he could not be acquitted 'of a certain extent of imprudence in his conduct towards and treatment of the elder girls of the school which has not been, we think, consistent with his position of headmaster of the establishment'.[57] Ewing was reprimanded and instructed not to allow the girls into his home.[58]

In spreading such allegations, the young women forced the issue of sexual impropriety to be named and exposed—an effective way in which to bring Ewing's suitability as head of the school into question. As 'private utterances', rumour can be a most expedient means of unsettling power relations. For the vulnerable and the powerless, such knowledge could render them resilient by giving them a voice and allowing them to make some impression on those who attempted to contain them.

Ewing claimed he was unnerved to hear that Wilson had spread the report of his alleged behaviour, and to his 'horror' learnt of the allegations that he had 'connection with the girl'. He was keen to air the matter and asked that it be investigated, so he could not be 'accused of hushing it all up'. By the time Ewing had agreed to confront the allegations against him, his behaviour, according to the witnesses was 'well known'. While Mary Ann Read reassured the board of inquiry that his overtures to Wilson had been talked about in the school for about two months, Mary Ann Wood believed that such 'talk' had been in circulation for four to five months.

Ewing did have a supporter. The surgeon of the school, John Learmouth, was alarmed to hear of such 'talk' and 'said it was of utmost importance to stop such reports'. Ewing said Learmouth had asked 'if I had heard anything of the report which had been circulating respecting myself'. Learmouth believed that the informant, Sarah Lawson, had contradicted herself and should be punished for telling 'lies'. Nothing, he claimed, had been proved against Ewing and when he cross-examined Wilson she denied Ewing had touched her or 'put anything into her'. Learmouth suggested to Ewing that he approach the police, but Ewing claimed this would only assist 'in the spread of falsehood'. The doctor's testimony in favour of Ewing was, however, a lone voice in a roll-call of witnesses who testified in support of Wilson. But even Learmouth was disturbed. While his examination of Wilson did not indicate any 'criminal intercourse', he was disturbed that Wilson claimed 'you have been in the habit of taking up her clothes and putting your hands between her legs and other things'.[59] In his testimony to the inquiry, Learmouth claimed that he went to the parsonage with the 'kindest intentions' to tell Ewing of the reports he had 'heard in circulation the day before'. Since Ewing had 'denied it absolutely', he thought it no more than necessary 'to get the girl's denial of the story and to put it in writing after corroborating the statement by examination'. But he was 'quite shattered on finding that she accused him of gross improprieties ... that she had often mentioned this to others before and that it was believed throughout the schools'. Learmouth claimed he could do no more than to stop the report 'that there had been criminal connection' and advised Ewing to report it to the Colonial Secretary.[60]

Mary Millington, a servant of the orphan school, was also aware of the danger of such rumours. Such 'talk', she claimed, and 'spreading such rumours amongst the servants would get back to him'. The reports, she testified, were 'carried amongst the children' and that while she 'did not know these reports from any particular individual—they were carried on the whole Establishment'.[61] She also testified that she had heard Ellen Wilson deny that Ewing had kissed her, or that he had put his hands under her dress. All the talk had clearly upset Wilson. Captain Swanston, who conducted the inquiry, noted that Wilson had been crying, claiming that she was distressed because they had been 'saying wicked things of her [and of] her and Mr. Ewing'.[62]

From the outset, Ewing denied the charges, dismissing them as attempts 'to destroy my character for reasons with which I am ... unacquainted ...'.[63] He claimed he adopted a paternalistic behaviour towards the girls, believing that they 'had no other friend to look for kindness', and he considered it his duty to treat them 'with great kindness' and so he allowed them into the garden and his house. He insisted that he had 'acted by a kindly feeling and a good motive', but that this generosity had 'given rise to the unpleasant reports which have led to the recent investigation'. Ewing attempted to discredit Wilson by claiming that 'little reliance can be placed on the word of this girl where any other person's testimony can be brought to bear ...'.[64]

Interestingly, it was not only the girls for whom this story was a source of some fascination. It had clearly captured the imagination of the boys in the orphan school. But whereas the girls were clearly distressed by it, the boys saw it as a source of fun. Eliza Livsey, the beadle of the school, confessed that 'it was ... known amongst the boys' and that the 'boys sing songs about it'. The cook at the boys school confirmed this, claiming that the 'boys have songs about it'. One of the boys, Edward Lord Fry, testified that all 'the boys say and talk about Mr. Ewing committing adultery with one of the girls Ellen Wilson. I saw Mr. Ewing buttoning up one side of his breeches when Ellen Wilson ran away'. He stressed the validity of his own testimony, assuring the investigation that this 'is no story—it is what I saw—All the boys talk about Mr. Ewing and Ellen Wilson—when I first saw Mr. Ewing he was gathering up from the ground and buttoning one side of his breeches'.[65]

Any claims in Ewing's favour could not compete with the force of the girls' 'talk'. Susan Cullyford, an inmate, testified that all 'the girls now talk of it' and they now 'all believe' that 'Mr. Ewing has done something to Ellen Wilson'. These proceedings, then, were the end and not the beginning of the matter. The girls' talk had circulated throughout the orphan school and that in itself became proof of Ewing's misdemeanours. The persistence of the rumour, and the knowledge it constructed, undermined Ewing's authority. It became articulated in such a way that it suggested a close network between some of the girls in the orphan school. Their own truth about the matter was confirmed as their talk circulated amongst themselves, and was challenged only when it became a public utterance.

It was not only white girls who were vulnerable in this way. Aboriginal girls were also the focus of the white man's sexual gaze. In August 1827 William Hall, the superintendent of the Female Orphan School in New South Wales, reported to the Committee of the Corporation that he had received 'several applications by Prisoners of the Crown for permission to marry Native girls belonging to the school', and asked whether 'there be any permission held forth to white men in such cases'.[66]

Orphan girls represented an anxiety about sexuality that did not characterise the concern surrounding the treatment of boys. Sexual abandonment informed the discussion on orphan girls and their vulnerability was a source of great concern. Despite efforts to establish a social and sexual order of cleanliness, purity and gender roles, instances of sexual impropriety undermined such efforts. The anxiety about sexuality was particularly evident in discussions about disease and dirt.

Dirt, Disease and the Body

The prevalence of disease and 'dirt' was an ongoing concern within the institutions. At the beginning of 1826, a large number of the girls in the Female Orphan School became ill with ophthalmia, or inflammation of the eyes. Archdeacon Thomas Scott noted with disgust the impact of this and other diseases. The children, he wrote, were covered 'with the Itch and Scald heads, which had been shamefully neglected'. About 120 children had been infected. This concern was exacerbated when a large number of children had been inflicted with the eye disease, 'which has continued through the extreme filth and negligence of the Master and Mistress [Mr and Mrs Walker] to this day'. The children had suffered 'shameful negligence and disease with scarcely any clothing to cover them'.[67] That January, a board was appointed to investigate the cause of the disease. The 'health, comfort and morals of the children were inspected' and the state and general conduct of the asylum were investigated. The board found that the ophthalmia had occurred because of a disease that was propagated by a number of the children 'washing their hands and faces in the same water and wiping their faces with the same towel'.[68] The children must have been healthy on arrival because the rules stipulated that 'no Child (would) be admitted without a certificate from the Attendant Surgeon, testifying that the Child has no infectious Disorder'.[69] The board recommended that a number of tin or pewter basins be provided, 'so that each child may have clean water' and that they be allowed separate towels.

Other illnesses were also being reported by the medical officer: the girls suffered from scalp ulcers, constipation, abscesses, and dysentery.[70] In terms of cleanliness, there were several aspects of the orphan schools that were in constant need of attention. Ventilation of the rooms was a problem, just as it was in the female factories; bedding was not regularly aired. The drainage in the building had been inefficient and the drains needed attention. It was recommended that children's sleeping rooms be kept aired and clean.[71] Instructions were given 'that the whole of the Bedding be carried out in the middle of the day . . . exposed to the influence of the sun and air'.[72] It was also believed that sleeping together further encouraged the spread of disease in the orphan schools. As the administrator for colonial education, and in his capacity as president of Trustees of Church and School Lands, Archdeacon Scott was thorough, 'tireless and exacting'.[73] The conditions he observed in the schools would have horrified him.

In his report, Scott noted with disgust that cleanliness and the standards of the schools had declined. He also commented, though, that the male and female orphan schools

> were placed on a very excellent footing, and were bidding fair to send forth to the Colony a number of young persons, whose habits of industry and morality would have proved the utility of those foundations, and their example would have operated strongly on others.

It was 'with regret' that he reported 'how shamefully these Institutions have been perverted'.[74] In a subsequent letter to Governor Darling, Scott noted that the children, who ought 'now to be well versed in those habits of industry and morality, are, at the age of 16 and 17 years, idle, profligate and immoral in the greatest degree'. In particular, he abhorred the 'loathsome and horrid state of disease and filth' of the orphan schools. [75] Disease and hygiene were also a problem in Van Diemen's Land, with the orphan school being infected with bugs. The school was in a 'diseased and filthy state' and Scott hoped that under the supervision of the Reverend Robert Cartwright, then master of the Male Orphan School, 'the children now in the school will turn out differently modelled'.[76] Cartwright had indeed improved the school in his four-year term from 1825 to 1829 and Scott spoke favourably of his efforts.[77]

The spatial arrangements of the orphan schools suggest the ways in which disease was discussed in relation to children's sexuality. In March 1821, the patroness complained to the Committee that, in some instances, three children were sleeping in the one bed. The medical 'gentleman' highly disapproved 'of even two children sleeping together' and of twenty to thirty children sharing the one apartment. He agreed with her that 'the "disease" currently prevalent will not exist', if first, the 'two children should not sleep together in one bed', a practice deemed 'highly improper'. Second, it was important for as few to sleep 'in one apartment as the accommodation would admit'. Space was at a premium, however. As Belcher has noted, 'it was common for children . . . parents and children and servants and children to share not only the same room but the same bed. In the orphanages, it was common for three children to sleep in one bed'. The school's response was swift on this matter. The Committee insisted that the accommodation in the house did not allow for the children to sleep in separate beds. It had worked to rectify the problem and now there was only one instance of more than one child sleeping in a bed.[78]

The diseased body and the stained body were sources of anxiety for the authorities, for whom cleanliness and purity were prescriptions for stable social order. Although these children were said to be stained, the orphan schools were greatly responsible for conditions that spread disease amongst these children. The anxiety about children's sexuality in these sleeping arrangements and the rules of the orphan schools,[79] as well as understandings of disease and disorder, coalesce around the discussion about the orphan's body.

It was stipulated in the rules of the orphan schools that each child had to be free of infectious diseases before being admitted, and records were kept of the children's state of health.[80] While the authorities were intent to eradicate the disease of the parents and the stain, they did much to perpetuate an unhealthy, unhygienic environment for the children.

In these discussions, the orphan's body became a focus of particular attention. Like the polluting and contaminating bodies of their parents, the orphan's body became a symbol of social disorder and disintegration.

Children were metaphorically diseased and stained by their parents. Yet they were also innocent and vulnerable, in need of protection. Orphans posed a danger to the social order, which was potential but nonetheless real. The orphan schools existed to eradicate and to contain the threat the orphans presented to the future colony.

The body of the child was an important point of reference for the authorities as it was through their bodies that authorities assessed, classified and analysed children. Sarah Anderson, at ten years old, was a 'small weakly child', while Bridget McNamara, aged nine, was 'subject to severe fits'. Aptitude was another way of identifying children. Mary Lenaghan, fourteen years old, 'seems without understanding tho' not by any means silly'. At nine years, Ann Larkin was a 'dirty thieving child'. The descriptions of the children are often conflated with those of their parents. Francis and Sarah Gowlet (aged ten and six respectively) had a mother at Port Macquarie, the penal settlement, and an 'immoral' father, while Amy Chilvers, aged ten, had an 'immoral' mother. A. Denning, it was noted suggestively, was born to a 'father soldier' and a 'vagabond' mother.[81]

In 1826 the superintendent of the Female Orphan School, the Reverend John Espie Keene, compiled a list in which the children in the various classes were identified and characterised by their bodily descriptions. Keene had temporarily taken over as master of the school after a heated dispute between Walker and Archdeacon Scott regarding Walker's competence, which had resulted in Walker's removal.[82]

This list contained descriptions of both Aboriginal and white children. Although segregation of white and black children was more common, there was a brief attempt made, during the mid-1820s, to educate the children together. Aboriginal girls were often identified as 'copper coloured' and there was reference made to their physical strength. Jane Walker was described as 'large and strong'. Fran Walker, a 'black' girl, was useful as a servant, but 'unmanageable' in school, while Ellen Shangley was 'pretty strong' and 'copper coloured'. White girls were also defined in terms of strength. M. Limbeck, Keene concluded, was 'strong and I think not a bad girl, eyes bad', while M. Sullivan was a 'very strong girl of strong feelings'. Elizabeth Wyatt was 'subject to fits', while Ann Allen was 'like a child every night in her bed', a 'weakness' that also inflicted Harriet Hall. M. Magrath was useful as a 'servant but has been much neglected' (he recommended retaining her), while Mary Murphy was a 'very good but not very quick girl'. Ann Larkin, the previously 'dirty thieving child', was, in Keene's estimation, 'a very wild but otherwise harmless child'. He noted, without qualification, that all 'the Larigans are dirty girls'. The divide between the intellectual and physical was made clear as there were girls who were given the 'first opportunity' to become teachers, while 'some girls of strength must be retained to keep the home clean and neat'.

The profiles of the children described by Keene present a picture of the children who entered these schools. His observations reveal the method of classification used by the authorities. Perceptions of 'the child' were informed by attention to bodily inscriptions that were also conflated with personality traits, cleanliness, skill in feminine tasks, aptitude and literacy. A. Kelly, aged twelve, 'reads well and sews', a 'lively and noisy but a good child', while E. Diggirew was a 'dirty and very obstinate girl but a girl of integrity'; she was the daughter of a soldier of the 73rd Battalion, born on the passage, whose parents were dead. E. Wyatt and M. O'Hara were clearly close, Keene noting that Wyatt 'reads a little, sews; a quiet girl; warm temperament; subject to fits' and that with O'Hara, 'has a relationship which they do not like to own'.

There are other patterns of behaviour that illuminate relations between the orphans and those who controlled them. Sulkiness was a form of withdrawal by children. It was recalcitrant behaviour that was extremely difficult to punish. The unsociability and resentment sulkiness connoted suggested a form of subversion by these children. By sulking, children registered a protest. Like rumour, sulkiness amongst children can be scrutinised as a means of exploring recalcitrance. Keene listed that R. Hynas was a 'gloomy sulky girl' and M. O'Hara was 'sometimes', but 'not often' sulky. M. Sullivan, aged twelve, who could spell and sew, was a 'very sulky bold girl'; another child of the same name was also a 'sulky girl of very warm temperament'. Stubbornness, carelessness and slowness were 'difficult' characteristics identified by Keene. M. Murphy was considered a 'very good girl, but slow', while S. Hall, who could scarcely spell, 'sews badly' and whom he considered 'stupid' was nonetheless an 'inoffensive' girl. A. Kennedy was a 'careless, giddy girl', and M. Devlin was inclined to be 'dirty and careless'. M. Ward was 'a stupid but a good girl, subject to fits'; and M. Browne was a 'dirty, inoffensive child', who had four sisters in the school. M. Bailey, who 'spells badly' was a 'dirty', quiet and 'idle' girl. There were girls who were described in a more favourable light. M. Limbor was a 'very good industrious girl', and S. Cooper was a 'good working girl' as was M. Tate. Ann Johnson was described as a 'tolerably good and useful girl'. M. Magrath was singled out because she 'does not know letters' and 'cannot sew', 'never found her bad, tho' I believe of warm temperament' and 'cannot account for her having been neglected'.[83]

Aboriginal children were also described in these terms. M. Gregory, who was thirteen, had entered the Orphan School in July 1817, and so had been an inmate for at least eight years. Described as 'copper coloured', and 'has much the New Zealand character of face', she was 'of a mild, passive character, who reads, but does not sew or write'. J. Walker 'could be said to read, but sews badly, often lazy, and when so, very sulky'. F. Walker, fifteen, did not read, and was 'doggedly obstinate'; E. Shangley was a 'clever and active girl' and A. Randle was 'rather quiet, suffered under ophthalmia which confined her'.

Despite these similarities, the contrast between white and Aboriginal children was made clear. The Reverend William Walker, who had requested to be superintendent of the Black Mission following his removal from the orphan school, observed 'children wearing clothes that had not been washed for three weeks or a month before; and they were so ragged as to make them not less indelicate than our wild aborigines'.[84] Parents of white children were keen to have their children separated from Aboriginal children. In 1828, Joseph Prye, a farmer, and Joseph Barsden, a district constable, each sent a 'little girl into the school to be boarded and lodged', expressing a wish to William Hall of the Committee that they be 'kept apart from the Aboriginal Natives as much as possible and to be at our table and treated as our own children—And for which they will allow something extra'.[85]

Aboriginal children were quarantined and isolated from other children. In the 1820s, moves were initiated to move the Native Institution from Parramatta to a location distant from the whites. The Reverend Robert Cartwright aimed to isolate the 'natives' to strengthen them to cope with the white community. Cartwright had long maintained an interest in the Aborigines and had been instrumental in developing Aboriginal welfare policy. As he wrote:

> The only security for their gradual and real improvement, and which is the opinion of many with whom I have conversed on the subject, is to keep them as much and as long separate as possible from the bad example of those around them.[86]

In Van Diemen's Land, the Aboriginal children were 'to be educated and trained in a manner fit [for them to mingle with] and to be ultimately absorbed into the community'.[87] This is not to suggest that Aboriginal children were not in demand as servants. Robert Clark wrote to the Colonial Secretary in 1842 requesting that an Aboriginal girl named Fanny, who had arrived from Flinders Island, be placed in his charge as he intended to educate the child as 'I do my own'. He was granted the request.[88]

The attempts to 'civilise' Aboriginal children have been well documented. J. J. Fletcher argues that the establishment of the Native Institution was inspired by William Shelley, a missionary, who claimed the reasons why Aboriginal children had deserted the missions was because of a need to be with their own 'people'. He advocated the establishment of an industrial school, which would teach occupational skills, so the children could be employed in the colony in farming. The main aim of this enterprise was to convert Aborigines to Christianity, although its success was 'negligible'.

Shelley and Governor Macquarie both agreed that the colony needed a racially segregated school for Aboriginal and European children. In the case of both the Native Institution and the orphan schools, it was assumed that the next generation would be regenerated only by being separated from their parents. The separation of European and Aboriginal children was also a characteristic of the Native Institution although there were some attempts to bring children together.[89] In 1821, the Institution was transferred from Parramatta to Blacktown. This too had limited success in achieving its aims. In 1824, most of the Aboriginal boys were transferred to the Male Orphan School. In 1825, the few Aboriginal girls from the Native Institution at Blacktown were merged with the Female Orphan School.

The orphan's body became the means by which Aboriginal and white children were classified, analysed and assessed. It became the measure of their obedience and conformity. Despite the stress on cleanliness and purity, disease and disorder more often characterised the conditions of schools. Cultural anxiety was understood in terms of stain and disease, but the orphans' schools created conditions that perpetuated these concerns. It was no wonder that orphans attempted to flee from such captivity.

Flight and Transgression

The orphan schools resembled the prisons of their parents because the children were incarcerated. It was stipulated that 'a high fence be erected in such a manner as to prevent the children getting to the water or the road'.[90] Restrictions on children were carefully enforced and their movement, especially, was monitored. The movement of children into and out of the orphan school in particular was curtailed. The separation of children from the colony was perceived as an important part of their reformation. 'In a convict colony', wrote Archdeacon Scott,

> where so many vicious examples exist, I was anxious to detach the Children as much as possible from . . . constant scenes of iniquity . . . although this may . . . at first [suggest] a tendency to destroy the natural ties between the parent and the offspring, yet where that offspring must necessarily become contaminated at so early a period of life, and imbibe all the horrid passions of its vicious parents, I cannot conceive that such arguments ought to avail here . . .[91]

Elizabeth Macquarie, who was a member of the Board of Management during the 1820s, noted with alarm that children had been permitted 'to go out and spend the evening in Parramatta'. She urged the prohibition of this, and suggested that leave be obtained from the Ladies of the Committee, two 'of whom I've so near that no inconvenience could be from the necessity of making the application'. Boundaries were established: 'The children are never permitted to go to the extent of the enclosure, nor near it, neither are they allowed to go down to the water'. One purpose of the schools was to train the children as domestic servants and apprentices, although there were girls who were indented to the institution as servants, some until 18 years of age. It was resolved that 'it appears improper that any girl once set apart for the Institution should be allowed to go out on any pretence whatever'.[92]

There were other boundaries established in order to scrutinise the habits of children. The Committee of the orphan schools monitored the distance children were sent as domestic servants. In February 1823 the Committee stated it could not approve of any of the girls being apprenticed to services in remote parts, 'improtected and unsettled'. The movement of children from the female factories was another such boundary. In May 1823, a letter from the factory doctor enclosed a list of eight children of prisoners in the factory with a view to them being admitted. The Committee resolved that it 'must be informed of the circumstances of each child' and to see the mothers and the children before they could 'sanction any admission'.[93]

Like their parents, children savoured momentary freedom by escaping from this incarceration. Mary Brown had run away three times from her master, Captain Moore. When she returned the final time she claimed 'that her mistress had severely beaten her'. Charles Wilton, the superintendent, confessed to Scott that she was not 'properly used'.[94] By the time she was apprenticed to another master, she was 'destitute of clothes' and the Ladies' Committee wished to know whether 'she may be allowed clothes from the Institution similar to those given to the girls who are apprenticed for the first time'. Sarah Sullivan, whose mother was in the factory and father at Port Macquarie, ran away from school and was found 'at the house of Mrs. Squires, a notorious character at Kissing Point'. Similarly, Caroline Dyer, or Doyle, was reported as having been ill-treated by her master, Mr Arndinant.[95]

Ill-treatment of children, who fled as a result, was a common theme in the orphan school records. Two incidents highlight this mistreatment. The first involved the complaint by the mother of James Darke about the treatment her son received at the hands of Giblin who, as we have seen, was later dismissed from the school for violence against the children. Giblin asserted that the blow was 'given accidentally in consequence of the boy's throwing himself upon the ground and turning the head suddenly while the Master was correcting him to destroying his clothes'.

James Darke 'ran away from the School', was found and returned. He was severely punished by being 'flogged before the whole school, the day after the offence was committed and in addition was confined for three days on bread and water'.[96] The second incident involved another master, who complained to the Committee about the behaviour of two female apprentices who had been recalcitrant. Elizabeth Smith from the School of Industry and Mary Tully from the orphan school absconded from service (for the second and third times respectively). They had, he reported, behaved 'very ill' for some months. They did not disguise 'their disgust at the idea of being compelled to live in the Country and expressed a fixed determination to get to Sydney or Parramatta'. They caused great mischief for the family that they were sent to. 'Girl Smith' had been punished with fourteen days solitary confinement but 'was in no way improved by it'. Tully had been a 'great favourite with her mistress' but had become 'a very vicious bad girl, no bounds to the annoyance and confusion she had caus'd with the children which has lessened to exist now that she is absent'.[97]

Martha Hillas reported to the Committee the disturbing behaviour of her servant from the Orphan School. She appeared to be 'rather deranged in her mood', she wrote, 'not fit to be trusted with the care of a child one moment out of sight and for which purpose I principally want her'. She was also, it was said, addicted to thieving, so much so 'that she pilfers everything that she can lay her hands on and her conduct and behaviour in General is so very indecent and improper that renders her unfit for my service'.[98] Aboriginal children also fled from masters who were violent and returned to their communities. In 1828 Orphan School Superintendent Hall noted dissent amongst Aboriginal groups. 'The Natives', he wrote, 'will not allow their children to be taught'.[99]

Establishing boundaries was imperative to maintaining discipline and control in the schools; children were quarantined from their parents but also insulated from the outside, despite movement into domestic service and apprenticeships. Wilton wrote to the Committee claiming that it was essential to obtain a constable 'by day as well as by night, who from the nature of his office, has it in his power to prevent improper persons coming near or up to the house and talking to the females'. It was crucial to keep such persons away, and the authorities were concerned when parents approached the orphan school. There was one case of a woman named Sullivan, who entered the house and abused the staff, 'demanding her children to be given up, as they should not be made Protestants'. After five months, Wilton had not yet received the extra personnel he demanded and the problem remained. A former employee of the school, Mrs Jenkins, entered the house without permission, would not leave 'the premises though repeatedly ordered to do so'. Wilson insisted that a 'day

Constable' was 'absolutely necessary', 'to prevent improper persons from entering these premises'. This would stop movement and contact with the outside world; it would prevent 'either men or women from holding communication with the children or women of the Institution which they may do through the . . . playground without coming up to the house'.[100] The Reverend Thomas Ewing, who was still headmaster in 1842, claimed that the parents

> scarcely ever come sober, and the children seeing their parents drunk, became accustomed to the vice. They sometimes bring spirits for their children, they have sometimes even made them drunk in spite of vigilance observed . . . Women sometimes represent themselves as having children at the school for the purpose of being permitted to go out.[101]

Convict servants who worked in the orphan schools were another source of concern about the children. They were perceived to have 'prevented their moral improvement', introducing spirits that intoxicated the girls and 'using licentious and profane language'.[102]

But the institutions provided no haven from these conditions in the colony. Like so many of the other institutions established in the colony, corruption was endemic within its walls. In 1828, it transpired that the master and matron, Mr and Mrs Walker, had been accused of negligence over the children's health. The children, it was discovered, had not been furnished with porridge, but a 'thin gruel', without bread at dinnertime. The servants also claimed that the 'children would sometimes pick up Bones, Turnip parings . . . thrown out from the kitchen, and pick the one and eat the other, and ask for bread and other things complaining of hunger'. The master and matron admitted to slapping the children, claiming that 'children should be kept quiet and orderly'.[103] The Committee concluded that the children had been 'deprived of their proper quantity of provisions . . .' and recommended that the master and matron be dismissed. Governor Arthur intervened, claiming that such action was necessary, as the 'footing on which the schools are now placed by the scrutiny of the Committee will no doubt influence them for many years to come'.[104] Ewing claimed that some children had been enticed into prostitution: 'I have known girls apprenticed from the school to most respectable Master and Mistresses who have afterwards been induced by their parents to abscond and become prostitutes'.[105]

The orphan schools were, as several commentators have noted, institutions that inculcated particular values of industry and sobriety. But they were also used by the poor as refuges for their children when they did not have the material conditions to care for them. The schools also show the ways in which the orphan became a particular source of anxiety for the authorities. Despite attempts to eradicate the stain inherited from their parents, the schools perpetuated disease and disorder. Within these structures, the children manipulated the circumstances to transgress the boundaries. This was done through the more conventional form of flight, but 'gossip' and sulking can also be seen as ways in which the inmates, of the female orphan schools in particular, registered their dissent. The state authorities both protected and punished the orphans who came under their charge. Within official discourse, they were keen to protect them as innocent and helpless victims of their parents' crimes, but in practice, they created conditions that made them even more vulnerable. It was no wonder that some parents, once free and able to retrieve their incarcerated children, did so with eager anticipation.

CHAPTER 7

Abandonment, Flight and Absence
Motherhood and Fatherhood During the 1820s and 1830s

In November 1826, James Mudie, the marine lieutenant and colonial magistrate, made an application on behalf of six-year-old William Waddle for him to be admitted to the Male Orphan School. His mother, who was a servant in the Mudie household, wrote Mudie, had, 'of late conducted herself in a very drunken and depraved manner', and was now in gaol. The boy's father was also a prisoner. The case appeared to be a straightforward one for the authorities, and Mudie's application was signed, simply, 'ordered to be admitted'. It was as uncommon for masters to apply for the entry of children into the orphan schools as it was for the orphan school Committee to be so immediately convinced of the appropriate course of action. This case was one amongst many hundreds which were documented in applications for children to be placed in the orphan schools.

These applications, lodged by convict and free parents to retrieve from or place their children in the schools, tell us much about the transitory nature of marriage, relationships and the family amongst the poor during the 1820s and 1830s in colonial society. An analysis of these applications points to the fluctuating fortunes and often desperate circumstances of convict men and women. The applications also suggest how the meanings of motherhood, fatherhood, masculinity and femininity were understood. They also shed light on the anxiety about abandonment by mothers, flight and absence of fathers, and roaming children. Before such considerations can be thrown into relief, the character of colonial marriage needs to be understood.

Marriage in the Colonies

The model of social control has shaped our understanding of marriage in colonial society. Historians agree that colonial administrators, governors and the clergy were unanimous that marriage would civilise convict men and purify convict women. For this purpose, they were given specific instructions to encourage marriage. Samuel Marsden announced that marriage was important for convicts' 'happiness and usefulness' and in preventing them from spending a 'vagrant and vicious life to the end of their days'.[1] The state promoted and encouraged marriage with a range of incentives introduced by a number of governors. In particular, Governor Macquarie was committed to offering 'every inducement to the formation of lasting and virtuous connexions'. Women who were not married could not, for example, claim the estate of their de facto husbands. In material terms, women were greatly disadvantaged if they were in de facto relationships.[2] Despite these measures, the marriage rate amongst convict women was not high and it was only after the end of transportation that marriage became the norm for this group of women. The Select Committee on Transportation accurately concluded in 1837 that 'marriages among convicts rarely turn out well'.[3] Within these marriages, Katrina Alford argues that women were in fact 'sexual victims',[4] and in her account, there appears to be little opportunity for women to escape such a predicament. Kociumbas similarly claims that for most women, marriage or cohabitation was the only way to alleviate their condition of poverty. They were the only 'possible solution' available to women, and the need for a male protector was imperative especially in the early years of white settlement.[5]

Colonialists perceived marriage as the acceptable way in which licentiousness and promiscuity could be contained. Davidoff and Hall have noted the importance of marriage to the British middle classes. Marriage, they argue, formed the economic and social 'building block' and was fundamental for the economic, social and emotional stability of middle-class men and women. It was understood, as Alford has noted, to have served a moralising and civilising function—the key to reform and purification—as well as an economic one, and reinforced the 'compelling association between legal marriage, private property and inheritance'.[6] For men, it was considered a means of 'containing potentially distracting sexual adventures';[7] for women, it marked their passage to adulthood and prepared them for motherhood. In this situation convict women were caught within a particular dilemma. Alford notes that although marriage was considered necessary to ensure moral reformation and moral respectability, it was also considered that, for convict women, their lack of moral worth made them unmarriageable. Reproduction was identified as women's primary function, their role within the family, and marriage was encouraged for demographic, social and economic reasons. Alford concludes that a combination of these factors— government policy supporting marriage and the promotion of a particular social role for women—'served to channel the energies and capabilities of colonial women increasingly into an essentially domestic and reproductive role'.[8]

Marriage patterns, however, suggest that the practice was more common amongst the elite, free and native born, than amongst the convicts. During the 1820s and 1830s, most were living in arrangements that were not bound by legal marriage.[9] By the mid-nineteenth century, marriage had become the dominant custom, and from the 1840s the family was established 'as one of the basic socio-economic institutions in the Australian colonies'. Colonial governments offered inducements for those from the lower orders to marry, such as land grants, although few ex-convict women succeeded in obtaining land grants.[10]

Efforts to impose this ordering of sexual relations were, as several commentators have noted, met with much 'passive opposition' amongst both middle-class and convict women.[11] Much of the scholarship on relationships and marriages has focused on the ways in which the state regulated the lives of convicts. Legal marriage was not common amongst the convicts and extra-legal marriages were the norm. Marian Aveling has written of the laws introduced by Darling, which privileged married couples.[12] In these discussions, the relationship between the state and marriage is drawn neatly and directly. It was the case that state laws shaped marriage practices, and convicts and others challenged these in a variety of ways, but in analysing the applications of orphan schools, I want to stress the instability of these relationships and the shifting meanings that were associated with them.

The middle and upper classes, for instance, may have aspired to reconstruct these ideals, but the regular absence of the husband and father in some of these marriages, and the practice of ruling-class men taking convict mistresses throw into question the extent to which colonial marriages were a 'partnership'. Such practices also highlight the extent to which relationships between the middle and upper classes assumed a particular expression within the colonial setting.[13] Middle-class and upper-class women did not always adhere to the prescriptive nature of marriage conventions. Women like Elizabeth Macarthur, Caroline Chisholm and Jane Franklin crossed the boundaries that aimed to circumscribe their behaviour while others created a space in the public work of philanthropy.[14]

Other historians have shown how this ideal was not upheld in relation to convict women. Alan Atkinson has considered the motives of convict women who married in terms of what purpose marriage served for them and how they managed to show an 'independence and cunning' in working the system.[15] Aveling also considers the ways in which women manipulated the marriage system to their benefit.[16] Portia Robinson has noted that 'not all colonial marriages were happy ones, nor were all wives dutiful and faithful'.[17] The fortunes and misfortunes of convict marriages are documented in the work of Babette Smith in her exploration of the ways in which women on the *Princess Royal* exploited the opportunities offered by marriage. She notes the ways in which marriage was considered as a way of reforming women, especially by clergymen such as Marsden, who considered marriage the 'path to reformation of the women'. Smith constructs a picture of the fate of convict women beyond official discourse on the *Princess Royal.* Her analysis reveals the range of women's responses and considers the ways in which marriage could offer women a liberating or oppressive situation, or a mixture of both.[18]

But her account is informed by a judgemental moralism. Smith considers the 'triumph' and 'failure' of marriage—implicitly defined in relation to the middle-class ideal—and asks to what extent did 'women's characters contribute to the violence and, in some instances, collapse of their marriage?'[19] For Robinson, this also becomes a morality tale of 'small percentage' of absconded wives and deserting husbands. She argues that it may have been the close involvement of the colonial authorities, 'especially the governor himself, in the everyday lives of the men and women of Botany Bay acted as a restraint'. The overall good conduct can be explained in terms of the alternatives to recalcitrant behaviour being less desirable.[20]

To move beyond such moral characterisations, we need to ask different questions. In what ways were relationships in the 1820s and 1830s transitory, and how were the meanings of masculinity, femininity, fatherhood, motherhood, childhood, and sexuality understood at this time?

Femininity/Motherhood: 'Abandonment'

The meaning and practice of 'free' motherhood were at stake in many of the applications lodged by parents for entry of their children into the orphan schools, and for parents attempting to retrieve their children. Mothering was central to nineteenth-century perceptions of bourgeois respectability. It was the mother who was expected to assume responsibility for the emotional support of children: maternal love was considered sacred.[21]

The 'abandoning mother'—both convict and free—was a powerful cultural symbol, especially in light of this idealisation of motherhood and the anxiety this produced within the context of the broader cultural abandonment of transportation. It is important to note that the applications relating to abandoning 'mothers' were made by men, usually the husbands or partners, who filed a complaint against the mother of their children. In such cases, men often harboured resentment. But more generally, perceptions of 'abandonment' by the mother—of being absent or being 'depraved'—became synonymous with the 'destitution' of children and the woman's flight from femininity. This applied not only to convict and free women but to Aboriginal women as well. The 'wandering' life was often conflated with freedom of choice, especially in sexuality. Wanderings by men evoked fear, envy and pity, but similar movements by women aroused anger and resentment.[22] In these records, the reasons why women fled are not stated, although it was probably because of physical assault or alcoholism by their male partners. Women's flight was considered in terms of recklessness, not only because they were seen to be neglecting their responsibilities as wives and mothers, but also because they were then autonomous. The prevailing perception of Aboriginal women and their 'wandering' life carried with it similar condemnation, although within discussions by white authorities this had the hallmark not only of cultural abandonment, but more disturbingly of 'savagery'.

Applications by husbands or guardians to place children into the schools were often premised on the assertion that the mother was incapable of nurturing the child and the father could not take full responsibility. The competence of these women as mothers was called into question. In February 1825, William Simpson applied on behalf of John King, whose father had deserted his regiment, and whose mother 'has wholly abandoned them leaving them destitute'. Andrew McQuire, a free man working as a labourer, was unable to care for his daughter, Ellen, because the mother of the child, to whom he had been married for about five years, 'absconded from him about two years since and is now living in adultery with a man'. This meant that he had been 'absent at his labour' and 'unable to take proper care of the girl'. Not surprisingly, men stressed women's incompetence as mothers—usually an effective means of ensuring a successful application. Francis Evans reported that after the expiration of his seven-year sentence he found 'the poor child in a shamefully neglected state'. The mother was 'incapable of providing for the child and of honestly setting her own living'. Similarly, Mary Goadby, the wife of a male prisoner, was deemed a 'worthless woman who has left the Girls wholly destitute of support and protection'.[23]

Cohabitation with other men was not often the cause of flight although the applications suggest it was prevalent. In 1828, Stephen Johnson elaborates how he 'cohabited' with a woman for twelve years and had three children with her. In his absence, 'this woman has eloped from my House and children, taking with her everything she thought was useful, together with receiving all debts due to me'. He pleaded that this situation had prevented him from providing the children with 'common necessities'. The woman, Elizabeth Durham, was subsequently apprehended for being 'illegally at large', her original sentence being fourteen years.[24]

Other women left without a trace, the children being—by definition of the mother being absent—destitute. Rebecca Harris's mother had 'absconded from her home about four years ago, abandoning her children', 'leaving them in a helpless condition', and had not been heard of since 'with any degree of certainty as to her way of life. Some say she cohabits with a man beyond the mountains and others that she is dead'. The eldest daughter, who was seventeen, cared for the other child, but it was said that both were 'in state of destitution and that the morals of the younger are much suspected'. In 1829, John Ramsay, in service, put in an application for his son because, although his wife was living, she was 'an abandoned woman living with another man'. An application from Pearce, a ticket of leave-holder, revealed that the mother of his two children was 'living in an abandoned way and totally unfit to have care of them'. Edward Ready applied for his daughter, Margaret Ready, to be placed in the orphan school, his wife Margaret having 'addicted herself to vicious causes . . . leaving the child destitute'. The father's work led him to be itinerant and therefore the girl could hear 'language and witness practices, that will contempt the mind—and render her through life a bad member of society'.[25]

Women fled for other reasons. The wife of Michael Minton was charged with being accessory to his murder; she had 'deserted the . . . two children, and gone to a distant part of the colony'. Minton left a wife and children in Ireland, who claimed his property. Others simply disappeared. In December 1828, Esther Dalton could not 'be found' and had not 'for the last two years and half seen nor has she enquired about the child'. Women, like children, were not supposed to be at large. Elizabeth Harris had 'deserted the family about three years since and it is uncertain whether she is living or dead'. In April 1829, the superintendent of police noted that Harriet Marsh, now a patient in the lunatic asylum, had been found wandering in town, 'in a very deplorable state, and so totally insane, as to be incapable of taking care of the infant belonging to her'. Her child was five months old.[26] Here, the itinerant, aimlessly wandering mother suggested a dislocated social order. Social anxiety derived not only from the deserted children, but also from expectations about the mother as the 'benign force or agent out there in the world looking out for us, our needs, and ensuring their satisfaction'.[27]

The death of a wife could also render men helpless. James Winter, since the death of his wife, was 'prevented from going out to earn a livelihood having no persons to take care of the children'. William Black, a private in the 39th Regiment, placed an application for his daughter Sarah in September 1830, his wife having died 'February last', 'leaving his child motherless and he having no means of taking the necessary care of her in the Barracks'.[28]

'Abandonment' and sexual promiscuity by mothers, however, were not always sufficient reason for children to be admitted to the orphan schools. In some cases, fathers were expected to assume family responsibilities. George Milward, a sergeant in the 39th Regiment, separated from his wife, 'who is now an abandoned prostitute on the streets of Sydney'. He applied for his two boys to be admitted, but the authorities were not convinced, querying his application, and the 'grounds he applies to have these boys admitted'.[29] In some cases, both parents could be considered abandoned. The Windsor children were deemed deserving members of the orphan school because both their parents were considered 'worthless characters' and 'abandoned'.[30]

Unstable domestic situations were often a cause for action. Margaret Barrett and her husband Charles Barrett 'live so unhappily, sometimes together and sometimes separate, that the said child is frequently without instruction and without a Home'. Catherine Farley was compelled to apply for two of her children (one was an infant) to become inmates of the orphan school because she was utterly unable to maintain her three children, 'in consequence of the conduct of their father, who has lately become so much addicted to drunken habits and idleness, as to leave his little helpless family destitute and forsaken'.[31]

Free women were also deemed to be innocent victims of circumstance, and the 'unprotected' mother became a central motif in many applications, usually with the death of the male breadwinner. Harriet Mackie was the widow of the late Sergeant Samuel Mackie, who had died of 'fever' and left his wife with three young boys, 'unprovided for and unprotected', and in a state of pregnancy. The only support she could obtain was through the officers of her husband's regiment, protection she would soon lose because they were embarking for India. In her application she requested that the orphan school house the two eldest sons. Similarly, when Sarah McGee's husband, Private John McGee, 'lost his health in this colony together with his intellects about two years ago, so that he was latterly in a complete state of idiocy', she had 'no friends to assist her' and because she was obliged to go to service, the main breadwinner being incapacitated, she 'finds it impossible to take care of her child, nor has she the means of supporting her'. In June 1827, Alice Williams was left with four girls, 'which since her husband's death she has endeavoured to support by carding and spinning of wool but finds she cannot get sufficient employment to enable her to keep the whole'. Sarah Radley was compelled to go to service to earn a living, feeling 'considerable stress from having no means for providing for her daughter, nine years of age'.[32] In 1832, Anne Ablett made a plea as a widow, having a family of two boys and four girls, waiting for her seventh child. She was paying off her husband's debts and was compelled to go into service.[33]

Sarah Mason was left with three children to care for following the death of her husband, Thomas Mason, 'who was shot by bushrangers in the South Creek Road'.[34]

The loss of the breadwinner could have devastating repercussions for the women concerned, although their status as single mothers did not carry the same denigrating connotations as the wandering or abandoning mother. The Act for the Maintenance of Deserted Wives and Children was passed in Van Diemen's Land in 1837 and in New South Wales in 1840. This law allowed women to apply for maintenance from their husband in the form of a weekly or monthly payment,[35] but it was difficult to enforce protection for women and benevolent institutions served the poor in Hobart and Launceston.[36] Relief for destitute families was offered by a range of such institutions during the 1820s and 1830s. The Benevolent Society in New South Wales was established in 1818, 'to relieve the Poor, the Distressed, the Aged, and Infirm'. In 1826, the Sydney Dispensary was formed, which was concerned with the plight of families. Four years later, the Sydney Dorcas Society aimed to 'relieve poor married women during the month of their confinement', while the Sydney Strangers' Friend, established in 1835, became an 'auxiliary' to the benevolent society.[37]

These charities and private benevolence, observes W. Nichol, 'became indispensable' for offering material support for the poor. Ann Brown's application illustrates how the absence of the breadwinner could easily affect family finances. She was the widow of Private William Brown, who was discharged from his regiment because he had 'become so completely deranged in his intellectuals—received into the Lunatic Asylum where he died'. As a widow of four, she was left in a state of destitution. Similarly, Sarah Matthews was left to support her children, and sustained herself by taking in washing, but was 'wholly unable to support the family'. Nicholas Delany, the main breadwinner of his family, was reduced to great poverty and distress, 'having some years broken his thigh and being unfit for labour'. Mary Chilvers' husband was killed in service of Mr Macarthur and the children were now 'wholly unprovided for and destitute'. Johanna Taylor applied because the father of her children had been transported for fourteen years, and herself seven weeks since confined 'she finds it impossible to maintain herself and three young children'. Shepherdess Agland's mother died in childbirth and soon afterwards her father also died. Her guardian reported that there was 'no means of further supporting the child'. Joseph Harris's wife died, 'some months', compelling him to leave them when he went into employment, 'without any protection'. Anne Reed was similarly left in despair, her husband having been transported to Moreton Bay for three years and, 'having two other children to support, with no fixed means of obtaining a livelihood is in very great distress'. Mary Weavers complained about her husband's 'breach of trust'. Her husband, Richard Weavers, 'some time Constable at Liverpool', was convicted of a 'breach of trust' and sentenced to six months imprisonment, during which time she had no other form of assistance. She was therefore 'reduced to great distress having four children, the two youngest only two years old, being twins, entirely dependent upon her labour for their support, which from her weak state she is unable to afford'.[38]

The absence of the mother created problems even when the father could find a surrogate mother. In the petition by John Hall, on behalf of John and Samual Laurence, four and a half and two years old respectively, Hall wrote that the mother had died, and the 'grandmother who has hitherto supported the children since the death of [their] mother' was 'convicted at the last quarter . . . and sentenced to be transported, which leaves the children quite destitute, and without any support'.[39]

The absent mother was a constant motif running through these applications. In being absent, these women challenged any idealisation or expectations of mothers. If a mother was considered abandoned or 'at large'—whether to escape wife-beating or alcoholism or both—her wandering status automatically became synonymous with her children being 'destitute' children. While marriage itself may not have been important amongst the poor, the abandoning and absent mother was cause for considerable anxiety for government authorities.

Masculinity/Fatherhood: Flight and Absence

Flight from fatherhood did not have the same moral repercussions as flight from motherhood, nor were those repercussions defined by such anxieties. Desertion, as Kay Daniels notes, was extremely common. This flight often left women in a position of helplessness. The case of Mary Starkey was typical. She was deserted by her husband and, because she was paralytic, was unable to 'maintain' her son, Thomas Starkey. Her application to place him in the orphan school reflected her desperation. Sarah Jones was left to look after her two infant children, Sarah, aged two and a half, and Elizabeth, three months old, after her husband had left the colony for England. Hers was a common tale of desertion. She wrote:

> I am in great poverty and nearly in want. My husband went to the Islands in a Sealing gang in Mr. McQueen's employ, but altho' I made my distressed case known to him he was not sure [if my] husband was on the island . . . I humbly hope you will forward my application—I am Sir really unable to support my children and pay house rent.

Her children were admitted and she was requested to pay a weekly contribution. In July 1828, Mary Johnston applied for her children to be placed in the orphan schools, noting simply that 'father of the children deserted his family'. In May 1829, Jane Stillwell, who had come to the colony under 'unfortunate circumstances', was unable to support herself and her family, since her husband, who had 'followed her a free subject', had left her with four children when 'he returned to England'.[40] The application for George Morgan, aged three years, was approved because his mother was deemed to be 'insane', 'and in great distress, deserted by her husband for some years'. Ann Webb attempted to support herself and her three children by washing. The father of her children had 'not been heard of for a considerable time and . . . [it was] supposed that he has left the colony'.[41] In one case, a father and his three children were transported to Moreton Bay for three years. The mother, having two other children to support with no fixed means of obtaining a livelihood, was 'in great distress'.[42]

While the absent father was a central concern in these applications he did not occupy the same cultural significance or elicit the same anxieties as the absent mother. Catherine Clark petitioned because the father of her children, Archibald Clark, a shoemaker, four years earlier had left her and her two female children. Sarah Jones reported that her husband had been absent from the colony in a sealing gang for nine or ten months. In May 1829, the application for John Worthy reported that his father had left the colony for England six years before in the *John Bull*, and had not been heard of since. His mother was dead.[43]

At Large: Roaming Homeless Children

Another central concern in these applications to the orphan schools was the way in which children would be influenced by 'corrupting' forces beyond their control. The roaming, homeless and helpless child with neither parent able to offer support was perceived as a problem. Idle children were cause for concern. In 1827, an application was placed by the inspector of police for a 'poor little boy named Thomas Holland, aged eight years', who was brought to him 'having been found in the street at the hour of nine last night'. Thomas stated that his mother had been sent to the factory and that he had no father (although it was scribbled in the margin of the application that in fact he did have a father, who was at Norfolk Island). The inspector of police advised that he 'not be left exposed to the vicious and depraved habits that children but too frequently imbibe by being left to roam about this Town'.[44] The fate of Jane Sullivan and her two sisters compelled the authorities to house them. Their mother, Catherine, was in the third class of the female factory, their father had been shot dead four years ago, while their mother's father-in-law was in an iron gang in Port Macquarie. Ten years further on, anxieties about such children had not reduced. The *True Colonist* expressed alarm about homeless children when it reported in 1837 'that the boys in particular, have been permitted to run about the neighbourhood, committing a variety of petty depredations'.[45]

Government authorities intervened to ensure that children's behaviour was circumscribed. Apprehending white children—as well as Aboriginal children—was a central motif in nineteenth-century Australia. Mary Ann Clark claimed that 'immediately upon her arrival in the Colony', her child, Margaret, then two years old, was taken from her and placed in the Female Orphan School. When Margaret was ten years old, both Clark and her husband ('a sober industrious man') were 'desirous to have Margaret returned to them'. It was not only women who experienced this sort of removal.[46] Men, too, had children taken from them. William Guthrie's child, Mary Ann Smith, was 'taken from me six years ago'. He was now free and could maintain her and was able to educate her.[47]

The orphanages also served as a means by which parentless couples could obtain children. In 1830, Mary Ann Wilson wrote to obtain Mary Jane Eddison, aged seven years, 'having no children of her own', she 'requests to maintain and support her'. Her husband was of 'industrious habits', holding a farm of twenty acres in the district, with 'no incumbrance' whatever. J. Hamilton similarly approached the Committee for a 'child at the age of 11–12 years, destitute of parents'.[48]

Bourgeois Respectability

J. Hicks wrote in 1831 that his sons John and Mark were placed in an orphan school in 1828, when he was a prisoner of the Crown. Since his 'emancipation he had been employed as a constable' and thus, 'able to provide for them he [requested] . . . that they may be placed again under his protection'.[49] The applications by parents for their children to be returned were informed by a reassurance that those who were now free had assumed a particular status and role. The paternalistic relationship between the applicants and the state was unmistakable in those applications to admit children into orphan schools. But when applying to retrieve their children, the applicants invariably did so with assuredness, confidence and bravado. Parents applied to have their children taken out of the orphan schools for a variety of reasons. In order to convince the authorities that they were respectable mothers and fathers, they were at pains to stress what they believed the state authorities would perceive as respectable virtues. The bases of many of these appeals to retrieve children were, first, that the applicants' circumstances had changed, and, second, that the applicants offered children the prospect of work or an apprenticeship.

Family

Family members often applied to retrieve relatives by employing them as servants and because the labour of children was needed to sustain the family.[50] Eliza O'Meara wrote in 1831 requesting her sister Sarah Bolton be apprenticed to her. She assured Charles Cowper, the superintendent, that the 'character of myself, and husband will bear the strictest investigation to support my Sister; whom I naturally wish to be under our protection'. Many of the applications came from husbands writing on behalf of their wives who had been prisoners and were now free. A letter from Richard Wilshire is typical of such cases. He wrote that 'about five years ago' he had married Louisa Thrusfield, who, while a prisoner, had placed her son from a previous marriage in the orphan school. As Wilshire was a tailor, and was 'competent to maintain and educate him', he asked that the boy now be 'placed under the charge of his mother'.[51]

Applicants exploited the goodwill and sympathy of the authorities by the appeal of the mothers' angst and anguish. James Hollorray wrote saying that his wife had placed her two children in the orphan school 'at a period when the mother was incapable of [providing] a sustenance for them'. He assured the authorities that he now had 'ample means' and was 'very willing to support the Girls as the mother . . . is languishing on account of their absence from her'. Mothers stressed this aspect in their applications. Jane Barns wrote in 1831 that 'with the feelings of a mother I am inclined to take under my care and protection a child' who had been in the orphan school for six years. In 1826, Sarah Hall tried this strategy, claiming that, having remarried, she had a 'good prospect of obtaining an honest and respectable subsistence' and therefore requested the release of her three children 'to the embraces of an affectionate parent'.[52]

Men, too, appealed in terms of their new status, attempting to convince the authorities of their worthiness as parents. John Owen wrote under 'an impulse of the strongest paternal affection I feel extremely anxious to have charge at least of my eldest Boy'. He promised that he could provide instruction in the boot and shoe business. Patrick McAuliffe reassured the authorities that he had the means to maintain 'my wife's children'. Mrs Quinn had put her son into the school at the time of his father's death, when she had been left alone with a small family. She had remarried, 'to a boot/shoemaker, who could provide him with a trade'.[53]

Women could make a claim for children through the respectability of marriage. In 1828, Mary Tennant wrote to the Committee of the Orphan School that her sister had been placed there, and she was confident that her married status and her husband's character bear the 'strictest investigation for honesty, sobriety and industry'. Honora Levy had now married a free man, John Finch, of 'honest, industrious, sober habits'. Ann Green reassured the authorities that five years ago she was left a widow with four small fatherless children. Now, she was a 'Married Woman, and has launched into a trade', and so requested that her children be restored to her.[54]

But not all applications involved convincing the authorities that a male breadwinner could support the family. Margaret Barrett wrote in 1830 that she had placed her son in the orphan school three years before and 'as it now lies in my power to provide for him', she hoped to retrieve him. Convincing the authorities of the respectability and legitimacy of one's position was a central part of attempting to retrieve the child. Bridget Welsh was transported for seven years and arrived with her daughter, who was duly placed in the orphan school. Once free, she hoped to retrieve her child, who was in service, and had evidently approached her child's master, who was willing to relinquish her, 'provided the sanction of the public authorities be obtained'. Mary Niblet's daughter, Ann Murphy, was also placed in the Female Orphan School on their arrival, Niblet had since married, lived with her husband and was 'now able to support and bring up her daughter comfortably'. John McAllister, a stonemason of Sydney who had recently married, wrote to Governor Darling on behalf of himself and his wife requesting the return of her three-year-old child, who was taken from her on arrival and put into the female factory, stating that he could 'well afford to maintain his wife and step child'. Elizabeth Cadman reassured the authorities that although in 1828 she had placed her two daughters in the school, her situation had improved; 'she now having the means of providing for them comfortably' and having married John Cadman, requested they be 'restored to her'.[55]

Work

Convincing the authorities that the applicants had the means by which to support the children was crucial in these applications. Acquiring respectability through learning a trade and skills was another theme in the applications to obtain orphans. When an employer apprenticed a child, he/she did not pay the child any wages; the child had to remain with the master for a number of years until they had learnt a trade in order to receive a return. Boys were apprenticed as tailors, carpenters, shoemakers, tobacco manufacturers and woollen weavers, while girls were apprenticed as nurses, domestics, and needleworkers.[56] Elizabeth Raine (a former matron of the Female Factory at Parramatta) wrote to Charles Cowper in February 1830 requesting the orphan M. Brooks for her service. 'I beg further to state', she wrote, 'that she will have an opportunity of improving her mind, as well as learning the business of a dressmaker and seamstress in general'. This was not the only time Raine applied for an apprentice. In January 1831 she requested the services of Mary Ann Long whom 'she brought up until she was four years'. Raine had since kept an 'establishment for the education of young ladies, where she will have the opportunity of improving herself . . . and make her if possible, an ornament to society'.[57]

The promise of religious education and high moral standards also assured a positive response from the authorities. Elizabeth Horne requested Mary Field as a servant, and promised that 'every care will be taken of her morals'. Similarly, George Green applied for a servant, with the assurance that every attention be paid 'to her morals'. A. Byrne reassured the Committee that in requesting a girl of fourteen years of age he pledged himself 'to allow her to attend the Church of England on all occasions'. Charles Farrell wrote to Charles Cowper requesting John Steward from the Male Orphan School 'to give him trade as a Carpenter'. 'Morals' were less of a concern for boys, although teaching them a trade was deemed important by the authorities who considered each application. John Jacob Sharpe wrote in 1831, requesting a 'youthful female servant' of 'industrious habits and steadiness' and 'every attention shall be paid in respect to her morals not being corrupted' and 'her Education in domestic affairs attended to'. E. L. Hall requested the services of a young girl, intending to train her, 'not to induce her to consider labour as degrading, which I have observed, the females of this County are too apt to consider'. James Barker applied for a servant to be employed in needlework. He was married and free, 'every care will be taken of the Girl's morals'. William Price promised he would teach two apprentices 'the Art or Mystery of a shoemaker'.[58]

In order to ensure that female servants would be obedient, applications often stipulated a desire to obtain a girl with no companions in the colony. Thomas Skeet wrote in November 1830 requesting a 'little girl about 10 years who is destitute of Friends'. Sarah Hitchcock made the same request, asking for a girl 'who has no friends in this town'. She promised an apprenticeship in her millinery business to a girl of 'good habits and teachable', and said she would 'feel pleasure in instructing her in my business'. Others requested those who possessed a skill. Mrs Wyatt asked for a girl who could 'work at her needlework'. Aboriginal children could also be obtained: Mrs Harriet Alwyn addressed the Ladies' Committee asking for an 'Aboriginal native girl named Mary Ann Robinson'.[59]

Parents often used the reason of 'work' and teaching them a trade to retrieve their children. Elizabeth Kenniwell wrote in 1826 requesting the release of her son, who had been in the orphan school for fourteen years, because of the 'frequent and unavoidable absence of her husband, whose business sometimes requires his presence in the country, so as to occasion an absence of 2 or 3 days successively; Petitioner must either trust to entire strangers to assist her, or neglect her business'. Robert Foulcher applied for his own son in August 1826 to teach him. Foulcher stated he was in 'Business as a Blacksmith and who is much inconvenienced for the want of a lad'. Mary Ann Caton applied to retrieve her daughter to assist her in her business as a laundress. She assured the authorities that her daughter would find a 'comfortable home and may be placed under the kind protection of a mother'. Unfortunately in this case, despite such reassurances, the child had been apprenticed elsewhere and could not be given out.[60]

These applications for children in and out of orphan schools indicate the ways in which femininity, sexuality, masculinity, motherhood and fatherhood assumed particular meanings and were contested both inside and outside of marriage. The stories they tell reflect how the social and moral anxiety about sexuality and gender relations was pervasive.

To consider these issues in this way is to depart from the existing approaches adopted by historians in analysing marriage and relationships in colonial Australia. Ideas about social control have been used here to suggest how marriage and relationships were shaped as part of public policy and infused with state ideology. Relationships between men and women are discussed in terms of the bourgeois ideal and whether convicts did or did not marry, why men and women did so and the benefits and problems this entailed. Marriage is considered in terms of how it was used to contain and order sexual relationships. But in reconstructing social and cultural meaning, we can look to other aspects of 'marriage' beyond the bourgeois dictum.

The shifting nature of these relationships also highlights the differences between the free and the bound. Once free, men and women acquired a new language and a new voice, as they redefined themselves in relation to their new place within the colony. We can see in applications from those who had become free, how the childlike dependency and sense of incompetence of the bound are replaced with assertiveness, confidence and self-esteem. In their applications, the free express the view that they now had a right to claim their children. If we consider these processes and interactions we can discern shifting understandings about fatherhood, motherhood and childhood, and how the applicants' identities were redefined in relation to these new identities.

Free and Bound

The themes of freedom and bondage emerge as important motifs in these applications. As Paula Byrne has noted, men and women in New

South Wales used the word free within the court of law to 'challenge magistrates and constables'.[61] While Hirst has argued that colonial society carried the hallmarks of a 'free society', there is no doubt that the psychology of what it meant to be free or bound was indelibly marked on its inhabitants. For women, freedom took on a particular meaning within a family context. Their new identity as free mothers and wives gave them a sense of pride and affirmation. These women assumed a new identity of legitimacy within a new family life.[62] Mary Bolton was transported in 1825 for seven years with four daughters, two of whom were placed in the Female Orphan School. Ellen had left the school after about two years and was serving an apprenticeship, and Sarah had also been apprenticed. Now free, Bolton was 'naturally anxious to have her youngest daughter . . . under her immediate care and superintendence'. David and Ann Patterson wrote in 1827 requesting that, in anticipation of becoming free, they should be allowed access to their child. The mother of the child would be free in a few months, and was holding a ticket of leave, while the husband was an assigned servant. But as they were not yet free, their application was refused on the grounds that both parents were still convicts. Catherine Darby, writing with confidence in 1831, claimed she was now free and 'capable of providing and protecting her daughter . . . in a comfortable and respectable manner'. Catherine Buck similarly wrote in 1827, that she was now a free woman of 'about a few months' and had married a free man. She now 'humbly begs that she be permitted to have her daughter out of the Orphan school' because she is 'fairly enabled to support her and give her education'.[63]

When convicts assumed the status of being free they assumed a confidence to assert a belief in their legal right to access to their children. A free identity became synonymous with assuming responsibility and an ability to provide and care. Unlike the patronising and childlike treatment of prisoners, once free, individuals were endowed with adult responsibility by the state authorities. Edward and Ann Raper wrote to Archdeacon Thomas Scott that they were both free, able to provide for her sisters, and were desirous to maintain them. Margaret Quinn wrote in 1831 that 'absolute necessity' compelled her and her husband as prisoners of the Crown to admit their three children, but now that they were free, they were in circumstances 'as will enable them to afford a sufficient and comfortable support'. Bridget Walsh reported in August 1830 that she had been transported for seven years and had placed her child in the orphan school on arrival. Since becoming free, she was now in circumstances which allowed her to maintain her child. Ann Howard assured the authorities that, as her term expired within a fortnight, she could now support her son in a 'comfortable way', by her own industry. Mary Ann Clark wrote in November 1832 that on her arrival in the colony in 1825 her child Margaret, who had been taken from her, had been placed in the orphan school. She had become free in April 1831, and now desired to have Margaret returned to her, for she had since had another child, with whom Margaret could assist, which would allow her to 'resume her usual work of washing'.[64]

It was less common for men to attempt to retrieve their children, but they did apply for them after becoming free. William Guthrie, a constable and free, applied for his daughter, Mary Ann Smith, 'who was taken from me six years ago and sent to the Orphan School' as he could now maintain her and was able to give her education.[65]

The applications by parents to obtain children in and out of orphan schools reveals the ways in which relationships were transitory during the 1820s and 1830s amongst the poor, convict and free. The applications lodged to retrieve children suggest that being free meant that former prisoners interacted in different ways with the state authorities. This new status gave them a confidence and belief in their right to gain access to their children. Furthermore, they understood that respectability and employment would be valued and recognised by the orphan school authorities in their endeavours to retrieve their children, in their quest for an emancipated life.

Conclusion

Each successive generation of historians has discarded, reformulated or asked new questions of the convict past in light of contemporary concerns. What preoccupies one generation of historians will inevitably be redefined by another. In this book I have suggested some new directions for broadening our understanding of convict history and of the experiences of convict women in particular. I have attempted to move the discussion beyond whether convict women were criminals or skilled labourers; whether they were whores or not; whether most of them became respectable citizens or not; whether they were victims of patriarchy or not; whether the conditions they endured were better in Australia or in Britain; and whether the prisons were a hell or a haven for female inmates. In order to shift the discussion away from these arguments we need to ask different questions of Australia's convict period. But if the task ahead is to be a profound revision, how can this revision be imagined?

Unravelling the cultural meaning of headshaving, of moments of laughter and play, of the language of pollution, purity and abandonment, of the inside/out nature of the prisons and the spatial arrangement on ships and within the towns, of the question of looking and seeing, of the perception of convict women as savage and other, of the abandoning and wandering mother and of the orphan, are new avenues for understanding colonial relationships.

The stories in this book are haunting and disturbing. They encapsulate some of the contradictions, tensions, and uncertainties that lay beneath the surface of cultural and personal expression during the nineteenth century. These stories point to the ways in which understandings about sexual and racial difference were crucial for both the maintenance and disturbance of colonial society and they suggest the way that these differences provided a pivot for the expression of cultural anxiety.

Often it is at those moments of ambiguity and tension that we can illuminate broader cultural and social meaning, in this case, to understand the dynamics that gave shape to relationships and meaning to behaviour. These are moments not usually of the public realm of political and military events, but rather of the private, related to the self, the body and the psyche. It is through an analysis of the interaction of these dynamics within the social and cultural context, that we can capture the relationship and interaction between the cultural, the social and the self.

Australian historians have generally been reluctant to examine these processes or to pursue the implications of this approach. In the writing of Australia's colonial past, they have often examined culture through accessible and seemingly self-explanatory events. We have come to understand colonial culture through frameworks that have recreated the past with a linear certainty and a closure about the meaning and expression of power and resistance, identity, sexuality, race and gender. But more can be revealed about the historical complexity of these issues by looking beyond surface meanings. We can look to those moments that crystallise the unstated, but prevailing, tensions and contradictions, which may be less visible to the historian's eye, but are no less real or profound in shaping, defining and giving meaning to colonial relationships.

Abbreviations

AONSW	Archives Office of New South Wales
AOT	Archives Office of Tasmania
CON	Convict Department Records
CSO	Colonial Secretary's Office
GO	Governor's Office, Tasmania
HRA	*Historical Records of Australia*
HRNSW	*Historical Records of New South Wales*
ML	Mitchell Library
PRO	Public Records Office
SLT	State Library of Tasmania

Notes

Introduction

1 'Proceedings of Inquiry, 10 September 1825', *Historical Records of Australia,* series 1, vol. XI, p. 819.
2 Carol Liston, 'New South Wales Under Governor Brisbane 1821–1825', PhD thesis, University of Sydney, 1980, p. 138.
3 'Proceedings of Inquiry', *HRA*, series 1, vol. XI, p. 819.
4 Ibid., pp. 820; 826–8.
5 Ibid., pp. 824; 828; 828–9.
6 Liston, 'New South Wales Under Governor Brisbane', p. 143.
7 Phillip Tardif, *Notorious Strumpets and Dangerous Girls: Convict Women in Van Diemen's Land 1803–1829,* Sydney, Angus & Robertson, 1990, p. 4.
8 Ibid., pp. 1; 3; 30.
9 For a detailed discussion of this literature see Joy Damousi, 'Beyond the "Origins" Debate: Theorising Sexuality and Gender Disorder in Convict Women's History', *Australian Historical Studies,* no. 106, April 1996.
10 Joan Scott, 'Gender: A Useful Category of Historical Analysis', *American Historical Review,* no. 5, vol. 91, December 1986, p. 1068.
11 Roger Chartier, *Cultural History: Between Practices and Representations,* translated by Lydia Cochrane, London, Polity Press, 1988, p. 104.
12 Regina Gagnier, *Subjectivities: A History of Self-Representation in Britain,* London, Oxford University Press, 1991, pp. 3–13.
13 Alan Atkinson, 'Four Patterns of Convict Protest', *Labour History,* no. 37, November 1979, p. 30.
14 Mary Douglas, *Natural Symbols: Explorations in Cosmology,* London, Penguin, 1970, p. 14.
15 Raphael Samuel, 'Reading the Signs', *History Workshop Journal,* no. 32, Autumn 1991, pp. 88–109.

1   Chaos and Order: Gender, Space and Sexuality on Female Convict Ships

1 Lloyd Robson, 'The Origin of the Women Convicts Sent To Australia, 1787–1852', *Historical Studies,* vol. 11, no. 41, November 1963, p. 43.
2 Tardif, *Notorious Strumpets and Dangerous Girls,* p. 15.

3 'Report of the Bench of Magistrates', *HRA*, p. 322.
4 Charles Bateson, *The Convict Ships 1787–1868*, Sydney, Reed, 1959, pp. 58–9.
5 Tardif, *Notorious Strumpets and Dangerous Girls*, pp. 1; 12.
6 'Lieutenant-Governor Arthur to Under-Secretary Hay, 20 June 1826', *HRA*, series 1, vol. V, pp. 285; 268.
7 'Governor Darling to the Commissioners of the Navy, 26 July 1826', *HRA*, series 1, vol. XII, p. 451.
8 'Mr Justice Field to Governor Macquarie, 1 December 1817', *HRA*, series 1, vol. IX, p. 510.
9 'Proceedings of the Bench of Magistrates, Testimony of Ann Moore', *HRA*, series 1, vol. X, p. 325.
10 'Testimony of Reverend Philip Connolly', ibid., pp. 326–7.
11 'Testimony of Reverend John Joseph Therry', ibid., pp. 328–9.
12 'Nicholas Bayly to Governor Macquarie, 24 May 1820', ibid., p. 319.
13 'Proceedings of the Bench of Magistrates, Testimony of Jacob Pistor', ibid., p. 331.
14 For a discussion of the conditions aboard ships that transported other groups, like emigrants and boy convicts, see A. J. Hammerton, ' "Without Natural Protectors": Female Immigration to Australia, 1832–36', *Historical Studies*, vol. 16, no. 65, October 1975, pp. 539–61; Kim Humphrey, 'Objects of Compassion: Young Male Convicts in Van Diemen's Land, 1834–1850', *Australian Historical Studies*, no. 98, April 1992, pp. 13–33; Andrew Hassam, *Sailing to Australia: Shipboard Diaries By Nineteenth Century British Emigrants*, Melbourne, Melbourne University Press, 1995; Emma Curtin, 'Gentility Afloat: Gentlewomen's Diaries and the Voyage to Australia, 1830–80', *Australian Historical Studies*, no. 105, October 1995, pp. 634–52. See Bateson, *The Convict Ships*; Babette Smith, *A Cargo of Women: Sussanah Watson and the Convicts of the Princess Royal*, Sydney, Sun Books, 1988, pp. 24–32; Greg Dening, *Mr. Bligh's Bad Language: Passion, Power and Theatre on the Bounty*, Cambridge, Cambridge University Press, 1992, pp. 19–28.
15 For a complete account of the incident on the *Friendship*, see 'Governor Macquarie to Earl Bathurst, 3 March 1818', and 'Depositions Respecting the Ship, *Friendship*' in *HRA*, series 1, vol. IX, pp. 750–8.
16 John West, *History of Tasmania*, vol. 2, Tasmania, Henry Dowling, 1852, p. 115.
17 Dening, *Mr. Bligh's Bad Language*, pp. 82–3.
18 John Haslem, *Convict Ships*, London, Taylor and Hessey, 1819, p. 15.
19 West, *History of Tasmania*, p. 116.
20 *Elizabeth* Inquiry, 1827–1828, Colonial Secretary Papers, 4/6981, AONSW.
21 Thrasycles Clarke, Journal, *Kains*, 1830–1, PRO 3199, AONSW.
22 See Bill Beatty, *Early Australia: With Shame Remembered*, Sydney, Angus and Robertson, 1962, p. 15.
23 Babette Smith, *A Cargo of Women*, p. 29.
24 Tardif, *Notorious Strumpets and Dangerous Girls*, p. 16.
25 Marian Aveling, 'Imagining New South Wales as a Gendered Society, 1783–1821', *Australian Historical Studies*, no. 98, April 1992, pp. 1–12.
26 Dening, *Mr. Bligh's Bad Language*, pp. 19–20; 83.
27 Doreen Massey, 'Politics and Space/Time', in Michael Keith and Steve Pile (eds), *Place and the Politics of Identity*, London, Routledge, 1993, p. 156.
28 Bateson, *The Convict Ships*, p. 123.
29 William Elyard, Journal, *John Bull*, 1821–1822, PRO 3199, AONSW, entries for 29 August 1821 and 22 October 1821.

30 Quoted in Bateson, *The Convict Ships*, p. 70.
31 Ibid., pp. 74; 188; 381; 188.
32 Tardif, *Notorious Strumpets and Dangerous Girls*, p. 12.
33 Ibid., pp. 381–94.
34 Bateson, *The Convict Ships*, p. 76; Paul Fildon and R. J. Ryan (eds), *The Journal of Philip Gidley King: Lieutenant R.N. 1787–1790*, Sydney, Australian Documents Library, 1980, pp. 184; 253; 283; 280.
35 William Rae, Journal, *Eliza*, 1822, PRO 3194, AONSW, 'General Orders'.
36 Ibid.
37 Thomas Roylance, Journal, *Hadlow*, 1818–1819, PRO 3197, AONSW.
38 William Evans, Journal, *Bencoolen*, 1819, PRO 3189, AONSW.
39 Dening, *Mr. Bligh's Bad Language*, p. 119.
40 *Instructions for Surgeons-Superintendents and Masters on Board Convict Ships*, London, 1838, item 13.
41 Robert Espie, Journal, *Lord Sidmouth*, 1822–1823, PRO 3201, AONSW, entry for 28 September 1822.
42 Ibid., 8 October; 18 October; 14 December 1822; 1 March 1823.
43 Elyard Journal, 20 August; 19 November 1821.
44 William Anderson, Journal, *City of Edinburgh*, 1828, PRO 3190, AONSW.
45 See Evans Journal, 5 May 1819.
46 Joseph Hughes, Journal, *Elizabeth*, 1827–1828, PRO 3194, AONSW, 'General Remarks'; 31 October; 16 November 1827.
47 Elyard Journal, 11 November; 12 November; 11 September; 17 July; 24 July 1821.
48 Thomas Reid, *Two Voyages to New South Wales and Van Diemen's Land*, London, 1822, pp. 132–3.
49 *Australian Dictionary of Biography*, vol. 1, Melbourne, Melbourne University Press, 1966, p. 376, 'Thomas Reid'.
50 Elyard Journal, 2 August; 31 August; 6 September; 11 November 1821.
51 Morgan Price, Journal, *Almorah*, 1824, PRO 3187, AONSW, entry for 21 April.
52 Espie Journal, *Lord Sidmouth*, 14 October; 3 October; 20 October 1822.
53 Elyard Journal, 9 September; 24 August; 6 October 1821.
54 Robert Hughes, *The Fatal Shore: A History of Transportation of Convicts to Australia 1787–1868*, London, Pan, 1987, pp. 144; 150–1; A. G. L. Shaw, *Convicts and Colonies: A Study of Penal Transportation from Great Britain and Ireland to Other Parts of the Empire*, London, Faber and Faber, 1966, p. 121.
55 Bateson, *The Convict Ships*, p. 51
56 Ibid., pp. 87; 53.
57 Alan Grocott, *Convicts, Clergymen and Churches: Changing Attitudes of Convicts and Ex Convicts Towards the Clergy and in New South Wales, 1788–1851*, Sydney, Sydney University Press, 1980, p. 47.
58 Shaw, *Convicts and Colonies*, pp. 110; 120–1.
59 *Australian Dictionary of Biography*, vol. 2, p. 369, 'William Redfern'.
60 Bateson, *The Convict Ships*, pp. 38–57.
61 Elyard Journal, 29 August; 28 September; 7 October; 5 November; 6 November; 14 November; 25 September; 13 September 1821.
62 Espie Journal, *Lord Sidmouth*, 13 January 1822.
63 William Leyson, Journal, *Henry Wellesley*, 1837–1838, PRO 3197, AONSW.
64 See Bateson, *The Convict Ships*, p. 277.
65 George Fairfowle, Journal, *Sovereign*, 1827, PRO 3210, AONSW.
66 Fairfowle Journal, 'General Remarks'.
67 *Australian Dictionary of Biography*, vol. 1, p. 268, 'Peter Cunningham'.

68 Peter Cunningham, *Two Years in New South Wales*, London, 1827, p. 317.
69 Thomas Reid, *Two Voyages to New South Wales and Van Diemen's Land*, London, 1822, pp. 173; 262; 304; 168; 172–3; 104.
70 Colin Arnott Browning, *The Convict Ship: A Narrative of the Results of Scriptural Instruction and Moral Discipline on Board the 'Earl Grey'*, London, Robert Craighead, 1856, p. 158.
71 *Australian Dictionary of Biography*, vol. 1, p. 169, 'Colin Arnott Browning'.
72 Browning, *The Convict Ship: A Narrative*, p. 200.
73 Leonore Davidoff and Catherine Hall, *Family Fortunes: Men and Women of the English Middle Class, 1780–1850*, London, Hutchinson, 1987, pp. 108–9.
74 Browning, *The Convict Ship: A Narrative*, pp. 206–8.
75 *Australian Dictionary of Biography*, vol. 1, p. 503, 'James Hall'.
76 'Proceedings of Bench of Magistrates, 19 August 1822', *HRA*, series 1, vol. X, p. 754.
77 'Proceedings of Bench of Magistrates, 29 May 1824', *HRA*, series 1, vol. XI, p. 299.
78 Ibid., pp. 291; 290.
79 'Governor Thomas Brisbane to Earl Bathurst, 24 June 1824', ibid., pp. 283–4.
80 Anne McClintock, *Imperial Leather: Race, Gender and Sexuality in the Colonial Contest*, New York, Routledge, 1995, p. 47.
81 William B. Jones, Journal, *Aurora*, 1851, PRO 3189, AONSW, 'General Regulations Adopted on Board'.
82 Hughes Journal, 31 October 1827.
83 Espie Journal, *Lord Sidmouth*, 'Copy of Regulations and Rules'.
84 *Instructions for Surgeons-Superintendents*, p. 22.
85 Surgeon-Superintendent Peter Leonard, Journal, *Atwick*, 1837–8, PRO 3189, AONSW.
86 Hughes Journal, 25 December 1827.
87 Fairfowle Journal, 'General Remarks'.
88 Dr. E. Ford Bromley, *Surry*, 1832–1833, PRO 3211, AONSW.
89 Jones Journal, *Aurora*; Clarke, Journal, *Kains*.
90 Jones Journal, 9 July 1851.
91 Leyson Journal, 'General Comments'.
92 Jones Journal, 18 July 1851.
93 See Bryan Gandevia and Simon Gandevia, 'Childhood Mortality and Its Social Background in the First Settlement at Sydney Cove, 1788–1792', *Australian Paediatric Journal*, vol. 11, no. 1, 1975, pp. 9–18; B. Gandevia and J. Cobley, 'Mortality at Sydney Cove, 1788–1792', *Australian and New Zealand Journal of Medicine*, vol. 4, no. 2, April 1974, pp. 111–25.
94 Lucia Zedner, 'Wayward Sisters: The Prison for Women', in Norval Morris and David J. Rottman (eds), *The Oxford History of the Prison: The Practice of Punishment in Western Society*, New York, Oxford University Press, 1995, p. 330.
95 Clarke Journal; Jones Journal, 'General Remarks'; Anderson Journal, 'General Remarks'.
96 Jones Journal, 12 June 1851.
97 Elyard Journal, 2 November 1821.
98 Espie Journal, *Lord Sidmouth*, 22 November 1822; Robert Espie, Journal, *Elizabeth*, 1836, PRO 3194, AONSW, 'General Remarks'.
99 Jones Journal, 'General Regulations Adopted on Board'; Morgan Price, Journal, *Almorah*, 1824, PRO 3187, AONSW.
100 Espie Journal, *Lord Sidmouth*, 1 October 1822.

101 Alan Grocott, *Convicts, Clergymen and Churches*, p. 56.
102 R. B. Walker, 'Tobacco Smoking in Australia, 1788–1914', *Historical Studies*, vol. 19, no. 75, October 1980, pp. 269; 279.
103 Elyard Journal, 20 August; 29 July 1821.
104 Leyson Journal, 'General Comments'.
105 Elyard Journal, 3 December 1821.
106 P. G. Fildon and R. J. Ryan (eds), *The Journal of Arthur Bowes Smyth, Surgeon, Lady Penthyn, 1787–1789*, Sydney, Australian Documents Library, 1979, p. 13, entry for April 1787.
107 Dening, *Mr. Bligh's Bad Language*, pp. 116–18.
108 Rae Journal.
109 Fildon and Ryan, *Journal of Arthur Bowes Smyth*, p. 70.
110 Espie Journal, *Elizabeth*.

2 'Depravity and Disorder': The Sexuality of Convict Women

1 Samuel Marsden, *An Answer to Certain Calumnies*, London, Hatchard and Son, 1826, p. 18.
2 James Jervis, *The Cradle City of Australia: A History of Parramatta 1788–1961*, Parramatta, City of Parramatta, 1961, pp. 6–26; 28–37.
3 3 September 1828.
4 Tardif, *Notorious Strumpets and Dangerous Girls*, pp. 17–18; Annette Salt, *These Outcast Women: The Parramatta Female Factory 1821–1848*, Sydney, Hale and Iremonger, 1981, p. 62
5 Salt, *These Outcast Women*, pp. 46–53.
6 Cunningham, *Two Years in New South Wales*, p. 323.
7 Tardif, *Notorious Strumpets and Dangerous Girls*, p. 2.
8 Laurel Heath, 'The Female Convict Factories of New South Wales and Van Diemen's Land: An Examination of their Role in the Control, Punishment and Reformation of Prisoners Between 1804 and 1854', MA thesis, Australian National University, 1978, pp. 19–27.
9 Elizabeth Wilson, *The Sphinx in the City: Urban Life, the Control of Disorder, and Women*, Virago, London, 1991, pp. 5–7; 28–38.
10 Samuel Marsden, *An Answer to Certain Calumnies*, pp. 19; 23.
11 See Lynda Nead, *Myths of Sexuality: Representations of Women in Victorian Britain*, London, Oxford University Press, 1988, p. 106.
12 'A Few Observations in the Situation of the Female Convicts in New South Wales', Marsden Papers, ML, MS 18.
13 A. T. Yarwood, *Samuel Marsden: The Great Survivor*, Melbourne, Melbourne University Press, 1977, pp. 50–3.
14 Smith, *A Cargo of Women*, pp. 60–6; Alan Atkinson, 'Convicts and Courtship', in Patricia Grimshaw, et al. (eds), *Families in Colonial Australia*, Sydney, Allen & Unwin, 1985, pp. 19–31.
15 See Nead, *Myths of Sexuality*, pp. 118–22; Judith Walkowitz, *City of Dreadful Delight: Narratives of Sexual Danger in Late Victorian London*, London, Virago, 1992, p. 22; Mary Poovey, 'Curing the "Social Body" in 1832: James Phillips Kay and the Irish in Manchester', *Gender and History*, vol. 5, no. 2, Summer 1993, pp. 196–211.
16 See Sandra Blair, 'The Revolt at Castle Forbes: A Catalyst to Emancipist Emigrant Confrontation', *Journal of the Royal Australian Historical Society*, vol. 64, part 2, September 1978, pp. 90–1.
17 *Australian Dictionary of Biography*, vol. 1, p. 266, 'James Mudie'.

18 'Report of the Select Committee on Transportation, 1837', in *British Parliamentary Papers, Crime and Punishment: Transportation*, vol. 2, *Session 1837*, Shannon, Irish University Press, 1968, p. 102.

19 James Mudie, *The Felonry of New South Wales: Being a Faithful Picture of the Real Romance of Life in Botany Bay*, London, Whaley and Co., 1837, p. 203.

20 15 June 1832, p. 2.

21 Cunningham, *Two Years in New South Wales*, pp. 287–8.

22 Peter Stallybrass and Allon White, *The Politics and Poetics of Transgression*, Ithaca, New York, Cornell University Press, 1986, pp. 126–33.

23 Nead, *Myths of Sexuality*, pp. 118–29.

24 1 March 1827, p. 2.

25 Michael Sturma, 'Eye of the Beholder: The Stereotype of Women Convicts 1788–1852', *Labour History*, no. 34, May 1978, pp. 3–10.

26 Jan Kociumbas, *The Oxford History of Australia*, vol. 2, *Possessions 1770–1860*, Melbourne, Oxford University Press, 1992, pp. 14–15.

27 John Ritchie, *Lachlan Macquarie: A Biography*, Melbourne, Melbourne University Press, 1986, pp. 34; 42.

28 Brian Fletcher, *Ralph Darling: A Governor Maligned*, Melbourne, Melbourne University Press, 1984, p. 24; Elizabeth Windschuttle, ' "Feeding the Poor and Sapping Their Strength": The Public Role of Ruling-Class Women in Eastern Australia, 1788–1850', in Elizabeth Windschuttle (ed.), *Women, Class and History: Feminist Perspectives on Australia 1788–1978*, Sydney, Fontana, 1980, pp. 53–79.

29 Leonore Davidoff, 'Regarding Some "Old Husbands' Tales": Public and Private in Feminist History', in Leonore Davidoff, *Worlds Between: Historical Perspectives on Gender and Class*, London, Polity Press, 1995, p. 235.

30 Nead, *Myths of Sexuality*, p. 141.

31 Davidoff and Hall, *Family Fortunes*, pp. 170–86.

32 Lyndal Ryan, ' "From Stridency to Silence": The Policing of Convict Women 1803–1853', in Diane Kirkby (ed.), *Sex, Power and Justice: Historical Perspectives on Law in Australia*, Melbourne, Oxford University Press, 1995, p. 74.

33 *Australian Dictionary of Biography*, vol. 1, p. 411, 'Jane Franklin'.

34 The Journal of Lady Franklin, vol. 2, 22 August to 9 September 1839, Franklin Papers, NS 279, State Library of Tasmania. I owe a very special thanks to Paul Patten for this reference.

35 From *Temperance Advocate*, 21 April 1841, quoted in Elizabeth Windschuttle, 'Women, Class and Temperance: Moral Reform in Eastern Australia, 1832–1857', *Push from the Bush*, no. 3, May 1978, pp. 5–25.

36 Ronald Hyam, 'Empire and Sexual Opportunity', *The Journal of Imperial and Commonwealth History*, vol. 14, no. 2, pp. 34–89.

37 Davidoff and Hall, *Family Fortunes*, p. 401.

38 Ryan, 'From Stridency to Silence', in Kirkby, *Sex, Power and Justice*, p. 72.

39 'Governor Macquarie to Viscount Castlereagh, 30 April 1810', in 'Appendix 33' of 'Report of the Select Committee on Transportation, 1812', in *British Parliamentary Papers, Crime and Punishment: Transportation*, vol. 1, *Sessions 1810–32*, Shannon, Irish University Press, 1969, p. 112.

40 Alison Alexander, *Governors' Ladies: The Wives and Mistresses of Van Diemen's Land Governors*, Hobart, Tasmanian Historical Research Association, 1987, pp. 17–35.

41 Paul Fildon and R. J. Ryan (eds), *The Journal and Letters of Lieutenant Ralph Clark, 1787–1792*, Sydney, Australian Documents Library, 1981, pp. 32; 19; 22; 27; 65; 97; 19; 68.

42 John White, *Journal of a Voyage to NSW*, Sydney, Angus and Robertson, 1962, pp. 30–31.

43 Ibid., pp. 95–6; 30–1.

44 *Australian Dictionary of Biography*, vol. 1, p. 595, 'John White'.

45 John Henderson, *Observations on the Colonies of New South Wales and Van Diemen's Land*, Calcutta, 1832, p. 22.

46 Davidoff, *Worlds Between*, p. 235.

47 'Passion and Power: Introduction', in Kathy Peiss and Christina Simmons (eds), *Passion and Power: Sexuality in History*, Philadelphia, Temple University Press, 1989, p. 10.

48 Carole Pateman, ' "The Disorder of Women": Women, Love, and the Sense of Justice', in Carole Pateman, *The Disorder of Women: Democracy, Feminism and Political Theory*, London, Polity Press, 1989, pp. 17–29.

49 Charles Zika, 'Fears of Flying: Representations of Witchcraft and Sexuality in Early Sixteenth Century Germany', *Australian Journal of Art*, vol. VIII, 1989/1990, pp. 19–47.

50 Michael Sturma, *Vice in a Vicious Society: Crime and Convicts in Mid-Nineteenth Century New South Wales*, St Lucia, University of Queensland Press, 1983, pp. 51–61.

51 Mary Douglas, *Purity and Danger: An Analysis of the Concepts of Pollution and Taboo*, Penguin, London, 1966, pp. 2–7.

52 See Portia Robinson, *The Women of Botany Bay: A Reinterpretation of the Role of Women in the Origins of Australian Society*, Melbourne, Penguin Books, 1988; Salt, *These Outcast Women*; Monica Perrott, *A Tolerable Good Success: Economic Opportunity for Women in New South Wales, 1788–1830*, Sydney, Hale and Iremonger, 1983; Smith, *A Cargo of Women*.

53 Portia Robinson, 'The First Forty Years', in Judy Mackinolty and Heather Radi (eds), *In Pursuit of Justice: Australian Women and the Law 1788–1979*, Hale and Iremonger, Sydney, 1979, p. 16.

54 Sturma, 'Eye of the Beholder', p. 4.

55 'Robert Lowe to Commissioner Bigge, 10 August 1820', in John Ritchie (ed.), *The Evidence to the Bigge Reports: New South Wales Under Governor Macquarie*, vol. 2, *The Written Evidence*, Melbourne, Heinemann, 1971, p. 48.

56 'John Macarthur to Commissioner Bigge, 7 February 1821', ibid., p. 74; 'Evidence of Archibald Bell', ibid., p. 56.

57 Sandra Blair, 'The Felonry and the Free? Divisions in Colonial Society in the Penal Era', *Labour History*, no. 45, November 1983, p. 9.

58 'Macarthur to Commissioner Bigge, 2 December 1819', in Ritchie, *The Evidence to the Bigge Reports*, pp. 75; 81.

59 G. Hammersley, 'A Few Observations on the Situation of the Female Convicts in New South Wales', Hammersley Papers, A657, Miscellaneous MSS 1820–1894, ML.

60 Stallybrass and White, *Politics and Poetics of Transgression*, p. 135.

61 Report of the Committee on Immigration, NSW Legislative Assembly, Parliamentary Papers, 1838.

62 *Australian Dictionary of Biography*, vol. 1, p. 269, 'Peter Murdoch'.

63 'Report of the Select Committee on Transportation, 1837', pp. 119; 12.

64 Paul Collins, 'William Bernard Ullathorne and the Foundation of Australian Catholicism 1815–1840', PhD thesis, Australian National University, 1989, p. 267.

65 William Ullathorne, *The Catholic Mission in Australasia*, Sydney, 1838, pp. 21; 20.

66 'Report of the Select Committee on Transportation, 1812', p. 12.
67 'Evidence of John Macarthur', in Ritchie, *The Evidence to the Bigge Reports*, p. 83; 'Report of the Select Committee on Transportation, 1837', p. 197.
68 'Report of the Commissioner of Inquiry into the State of the Colony of New South Wales, June 1822', *British Parliamentary Papers, Colonies: Australia*, vol. 1, *Sessions 1822–25*, Shannon, Irish University Press, 1968, p. 70.
69 'Governor Darling to Sir George Murray, 18 February 1829', *HRA*, series 1, vol. XIV, p. 652.
70 Tardif, *Notorious Strumpets and Dangerous Girls*, p. 26.
71 '3 July 1799', *Historical Records of New South Wales*, vol. III, pp. 685–6.
72 'Governor Darling to Under-Secretary Hay, 26 July, 1826', *HRA*, series 1, vol. XII, p. 450.
73 Roger Therry, *Reminiscences of Thirty Years' Residence in New South Wales and Victoria*, London, 1863, p. 219.
74 Ullathorne, *The Catholic Mission in Australasia*, p. 19.
75 Henderson, *Observations on the Colonies*, p. 20.
76 'Transcript of Evidence before R. P. Stuart and Benjamin Horne, 10 April 1851', Tasmanian Papers, no. 111, FM/4/8517, ML.
77 Stuart to Comptroller-General, 14 April 1851, in Transcript of Evidence, Tasmanian Papers, no. 111, 15163, FM 4/8517, ML.
78 Alphabetical List of Women Applying for Permission to Marry with Woman's Name and Decision, January 1854 to July 1857, CON 52/7, AOT, pp. 65; 363; 356.
79 *Town and Country Journal*, 18 May 1889, p. 28.
80 James Bonwick, *Curious Facts of Old Colonial Days*, London, 1870, p. 281.
81 Ibid., p. 282.
82 Henderson, *Observations on the Colonies*, p. 21.
83 R. C. Hutchinson, 'Mrs. Hutchinson and the Female Factories of Early Australia', *Tasmanian Historical Research Association*, vol. 11, no. 2, December 1963, p. 57.
84 'Report of the Select Committee on Transportation, 1837', p. 196.
85 Ibid., p. 39.
86 Ryan, 'From Stridency to Silence', in Kirkby, *Sex, Power and Justice*, p. 82.
87 Godfrey Charles Mundy, *Our Antipodes: Or, Residence and Rambles in the Australasian Colonies with a Glimpse of the Goldfields*, London, 1854, pp. 500; 501.
88 E. A. Kaplan, 'Is the Gaze Male?', in A. Snitow, et al. (eds), *Powers of Desire: The Politics of Sexuality*, New York, Monthly Review Press, 1983, p. 311.
89 See Stonequarry Benchbooks, 4/8/1831–9/12/1833, 4/7573, Reel 672, AONSW, 16 July 1832; 18 April 1833.
90 Stallybrass and White, *Politics and Poetics of Transgression*, p. 137.
91 Walkowitz, *City of Dreadful Delight*, p. 23.
92 Tardif, *Notorious Strumpets and Dangerous Girls*, p. 18.
93 James O'Connell, *A Residence of Eleven Years in New Holland and the Caroline Islands*, Boston, 1836, p. 70.
94 'Report of the Select Committee on Transportation, 1837', p. 39.
95 *Sydney Gazette*, 14 July 1832, p. 4.
96 Marsden, *An Answer to Certain Calumnies*, p. 27.
97 Poovey, 'Curing the "Social Body" in 1832', p. 196.
98 Catherine Hall, *White, Male and Middle Class: Explorations in Feminism and History*, London, Polity Press, 1992, p. 206.
99 Poovey, 'Curing the "Social Body" in 1832', p. 197.

100 Bonwick, *Curious Facts of Old Colonial Days*, p. 156

101 Therry, *Reminiscences*, p. 217.

102 Nead, *Myths of Sexuality*, p. 91.

103 Hammersley, 'A Few Observations', Hammersley Papers.

104 Henderson, *Observations on the Colonies*, p. 19.

105 L. Perry Curtis Jr, *Apes and Angels: The Irishman in Victorian Caricature*, London, David and Charles, 1971, p. 95; John Williams, 'Irish Female Convicts and Tasmania', *Labour History*, no. 44, May 1983, p. 10.

106 'Report of the Select Committee on Transportation, 1837', p. 169.

107 'Testimony, Josiah Spode', Report of the Committee of Inquiry into Female Convict Prison Discipline, CSO 22/50, AOT.

108 Lieutenant Breton, *Excursions in New South Wales, Western Australia and Van Diemen's Land During the Years 1830, 1831, 1832, and 1833*, London, Richard Bentley, 1833, pp. 79; 319.

109 Reverend Daniel Tyerman and George Bennett, *Journal of Voyages and Travels*, vol. 2, London, 1831.

110 G. Bond, *A Brief Account of the Colony of Port Jackson in NSW: Its Native Inhabitants, Productions, etc.*, London, 1809, p. 3; 'Reverend Robert Cartwright to Governor Macquarie, 6 December 1819', and 'Governor Darling to Earl Bathurst, 22 December 1826', in *British Parliamentary Papers, Colonies: Australia*, vol. 4, *Sessions 1830–36*, pp. 4; 11; 'Lord John Russell to Sir George Gipps, 25 August 1840', in *British Parliamentary Papers, Colonies: Australia*, vol. 8, *Session 1844*, p. 74.

111 Lyndal Ryan, *The Aboriginal Tasmanians*, St Lucia, University of Queensland Press, 1981, pp. 85; 87–97. See also Henry Reynolds, *Frontier: Aborigines, Settlers and Land*, Sydney, Allen & Unwin, 1987, pp. 42–52.

112 Henry Reynolds, *Fate of a Free People: A Radical Re-examination of the Tasmanian Wars*, Melbourne, Penguin, 1995, pp. 29; 55–60.

113 Captain Watkin Tench, *A Narrative of the Expedition to Botany Bay*, London, 1789, p. 84

114 *Australian Dictionary of Biography*, vol. 2, p. 506, 'Watkin Tench'.

115 'Report of the Select Committee on Transportation, 1837', p. 43.

116 See Ann McGrath, 'The White Man's Looking Glass: Aboriginal–Colonial Gender Relations at Port Jackson', *Australian Historical Studies*, vol. 24, no. 95, October 1990, pp. 189–206.

117 'Report of the Commissioner of Inquiry into the State of the Colony of New South Wales, June 1822', p. 70.

118 Hutchinson, 'Mrs. Hutchinson and the Female Factories', p. 53.

119 Robert Hughes, *The Fatal Shore*, p. 95.

120 'Report of the Select Committee on Transportation, 1837', p. 42.

121 Lieutenant Breton, *Excursions*, p. 195.

122 Stallybrass and White, *Politics and Poetics of Transgression*, p. 23.

3 Disrupting the Boundaries: Resistance and Convict Women

1 *Australian Dictionary of Biography*, vol. 1, p. 77, 'William Bedford'.

2 Robert Crooke, *The Convict*, Hobart, 1958, pp. 23; 25; 26.

3 Kathleen Fitzpatrick, *Sir John Franklin in Tasmania, 1837–1843*, Melbourne, Melbourne University Press, 1949, pp. 80–1.

4 Report, Inquiry into Female Convict Prison Discipline, 24 March 1842.

5 Ibid., August 1842. Reprimanded were Bridget Toomey, Mary Roberts, Mary Smith, Caroline Justin, Martha Hodgson, Jane Charlton; extended

sentences, Ann McKenna and Cath Jane Downey; hard labour and solitary confinement, Fanny Jarvis, Mary Cunningham, Janet McLean, Elizabeth Thomas, Mary Matthews, Mary Rafter, Elizabeth Clayton, Sarah Griffiths, Elizabeth Reid.

6 Report, Inquiry into Female Convict Prison Discipline, 'Evidence of Mrs. Hutchinson, 8 December 1841'.

7 Ibid., 'Testimony of John Price, Police Magistrate'; *Australian Dictionary of Biography*, vol. 2, p. 351, 'John Price'.

8 *True Colonist*, 26 May 1837, p. 578.

9 Zedner, 'Wayward Sisters', Morris and Rottman, *The Oxford History of Prison*, p. 350.

10 Douglas, *Natural Symbols: Explorations in Cosmology*, p. 14.

11 See Alastair Davidson, *The Invisible State: The Formation of the Australian State 1788–1901*, Cambridge, Cambridge University Press, 1991, pp. 19–64.

12 Robert Hughes, *The Fatal Shore*, p. 367.

13 Davidoff, 'Regarding Some "Old Husbands' Tales" ', Davidoff, *Worlds Between*, p. 231.

14 Yarwood, *Samuel Marsden*, p. 51.

15 Michael Ignatieff, *A Just Measure of Pain: The Penitentiary in the Industrial Revolution 1750–1850*, New York, Columbia University Press, 1978, p. 187.

16 See Davidson, *The Invisible State*, pp. 35–8.

17 Michel Foucault, *Power/Knowledge: Selected Interviews and Other Writings 1972–1977*, Susse, Harvester, 1980, p. 142.

18 Atkinson, 'Four Patterns of Convict Protest', p. 30.

19 W. Nichol, '"Malingering" and the Convict Protest', *Labour History*, no. 47, November 1984, pp. 18–27; 32.

20 *Sydney Herald*, 24 February 1834.

21 Ken Buckley and Ted Wheelwright, *No Paradise for Workers: Capitalism and the Common People in Australia 1788–1914*, Melbourne, Oxford University Press, 1988, pp. 57; 58; 59.

22 Smith, *A Cargo of Women*, p. 170; John Williams, 'Irish Female Convicts and Tasmania', p. 14; Robinson, 'The First Forty Years', Mackinolty and Radi, *In Pursuit of Justice*, pp. 7–8.

23 For a discussion along these lines, see Biddy Martin, 'Feminism, Criticism and Foucault', in Irene Diamond and Lee Quinby (eds), *Feminism and Foucault: Reflections on Resistance*, Boston, Northeastern University Press, 1988, pp. 9–10.

24 Michel Foucault, *A History of Sexuality: An Introduction*, Harmondsworth, Penguin, 1976, pp. 95–6; Foucault, *Power/Knowledge*, p. 142.

25 Steven Foster, 'Convict Assignment in New South Wales in the 1830s', *Push from the Bush*, no. 15, 1983, pp. 35–80.

26 'Report of the Select Committee on Transportation 1812', p. 12.

27 Tardif, *Notorious Strumpets and Dangerous Girls*, p. 19.

28 Patricia Grimshaw, et al., *Creating a Nation 1788–1990*, Melbourne, Penguin, 1994, pp. 68–9.

29 Ryan, 'From Stridency to Silence', Kirkby, *Sex, Power and Justice*, p. 74.

30 Tardif, *Notorious Strumpets and Dangerous Girls*, p. 19.

31 J. B. Hirst, *Convict Society and Its Enemies: A History of Early New South Wales*, Sydney, Allen & Unwin, 1983, pp. 56–7.

32 'Assignment of Female Convicts', 25 November 1840, Colonial Secretary Inward Letters, 4/2610.1, AONSW.

33 Davidson, *The Invisible State*, p. 42.

34 Report, Inquiry into Female Convict Prison Discipline.

35 Stonequarry Benchbooks, entry for 16 July 1832.

36 Ibid., entries for 18 April; 26 September 1833.

37 Ibid., entries for 4 August 1831; 6 July 1832; entry for 21 June 1839, Police Records, 1839–40, Tasmanian Papers, no. 238, ML, 21 June 1839; entries for Waterloo Point Police Court, 1837–39, Tasmanian Papers, no. 339, ML, 26 December 1837; 17 April 1838; entry for Campbelltown Police Court, 1831–1833, Tasmanian Papers no. 253, ML, 1 April 1833; entry for Richmond Police Court, Tasmanian Papers, no. 324, ML, 13 February 1833; entry for Spring Bay Police Court, 1838–1846, Tasmanian Papers no. 334, ML, 8 June 1839; entry for Oatlands Police Court 1839–1842, Tasmanian Papers no. 291, ML, 5 September 1835; entry for Richmond Police Court, Tasmanian Papers, no. 324, ML, 20 September 1833.

38 Police Report of Prisoners, 8/7/1828, x821, Reel 660, AONSW; Stonequarry Benchbooks, 15 August 1831; 13 May 1833; Hall on 18 July 1833; Callaghan on 10 September 1834; Munay on 19 September 1840; entry for 16 February 1836, Police Department, Police Court Records, Minutes, 1835–36, Tasmanian Papers, no. 237, ML.

39 'Report of the Select Committee on Transportation, 1837', p. 318.

40 Report, Inquiry into Female Convict Prison Discipline.

41 'An Indecent Assault upon the Person of Mary Newell', in ibid., 18 January 1843.

42 Report, Inquiry into Female Convict Prison Discipline.

43 W. J. Irvine to Comptroller-General, Tasmanian Papers, no. 93, Doc. 11037/1, FM/8508, ML.

44 W. J. Irvine to Comptroller-General, Tasmanian Papers, no. 107, FM 4/8515, ML.

45 Martha Vicinus, ' "They Wonder to Which Sex I Belong": The Historical Roots of the Modern Lesbian Identity', *Feminist Studies*, vol. 18, no. 3, Fall 1992, p. 479.

46 Jeffrey Weeks, *Coming Out: Homosexual Politics in Britain, From the Nineteenth Century to the Present*, London, Quartet Books, 1977, p. 88.

47 This link was made in the reformatory system for girls in Britain. See Michelle Gale, 'Girls and the Perception of Sex and Danger in the Victorian Reformatory System', *History*, vol. 78, no. 253, June 1993, pp. 212–14.

48 Benches of Magistrates, Police Court, Sydney, 1815–1816, 7/2643, Reel 660, AONSW; Bench of Magistrates, Parramatta, Jan. to Sept. 1822, Reel 660, AONSW, entry for 19 August 1822; Bathurst Benchbooks, 1825–6; 1832–3, Volume 2/8324, Reel 663, AONSW; Stonequarry Benchbooks.

49 Tardif, *Notorious Strumpets and Dangerous Girls*, pp. 32; 33.

50 See Paula Byrne, *Criminal Law and the Colonial Subject*, Cambridge, Cambridge University Press, 1993, pp. 106–24.

51 Minutes of Proceedings in the Court of Quarter Sessions, January 1832–June 1833, LC 216/1, AOT, entry for 23 March 1832; Record of Cases Heard in Petty Sessions, Sept 1836–April 1837, ML, entry for 8 October 1836; Magisterial Records, Launceston Court, 1833–1834, Tasmanian Papers, no. 277, CY 1966, ML, entry for 17 December 1833.

52 Benches of Magistrates, Police Court Sydney, entry for 16 April 1816; Bathurst Benchbooks, entry for 4 March 1833.

53 Return of Proceedings Taken at the Court House Parramatta for Quarter Ending 30 September 1824, 4/6671, Reel 660, AONSW, entries for 13 September 1824; 24 September 1824.

54 Bench of Magistrates, Stonequarry, 8/6/1829–1/8/1831, 4/7572, Reel 671, AONSW; 4/8/1831–9/12/1833, 4/7573, Reel 672, AONSW, entries for 28 November 1833; 6 December 1832.

55 Ibid., 24/6/1837–1/7/1843, 4/5627, Reel 672, AONSW, entry for 5 January 1841.

56 Ibid., entries for 18 July 1840; 23 February 1841.

57 Richmond Police Court, entry for 2 January 1833.

58 Bench of Magistrates, Stonequarry, entry March 1831; Stonequarry Benchbook, entries for 21 May 1832; 11 March 1833.

59 Ibid., entries for 15 May 1833; 3 June 1833; 2 January 1834; 11 August 1840; Magisterial Records, Launceston Court, entry for 25 January 1834.

60 Stonequarry Benchbooks, entry for 28 May 1832.

61 For a discussion of language, see Peter Burke and Roy Porter (eds), *The Social History of Language*, Cambridge, Cambridge University Press, 1987.

62 Sturma, *Vice in a Vicious Society*, pp. 129–31.

63 For a discussion of the relationship between language, gender and sexuality, see Laura Gowing, 'Gender and the Language of Insult in Early Modern London', *History Workshop Journal*, no. 35, Spring 1993, pp. 1–21.

64 Record of Cases Heard in Petty Sessions; entry for 27 September 1836, Police Court, Hobart Town, Record of Charges laid, September 1836–April 1837, AOT.

65 Stonequarry Benchbook, entries for 26 March 1832; 8 August 1833.

66 Richmond Police Court, entry for 8 January 1833.

67 Ibid., entry for 12 August 1833.

68 Michael Sturma, 'Policing the Criminal Frontier in Mid-Nineteenth Century Australia, Britain and America', in Mark Finnane (ed.), *Policing in Australia: Historical Perspectives*, Sydney, University of New South Wales Press, 1987, p. 22.

69 Michael Sturma, 'Police and Drunkards in Sydney 1841–1851', *Australian Journal of Politics and History*, no. 27, 1981, pp. 52–4.

70 See Police Report of Prisoners.

71 Tardif, *Notorious Strumpets and Dangerous Girls*, p. 5.

72 Deborah Oxley, *Convict Maids: The Forced Migration of Women to Australia*, Cambridge, Cambridge University Press, 1996, p. 49.

73 Beverley Lemire, 'The Theft of Clothes and Popular Consumerism in Early Modern England', *Journal of Social History*, vol. 24, no. 2, pp. 255–76; Margaret Maynard, *Fashioned from Penury: Dress as Cultural Practice in Colonial Australia*, Cambridge, Cambridge University Press, 1995, p. 10.

74 Ryan, 'From Stridency to Silence', Kirkby, *Sex Power and Justice*, p. 74.

75 *True Colonist*, 26 May 1837, p. 578.

76 Stonequarry Benchbooks, entry for 8 August 1833; Minutes of Proceedings in the Court of Quarter Sessions, entries for 31 May 1834; 23 March 1832; 4 February 1834.

77 Stonequarry Benchbooks, 14 December 1833–29 April 1835, Reel 672, AONSW; entries for 15 October 1834; 22 March 1832; Magisterial Records, Hobart Branch, 1819–1820, Tasmanian Papers, no. 271, CY 1878, ML, entry for 2 October 1819; Magisterial Records, Launceston Court; Richmond Police Court 1838–1839, Tasmanian Papers, no. 326, ML, entry for 4 March 1839; Campbelltown Police Court, entry for 19 April 1833.

78 *Sydney Gazette*, 10 February 1825, p. 3.

79 Ibid., 20 January 1825, pp. 3; 2.

80 Richmond Police Court, 1832–1841, entries for 25 September 1832; 8 January 1833; 8 April 1833; Magisterial Records, Hobart Branch, entry for 4 December 1819; Magisterial Records, Launceston Court, entry for 14 April 1834.
81 Police Department, Police Court Records, entry for 19 March 1836; Richmond Police Court 1838–1839, entry for 4 April 1838; Waterloo Police Court, entry for 4 June 1838.
82 *Australian*, 31 October 1827, p. 3.
83 Undated letter, 1830, Piper Papers, vol. 3, CYA256, p. 753, ML.
84 *Sydney Monitor*, 5 February 1831.
85 *Colonial Times*, 7 May 1839.
86 *Sydney Gazette*, 31 October 1827, p. 2.
87 Mundy, *Our Antipodes.*
88 *Sydney Gazette*, 30 September 1830, p. 2.
89 Hirst, *Convict Society and Its Enemies*, p. 133.
90 Robert Hughes, *The Fatal Shore*, p. 476.
91 See Anne Summers, 'Factory Girls, Refractory Girls', *Refractory Girl*, no. 1, Summer 1972/3, pp. 15–17; David Kent, 'Customary Behaviour Transported: A Note on the Parramatta Female Factory Riot of 1827', *Journal of Australian Studies*, no. 40, March 1994, pp. 75–9.
92 For coverage of male rebellion, see Sandra Blair, 'The Revolt at Castle Forbes'.
93 Colonial Secretary Outward Letters, 4/3719, 31/39; 31/84; Reel 1057, AONSW.
94 Police Office to Governor Gipps, 19 February 1843, 43/1347, AONSW.
95 Colonial Secretary Outward Letters, 4/3725, 42/37.
96 Colonial Secretary Inward Letters, 17 February 1843, no. 43/1448, 4/2610.1.
97 Ibid., February 1843, 4/2610.1, no. 43/1448, 27 July 1843.
98 Report prepared by the principal superintendent, 3 February 1843, Colonial Secretary's Office, 22/50, AOT.
99 Return of Punishments at the Female Factory Parramatta, 1 January to 30 June 1828, 2/8211, Reel 2278, AONSW; Return of Punishments at the Female Factory, Parramatta, 1/1–30/6/1829, in Reports of Boards and Inquiries, 1829–30, 4/2094, AONSW.
100 Abstract of Punishment at the Female Factory Parramatta, for Half Year Ending 31 December 1827, 2/8211, Reel 2278, AONSW.
101 Return of Punishments at the Female Factory, Parramatta, 1/1/–30/6/1829, in Reports of Boards and Inquiries 1829–30, 4/2094, AONSW.
102 Abstract of Punishment, for Half Year Ending 31 December 1827; Return of Punishments, Parramatta.
103 Return of Punishments, Parramatta.
104 Abstract of Punishment, for Half Year Ending 31 December 1827.
105 Return of Punishments, Parramatta.
106 Ibid.
107 Heath, 'The Female Convict Factories', p. 263.

4   Defeminising Convict Women: Headshaving as Punishment in the Female Factories

1 *Colonial Times*, 7 May 1839.
2 Report, Inquiry into Female Convict Prison Discipline.
3 Hirst, *Convict Society and Its Enemies*, p. 17.

4   Ryan, 'From Stridency to Silence', Kirkby, *Sex, Power and Justice*, p. 76.
5   Waterloo Point Police Court, 1834–1837, Tasmanian Papers, no. 338, ML, entry for 24 February 1837.
6   See Philip Priestley, *Victorian Prison Lives: English Prison Biography, 1830–1914*, London, Methuen, 1985, pp. 22–23; Ignatieff, *A Just Measure of Pain*, p. 6.
7   Rules and Regulations for the Conduct of the Female Factory and Recommended by the Committee of Inquiry in their Report, in Governor's Minutes 1826 4/990, AONSW.
8   Shane White and Graham White, 'Slave Hair and African American Culture in the Eighteenth and Nineteenth Centuries', *The Journal of Southern History*, Volume LXI, no. 1, February 1995, p. 54.
9   O'Connell, *A Residence of Eleven Years in New Holland and the Caroline Islands*, p. 68.
10 *Australian Dictionary of Biography*, vol. 1, p. 45, 'James Backhouse'.
11 James Backhouse and George Walker, *A Narrative of a Visit to the Australian Colonies*, London, 1843, p. 21.
12 Yvonne Knibiehler, 'Bodies and Hearts', in Genevieve Fraisse and Michelle Perrot (eds), *A History of Women: Emerging Feminism from Revolution to World War*, Cambridge, Harvard University Press, 1993, p. 326.
13 *Blossom*, May 1828, no. 1, p. 64.
14 Ignatieff, *A Just Measure of Pain*, pp. 143–4.
15 Estelle Freedman, *'Their Sisters' Keepers': Women's Prison Reform in America 1830–1930*, Michigan, University of Michigan Press, 1981, pp. 23; 25.
16 Russell Dobash, R. Emerson Dobash and Sue Gutteridge, et al., *The Imprisonment of Women*, London, Basil Blackwell, 1986, pp. 42–51.
17 Ibid., p. 55.
18 Ibid., p. 54.
19 'Report of the Select Committee on Transportation, 1832', in *British Parliamentary Papers, Crime and Punishment: Transportation*, vol. 1, *Sessions 1810–1832*, p. 123.
20 'Report of the Select Committee on Transportation, 1837', p. 49.
21 Report, Inquiry into Female Convict Prison Discipline.
22 Female Orphan School, Minutes of Meetings, 1818–1824, 4/403, AONSW, p. 77, 17 October 1821.
23 Quoted in Robert Hughes, *The Fatal Shore*, pp. 257–8; 258.
24 Samuel Marsden to Colonial Secretary, 7 March 1833, Colonial Secretary Inward Letters, 1833, 4/2191.3, AONSW.
25 *Sydney Monitor*, 5 February 1831.
26 Judith Butler, *Bodies That Matter: On the Discursive Limits of 'Sex'*, London, Routledge, 1993, p. 233.
27 David Collins, *An Account of the English Colony in New South Wales*, vol. 1, (1798), Sydney, Reed, 1975, p. 39.
28 For an analysis along these lines of women, crime and punishment, see Dobash, et al., *The Imprisonment of Women*, pp. 104–8.
29 Return of Proceedings taken at the Court House Parramatta for Quarter Ending 30 September 1822, Reel 660, AONSW.
30 Henderson, *Observations on the Colonies*, p. 20.
31 See Kay Daniels, 'The Flash Mob: Rebellion, Rough Culture and Sexuality in the Female Factories of Van Diemen's Land', *Australian Feminist Studies*, no. 18, Summer 1993, pp. 133–50.
32 Testimony of Mary Haigh, Report, Inquiry into Female Convict Prison Discipline.

33 Testimony of John Price, ibid.
34 Alphabetical List of Women Applying For Permission to Marry, CON 52/2, AOT, p. 245.
35 'Testimony of Grace Heinbury', Report, Inquiry into Female Convict Prison Discipline.
36 Alan Atkinson and Marian Aveling (eds), *Australians 1838*, Sydney, Fairfax, Syme and Weldon, 1987, pp. 281–3.
37 Hutchinson, 'Mrs. Hutchinson and the Female Factories', p. 57.
38 *Sydney Gazette*, 29 December 1836, p. 3.
39 Stonequarry Benchbooks.
40 *Colonial Times*, 3 April 1838, p. 10.
41 Robyn Cooper, 'Victorian Discourses on Women and Beauty: The Alexander Walker Texts', *Gender and History*, vol. 5, no. 1, Spring 1993, pp. 34–55.
42 Yvonne Knibiehler, 'Bodies and Hearts', Fraisse and Perrot, *A History of Women*, p. 327.
43 Tardif, *Notorious Strumpets and Dangerous Girls*, p. 9.
44 'Governor Darling to W. Huskisson', *HRA*, series 1, vol. XIV, p. 131.
45 *Hobart Town Gazette*, 30 December 1836, p. 1294.
46 Ibid., 6 January 1837, p. 25; 24 February 1837, p. 163; 17 March 1837, p. 215.
47 Ibid., 10 March 1837, p. 196; 4 August 1837, p. 713; 4 August 1837, p. 712; 16 December 1836, p. 1237; 4 August 1837, p. 712.
48 *Sydney Gazette*, 17 September 1828, p. 14; 22 October 1827, p. 4; 2 December 1826, p. 4; 5 November 1827, p. 3; 2 December 1826, p. 4.
49 Espie Journal, *Lord Sidmouth*.
50 Hirst, *Convict Society and Its Enemies*, p. 41.
51 Hilary Weatherburn, 'The Female Factory', in Mackinolty and Radi, *In Pursuit of Justice*, pp. 26; 23.
52 Heath, 'The Female Convict Factories', pp. 273; 271–6.
53 Summers, 'Factory Girls, Refractory Girls', p. 16; Anne Summers, *Damned Whores and God's Police: The Colonization of Women in Australia*, Melbourne, Penguin, 1975, p. 282.
54 Dobash, et al., *The Imprisonment of Women*, pp. 1–12.
55 Freedman, *'Their Sisters' Keepers'*, pp. 10–21.
56 Hirst, *Convict Society and Its Enemies*, p. 9.
57 Ibid., pp. 38–40; see also Michel Foucault, *Discipline and Punish: The Birth of the Prison*, Harmondsworth, Penguin, 1987, pp. 200–28; Ignatieff, *A Just Measure of Pain*, pp. 109–13.
58 Ignatieff, *A Just Measure of Pain*, pp. 112–13.
59 Hirst, *Convict Society and Its Enemies*, pp. 10–22.
60 J. S. Kerr, *Out of Sight, Out of Mind: Australia's Places of Confinement 1788–1988*, Sydney, Library of Australian History, 1988, pp. 37–45.
61 Kociumbas, *The Oxford History of Australia*, vol. 2, pp. 169–70.
62 'Governor King to Lord Hobart, 14 August 1804', *HRA*, series 1, vol. V, p. 12.
63 Salt, *These Outcast Women*, pp. 43–46; 46–53.
64 Hutchinson, 'Mrs. Hutchinson and the Female Factories', p. 61.
65 Foucault, *Discipline and Punish*, p. 242.
66 Oxley, *Convict Maids*, pp. 118–22.
67 'Washing', 19 January 1841, Colonial Secretary's Office, Colonial Secretary Inward Letters.
68 'Needlework', 18 October 1841, Colonial Secretary's Office, Colonial Secretary Inward Letters.
69 Report, Inquiry into Female Convict Prison Discipline.

70 Davidson, *The Invisible State*, p. 39; Atkinson and Aveling (eds), *Australians 1838*, p. 283.
71 Lachlan Macquarie, *Rules and Regulations for the Management of the Female Convicts in the New Factory at Parramatta*, Sydney, 1821, pp. 1–11.
72 Fletcher, *Ralph Darling: A Governor Maligned*, pp. 117–18.
73 Governor's Minutes 1826, 4/990, AONSW.
74 Dobash, et al., *The Imprisonment of Women*, p. 54.
75 Foucault, *Discipline and Punish*, pp. 146–9.
76 *Hobart Town Gazette*, 3 October 1829, pp. 220; 219.
77 Maynard, *Fashioned from Penury*, pp. 20–4.
78 Dobash, et al., *The Imprisonment of Women*, p. 75.
79 Zedner, 'Wayward Sisters', Morris and Rottman, *The Oxford History of Prison*, p. 342.
80 *Hobart Town Gazette*, 3 October 1829, pp. 221; 220.
81 Ibid.
82 Atkinson and Aveling (eds), *Australians 1838*, p. 280.
83 Foucault, *Discipline and Punish*, p. 137.
84 J. D'Arcy to J. Burnett, Colonial Secretary, 31 January 1829, CSO 1/19/340, AOT.
85 Mr Clapham, 26 March 1838, 'Correspondence relating to the deplorable state of the factory, pre the arrival of Governor Gipps', Parramatta Female Factory Papers, A1813, ML.
86 *True Colonist*, 26 May 1837, p. 578.
87 *Colonial Times*, 6 July 1827, p. 3; 29 June 1827, p. 3.
88 Ibid., 29 June 1827, p. 3.
89 Zedner, 'Wayward Sisters', Morris and Rottman, *The Oxford History of Prison*, pp. 334–5.
90 Objects of the Formation of the Proposed Committee of Ladies for the Charitable Superintendence of Female Convicts, 21 October 1836, 36/8000, in ML Dixson Library Add 64.
91 Fletcher, *Ralph Darling: A Governor Maligned*, p. 18.
92 Robinson, 'The First Forty Years', Mackinolty and Radi, *In Pursuit of Justice*, p. 11.
93 Freedman, 'Their Sisters' Keepers', p. 2; Elizabeth Windschuttle, 'Feeding the Poor', Windschuttle, *Women, Class and History*.
94 'Governor Darling to Sir George Murray, 18 February 1829', *HRA*, series 1, vol. XIV, p. 657.
95 Report of the Board of Management of the Female Factory for the Half Year Ended 30 June 1829, in Reports of Boards and Inquiries, 1829–30, 4/2094, AONSW.
96 'Governor Gipps to Lord John Russell, 1 October 1840', *HRA*, series 1, vol. 21, p. 6.
97 Mrs Hutchinson, Testimony, Report, Inquiry into Female Convict Prison Discipline.
98 Sisters of Charity Archive, St Vincents Place, College Convent, Potts Point, p. 6, 9 April 1839. I owe a special thanks to Dr Paul Collins for directing me to this source.
99 Ibid., p. 22.
100 Daniels, 'The Flash Mob', pp. 133–50.
101 Report, Inquiry into Female Convict Prison Discipline.
102 Hutchinson, 'Mrs. Hutchinson and the Female Factories', p. 61.
103 Testimony of Robert Person, 1841, Report, Inquiry into Female Convict Prison Discipline.

104 *Colonial Times*, 3 April 1838, p. 10.
105 Dobash, et al., *The Imprisonment of Women*, pp. 57–8.
106 Heath, ' "A Safe and Salutary Discipline": The Dark Cells of the Parramatta Female Factory 1838', *Push From the Bush*, no. 9, 1981, p. 25.
107 Ryan, 'From Stridency to Silence', Kirkby, *Sex, Power and Justice*, pp. 80–4.
108 J. S. Kerr, *Design for Convicts: An Account of Design for Convict Establishments in the Australian Colonies During the Transportation Era*, Sydney, Library of Australian History, 1984, pp. 85–105.
109 Comptroller-General Report, 1 May to 31 December 1848, GO 33/66, AOT.
110 *Austral Asiatic Review*, 29 October 1841, p. 2.
111 Heath, 'A Safe and Salutary Discipline', pp. 22; 24.
112 Report, Inquiry into Female Convict Prison Discipline.

5 Convict Mothering

1 *Colonial Times*, 20 March 1838, pp. 92; 93; 94.
2 Letter from Josiah Spode to Colonial Secretary, CSO 5/114/2605.
3 Kociumbas, *The Oxford History of Australia*, vol. 2, p. 173; Weatherburn, 'The Female Factory', Mackinolty and Radi, *In Pursuit of Justice*, p. 29.
4 Davidoff and Hall, *Family Fortunes*, p. 399.
5 Weatherburn, 'The Female Factory', Mackinolty and Radi, *In Pursuit of Justice*, p. 28.
6 *Colonial Times*, 8 May 1838, p. 148; 3 April 1838, p. 108.
7 Ibid., 29 May 1838, p. 174.
8 Testimony by William Cato, Inquiry into the Death of Barbara Hemming, CSO 5/114/2608, AOT.
9 Testimony by Elisabeth Inchbald, ibid.
10 Testimony by Mary Owen, ibid.
11 *Colonial Times*, 13 March 1838, p. 95.
12 Jane Flax, *Disputed Subjects: Essays on Psychoanalysis, Politics and Philosophy*, New York, Routledge, 1993, pp. 67; 64.
13 'Report of the Select Committee on Transportation, 1812', p. 12.
14 Kociumbas, *The Oxford History of Australia*, vol. 2, p. 27.
15 Ibid., p. 28
16 Mrs Slea, Testimony, 8 December 1841, Report, Inquiry into Female Convict Prison Discipline.
17 J. C. Byrne, *Twelve Years' Wanderings in the British Colonies from 1835 to 1847*, vol. 1, London, 1848, p. 232.
18 John Price, Testimony, Report, Inquiry into Female Convict Prison Discipline.
19 Reverend Thomas Ewing, Testimony, Report, Inquiry into Female Convict Prison Discipline.
20 'Governor Darling to Under-Secretary Twiss, 13 August 1829', *HRA*, series 1, vol. XV, p. 117.
21 Michael Belcher, 'The Child in New South Wales 1820–1837', PhD thesis, University of New England, 1982, p. 83.
22 H. S. Payne, 'A Statistical Study of Female Convicts in Tasmania 1843–53', *Tasmanian Historical Research Association*, vol. 9, no. 2, June 1961, p. 60.
23 Mrs Slea, Testimony, 27 December 1841, Report, Inquiry into Female Convict Prison Discipline.
24 Joan C. Brown, *'Poverty Is Not a Crime': Social Services in Tasmania 1803–1900*, Hobart, Tasmanian Historical Research Association, 1972, p. 65.

25 Instructions for the Medical Officer Attending the Female House of Correction, CSO 1/902/19161, AOT.

26 Instructions for the Nurse or Midwife at the Female House of Correction, CSO 1/902/19161, AOT.

27 Belcher, 'The Child in New South Wales', p. 77.

28 Knibiehler, 'Bodies and Hearts', Fraisse and Perrot, *A History of Women*, pp. 332; 334.

29 Instructions for the Nurse or Midwife at the Female House of Correction, CSO 1/902/19161, AOT

30 'Principal Surgeon Bowman to Governor Macquarie, 6 October 1821', *HRA*, series 1, vol. X, p. 668.

31 'Report of Board of Management of Female Factory', *HRA*, series 1, vol. XIV, p. 654.

32 Ibid., p. 656.

33 'Report of Board of Inquiry of Female Orphan School, 16 January 1826', *HRA*, series 1, vol. XII, p. 163.

34 Dr Dermer, Medical Charge of the Factory and Nursery, 1841, Report, Inquiry into Female Convict Prison Discipline.

35 Ewing, 1841, ibid.

36 Belcher, 'The Child in New South Wales', pp. 81; 83; 87.

37 Knibiehler, 'Bodies and Hearts', Fraisse and Perrot, *A History of Women*, p. 351.

38 Inquiry into the Death of Barbara Hemming, CSO 5/114/2608, AOT, pp. 203; 204

39 Samuel Sherlock to George Arthur, 15 January 1831, CSO 1/19/340, AOT.

40 Ibid.

41 Brown, *'Poverty Is Not a Crime'*, pp. 63–5.

42 Acting Assistant Surgeon's Report, 14 April 1834, CSO1/902/19161, AOT.

43 Knibiehler, 'Bodies and Hearts', Fraisse and Perrot, *A History of Women*, p. 332.

44 Acting Assistant Surgeon's Report, CSO 1/902/19161, AOT.

45 Acting Assistant Surgeon's Report; Committee Inquiry, June 1834, CSO 1/902/19161, AOT.

46 Coroner's Report, October 1834, CSO 1/902/19161, AOT.

47 Deputy Superintendent-General of Hospitals, John McClarke, to Colonial Secretary, 27 September 1842, CSO 22/63/943, AOT.

48 John McClarke to Colonial Secretary, 15 September 1842, CSO 22/63/943, AOT.

49 CSO 5/216/5423, AOT.

50 Josiah Spode to Colonial Secretary, 22 May 1843, Report, Inquiry into Female Convict Prison Discipline.

51 2 March 1848, GO 33/63, AOT, pp. 162; 482.

6 'Wretchedness and Vice': The 'Orphan' and the Colonial Imagination

1 Samuel Marsden to William Wilberforce, Parramatta 1799, Bonwick Transcripts, ML.

2 *HRNSW*, vol. 4, p. 113.

3 Ibid.

4 'Lieutenant Governor King to Lieutenant Kent, 23 May 1800', *HRNSW*, vol. IV, p. 87.

5 John Ramsland, *Children of the Back Lanes: Destitute and Neglected Children in Colonial New South Wales*, Sydney, University of New South Wales Press, 1986, pp. 1–2.

6 'Lieutenant King to the Reverend Richard Johnson', *HRNSW*, 7 July 1800, vol. V, p. 135.

7 'State of the Colony, 1801', *HRNSW*, vol. IV, p. 658.

8 'Macquarie to Bathurst 27 July 1822', *HRA*, series 1, vol. X, p. 678.

9 Ramsland, *Children of the Back Lanes*, pp. 16–17.

10 Jan Kociumbas, 'The Best Years', in Verity Burgmann and Jenny Lee (eds), *Making a Life: A People's History of Australia since 1788*, Melbourne, Penguin, 1988, pp. 140–1.

11 Ramsland, *Children of the Back Lanes*, p. 21.

12 Minutes of Meetings of the Committee of Management, King's Orphan Schools, 1826–1833, SWD 24, AOT, 26 April 1828; Brown, 'Poverty Is Not a Crime', pp. 26; 28; 26–7.

13 Samuel Marsden to William Wilberforce, 11 August 1819, Hassall Correspondence, vol. 2, CY 913 (A1677–2), ML.

14 *Australian Dictionary of Biography*, vol. 1, p. 521, 'Rowland Hassall'.

15 'The Reverend Rowland Hassall to Reverend G. Burder, Coventry', *HRNSW*, vol. IV, p. 447.

16 Samuel Marsden, 24 August 1801, Hassall Correspondence, vol. 2, CY 913 (A1677–2).

17 Female Orphan Institution Parramatta: Rules and Regulations for the Future Management and Improvement of the Female Orphan Institution, including Minutes of Meetings, 1818–1825, 4/403, AONSW.

18 'Archdeacon Scott to Governor Darling', *HRA*, series 1, vol. XV, p. 219.

19 Circular sent establishing Orphan Schools, CSO 1/122/3073, AOT.

20 *True Colonist*, 28 July 1837, p. 651.

21 *Colonial Times*, 24 February 1826, p. 2.

22 Female Orphan Institution Parramatta: Rules and Regulations.

23 Susan Magarey, 'The Invention of Juvenile Delinquency in Early Nineteenth Century England', *Labour History*, no. 34, 1978, pp. 11–25; 16–17.

24 John R. Gillis, *Youth and History: Tradition and Change in European Age Relations 1770–Present*, Harcourt, Brace, Jovanovich, 1981, pp. 61–4.

25 Humphrey, 'Objects of Compassion', pp. 33; 14; Beverly Earnshaw, 'The Convict Apprentices 1820–1838', *Push from the Bush*, no. 5, 1979, pp. 82–95.

26 Kim Humphrey, 'The Remaking of Youth: A Study of Juvenile Convicts and Orphan Immigrants in Colonial Australia', MA thesis, University of Melbourne, 1987, pp. 114–15.

27 Brown, *'Poverty Is Not a Crime'*, p. 24.

28 Ibid., p. 25.

29 Humphrey, 'The Remaking of Youth', p. 29

30 See Jan Kociumbas, 'Childhood History as Ideology', *Labour History*, no. 47, November 1984, pp. 14–16.

31 A. McRobbie, *Postmodernism and Popular Culture*, London, Routledge, 1994, p. 180.

32 J. J. Fletcher, *Clean, Clad and Courteous: A History of Aboriginal Education in New South Wales*, Sydney, 1989, p. 20.

33 For these arguments, see Barry Bridges, 'The Sydney Orphan Schools 1800–1830', M.Ed thesis, University of Sydney, 1973; Ramsland, *Children of the Back Lanes;* Brown, *'Poverty Is Not A Crime'*; Helen Heney, *Australia's Founding Mothers*, Melbourne, Nelson, 1978.

34 Female Orphan Institution, Parramatta, Minutes of Meetings, 4/403, AONSW, 3 July 1821; 14 February 1821; 13 February 1822.

35 Josiah Spode to Colonial Secretary, 26 March 1836; 18 August 1835, CSO 1/802/17152, AOT pp. 101; 89.

36 Minutes of Meetings of the Committee of Management, King's Orphan Schools, SWD 24, AOT, 12 June 1828; 15 November 1828.

37 Belcher, 'The Child in New South Wales', p. 206.

38 Female Orphan Institution, Parramatta: Rules and Regulations.

39 Female Orphan Institution, Parramatta: Minutes, 14 July 1820, Rules and Regulations.

40 Male Orphan School Rules and Regulations and Minutes of Meetings 1819–1823, 4/400, AONSW.

41 Female Orphan Institution, Parramatta: Minutes, 14 August 1822.

42 Minutes of Meetings of the Committee of Management, King's Orphan Schools, 17 January 1831; 18 January 1831.

43 Belcher, 'The Child in New South Wales', pp. 50–3.

44 *HRNSW*, Volume IV, p. 658.

45 Bonwick Transcripts 28, 'Bigge's Appendix', CY 1546, p. 7064.

46 Ramsland, *Children of the Back Lanes*, p. 30; *Australian Dictionary of Biography*, vol. 2, p. 613, 'Charles Wilton'.

47 Charles Wilton to the Committee of the Corporation, 23 November 1827, 4/326, Female Orphan School Letters, 1825–1829.

48 *Sydney Gazette*, 24 November 1805, p. 1.

49 W. Walker to the Rev. R. Watson, 7 July 1825, Bonwick Transcripts, Box 53, CY 1529, p. 1471.

50 Charles Wilton to the Committee of the Corporation, 31 March 1828, Female Orphan School Letters.

51 Belcher, 'The Child in New South Wales', pp. 282; 285.

52 *Sydney Herald*, 6 February 1837, p. 2.

53 Ibid., 2 September 1833, p. 2.

54 'Robert Kirkwood Ewing', in Brian Dickey (ed.), *The Australian Dictionary of Evangelical Biography*, Sydney, Evangelical History Association, 1994, p. 107.

55 Ibid., p. 108.

56 Brown, *'Poverty Is Not a Crime'*, pp. 67; 68.

57 Inquiry into Thomas Ewing, CSO 8/2/420, AOT.

58 Brown, *'Poverty Is Not a Crime'*, p. 67.

59 Thomas Ewing to Colonial Secretary, 17 July 1841, Inquiry into Thomas Ewing.

60 Ibid., Testimony of John Learmouth, Surgeon, 23 July 1841.

61 Ibid., Testimony of Mary Millington, 8 July 1841.

62 Ibid., Testimony of Swanston, 8 July 1841.

63 Reverend Ewing to Colonial Secretary, 26 July 1841.

64 Ibid.

65 Ibid., Testimony of Edward Lord Fry, 10 July 1841.

66 William Hall to Committee of the Corporation, 8 August 1827, Black Town Correspondence and Returns of Stock 1826–9, 4/345, AONSW.

67 'Report on the Church and School Establishments by Archdeacon Scott', *HRA*, series 1, vol. XII, p. 313.

68 'Report of Board of Inquiry on Female Orphan School, 16 January 1826', ibid., p. 163.

69 'General Rules for the Female Orphan House', *HRA*, series 1, vol. XII, p. 281.

70 Ramsland, *Children of the Back Lanes*, p. 30.
71 16 January 1826, 'Proceedings of a Board assembled at the Female Orphan Institution at Parramatta', Female Orphan School Letters.
72 'Report of Board of Inquiry on Female Orphan School, 16 January 1826', *HRA*, series 1, vol. XII, p. 163.
73 *Australian Dictionary of Biography*, vol. 2, p. 431, 'Thomas Scott'.
74 'Report on the Church and School Establishments by Archdeacon Scott, 1 May 1826', *HRA*, series 1, vol. XII, p. 312.
75 'Archdeacon Scott to Governor Darling, 1 September 1829', *HRA*, series 1, vol. XV, p. 219.
76 CSO 1/855/18093, AOT.
77 *Australian Dictionary of Biography*, vol. 1, p. 212, 'Reverend Robert Cartwright'.
78 Female Orphan Institution, Parramatta: Minutes, 25 April 1821; Belcher, p. 66.
79 Foucault, *A History of Sexuality*, pp. 27–8.
80 Bridges, 'The Sydney Orphan Schools 1800–1830', p. 437.
81 Female Orphan School Letters, 26 January 1826.
82 Ramsland, *Children of the Back Lanes*, pp. 28–30; '20 May 1826, List Compiled by J. E. Keene, Chaplain Superintending the Female Orphan School', Female Orphan School Letters.
83 Ibid.
84 W. Walker to the Rev. R. Watson, 7 July 1825, Bonwick Transcripts, Box 53, p. 170.
85 William Hall to Committee of the Corporation, 25 January 1828, Black Town Correspondence.
86 Quoted in B. J. Bridges, 'The Native Institution, Parramatta and Blacktown, Part II 1820–1829', *The Forum of Education: An Australian Journal of Teacher Education*, vol. XXXI, no. 2, September 1972, p. 158.
87 Colonial Secretary's Office, 4 November 1847, CSO 24/32/992, AOT.
88 Robert Clark to Colonial Secretary, 8 December 1842, CSO 8/72/1642, AOT.
89 J. J. Fletcher, *Clean, Clad and Courteous*, p. 20.
90 Female Orphan Institution, Parramatta: Minutes, 14 October 1818.
91 'Archdeacon Scott to Governor Darling', *HRA*, series 1, Vol. XV, p. 210.
92 Female Orphan Institution, Parramatta: Minutes, 25 August 1819; 5 July 1820; 7 August 1821.
93 Ibid., 12 February 1823; 14 May 1823.
94 Charles Wilton to Archdeacon Scott, 13 August 1827, Female Orphan School Letters; see also letters from Wilton to Committee of the Corporation, 3 July 1827; 26 July 1827.
95 Charles Wilton to Committee, 5 November 1817; 9 November 1817; 25 September 1829, Female Orphan School Letters.
96 Minutes of Meetings of the Committee of Management, King's Orphan Schools, 23 October 1830; 6 November 1830.
97 Letter from (name illegible) to Charles Cowper 25 October 1830, Application for Children out of the Orphan Schools, 4/334, AONSW.
98 Letter from Martha Hillas to the Committee, ibid., 4/333.
99 William Hall to Committee of the Corporation, 10 September 1828, Black Town Correspondence, 4/345, AOT.
100 Charles Wilton to Committee, 31 March; 22 August 1828, Female Orphan School Letters.

101 Testimony of the Reverend Thomas Ewing, 1 January 1842, Report, Inquiry Into Female Convict Prison Discipline.
102 *True Colonist*, 28 July 1837, p. 651.
103 Minutes of Meetings of the Committee of Management, King's Orphan Schools, 26 July 1828.
104 Ibid., 9 August 1828.
105 Testimony of the Reverend Thomas Ewing, 1 January 1842, Report, Inquiry into Female Convict Prison Discipline.

7   Abandonment, Flight and Absence: Motherhood and Fatherhood During the 1820s and 1830s

1 Robinson, *The Women of Botany Bay*, pp. 252; 265.
2 Katrina Alford, *Production or Reproduction? An Economic History of Women in Australia 1788–1850*, Melbourne, Oxford University Press, 1984, p. 40; ibid., pp. 253–4.
3 'Report of the Select Committee on Transportation, 1837'.
4 Alford, *Production or Reproduction?*, p. 76.
5 Kociumbas, *The Oxford History of Australia*, pp. 23–4.
6 Alford, *Production or Reproduction?*, p. 39.
7 Leonore Davidoff and Catherine Hall, *Family Fortunes*, p. 323.
8 Alford, *Production or Reproduction?*, pp. 28–30; 53; 54; 58.
9 Marian Aveling, 'She Only Married To Be Free; Or, Cleopatra Vindicated', *Push from the Bush*, no. 2, 1978, p. 118.
10 Alford, *Production or Reproduction?*, pp. 31; 76.
11 Alan Atkinson, 'The Moral Basis of Marriage', *Push from the Bush*, no. 2, November 1978, p. 105.
12 Aveling, 'She Only Married to be Free', p. 118; Grimshaw, et al., *Families in Colonial Australia*, pp. 58–9.
13 See Penny Russell (ed.), *For Richer, For Poorer: Early Colonial Marriages*, Melbourne, Melbourne University Press, 1994; Alison Alexander, *Governors' Ladies: The Wives and Mistresses of Van Diemen's Land Governors*.
14 Penny Russell, 'Paradise Lost: Sir John Franklin and Lady Jane Franklin', pp. 50–72; Patricia Grimshaw, 'The Moral Reformer and the Imperial Major: Caroline and Archibald Chisholm', pp. 94–113, in Russell (ed.), *For Richer, For Poorer*.
15 Atkinson, 'The Moral Basis of Marriage', p. 28.
16 Aveling, 'She Only Married To Be Free', p. 121.
17 Robinson, *The Women of Botany Bay*, p. 291.
18 Smith, *A Cargo of Women*, pp. 68; 82–3; 92–3.
19 Ibid., p. 97.
20 Robinson, *The Women of Botany Bay*, p. 292.
21 Davidoff and Hall, *Family Fortunes*, pp. 335–43.
22 M. A. Crowther, 'The Tramp', in Roy Porter (ed.), *Myths of the English*, London, Polity Press, 1993, pp. 92–3.
23 Petition of William Simpson for John King, Applications for Admission into the Orphan Schools 1825–8, 4/330, AONSW; Petition of Andrew McQuire for Ellen McGuire, ibid; Minutes of Meetings of Committee of Management, King's Orphan Schools, 22 September 1831; 3 November 1831.
24 Letter from Stephen Johnson to Charles Cowper, 10 July 1828, Applications for Admission into the Orphan Schools.

25 Letter from Archdeacon Bell to Charles Cowper, 17 September 1828; Petition of John Ramsay, n.d. (1829–1832), Applications for Admission into Orphan Schools; Minutes of Meetings of Committee of Management, King's Orphan Schools, 3 March 1831; Petition of Edward Ready, 9 July 1829, Applications for Admission to Orphan Schools 1829–1832.

26 Application from Court, 2 October 1828; Petition of Jane Bolton, 16 December 1828; Petition of Sarah Pearce, n.d.; Superintendent of Police to Charles Cowper, 15 April 1829, Applications for Admission to Orphan Schools.

27 Flax, *Disputed Subjects*, p. 70.

28 Petition of James Winter, 16 July 1828; Petition of Joseph Harris, 22 July 1828; Petition of William Black, 1 September 1830, Applications for Admission to Orphan Schools.

29 Petition of George Milward, 22 April 1832, ibid.

30 Minutes of Meetings of Committee of Management, 13 September 1828.

31 Petition of Margaret Barrett, 2 May 1828; Letter from Catherine Farley to Committee of the Female Orphan School, 11 February 1831, Applications for Admission to Orphan Schools.

32 Petition of Harriet Mackie, 19 February 1827; Petition of Sarah McGee, 19 March 1827; Petition of Alice Williams, 20 June 1827; Petition of Sarah Radley, 16 October 1827, ibid.

33 Letter from Anne Ablett to Archdeacon of New South Wales, 12 January 1832, ibid.

34 Petition of William Cox, 10 March 1830, ibid.

35 Belcher, 'The Child in New South Wales', p. 265.

36 Kociumbas, *The Oxford History*, p. 229.

37 Quoted in W. Nichol, 'Medicine and the Labour Movement in New South Wales, 1788–1850', *Labour History*, no. 49, November 1985, pp. 21; 22.

38 Petition of Ann Brown, n.d. (1829–1832), Applications for Admission to Orphan Schools; Minutes of Meetings of Committee of Management, King's Orphan Schools, 12 June 1828; Petition of Nicholas Delany, 1820; Petition of Mary Chilvers, n.d. (1829–1832); Petition of Johanna Taylor, n.d. (1829–1832); Petition of Agland, 3 March 1828; Petition of Joseph Harris, 22 July 1828; Petition of Anne Reed, 10 November 1827; Petition of Mary Weavers, Applications for Admission to Orphan Schools.

39 Petition of John Hall, 2 May 1827, ibid.

40 Petition of Mary Starkey, n.d. (1825–1828); Petition of Sarah Jones; Petition of Mary Johnston, 23 July 1828; Petition of Jane Stillwell, 28 May 1829, ibid.

41 Minutes of Meetings of Committee of Management, King's Orphan Schools, 11 July 1829; 17 April 1830.

42 Petition of Catherine Breckly, n.d., Applications for Admission to Orphan Schools.

43 Petition of Catherine Clark, 31 December 1829; Petition of Sarah Jones, 22 September 1829, ibid.

44 Letter by Inspector of Police to Archdeacon Scott, 13 July 1827, ibid.

45 *True Colonist*, 14 July 1837, p. 632.

46 Letter from Mary Ann Clark, n.d. (1830–2), Applications for Children Out of the Orphan Schools.

47 Letter from William Guthrie, 5 March 1833, ibid.

48 Letter from J. Hamilton, 18 November 1830, ibid.

49 Letter from J. Hicks to Committee, 15 February 1831, ibid.

50 Belcher, 'The Child in New South Wales', p. 212.

51 Letter from Eliza O'Meara to Charles Cowper, 4 February 1831; Letter from Richard Wilshire to the Committee, n.d. (1830–2), Applications for Children Out of the Orphan Schools.

52 Letter from James Hollorray,18 November; Letter from Jane Barns, 1 July 1831; Letter from Sarah Hall, c. 1826, to Archdeacon Scott, ibid.

53 Letter from Patrick McAuliffe, 10 July 1832; Letter from Mrs Quinn, 2 September 1832, ibid.

54 Letter from Mary Tennant to Committee of the School, 21 August 1828; Letter from Honora Levy, September 1832; Letter from Ann Green to the Committee of Male Orphan Institute, 30 June 1825, ibid.

55 Letter from Margaret Barrett, 19 October 1830; Letter from Bridget Welsh, n.d. (1830–1832); Letter from Mary Niblet, 18 July 1831; Letter from John McAllister, to Governor Ralph Darling, n.d. (1825–1829); Letter from Elizabeth Cadman, 21 February 1831, ibid.

56 Belcher, 'The Child in New South Wales', pp. 208, p. 209.

57 Letter from Elizabeth Raine to Charles Cowper, 2 February 1830; Letter from Elizabeth Raine to Archdeacon of NSW, 7 January 1831, Applications for Children Out of the Orphan Schools.

58 Application from Elizabeth Horne, 3 November 1831; Application from George Green 30 November 1832; Letter from A. Byrne, 1 February 1830; Charles Farrell to Charles Cowper, 28 September 1830; John Jacob Sharpe to Committee of Female Orphan Institution, 14 January 1831; Letter from E. L. Hall, 22 November, 1831; Application from James Barker, April 1833; William Price to the Committee of Male Orphan Institution, 22 March 1825, ibid.

59 Letter from Thomas Skeet, 3 November 1830; Letter from Sarah Hitchcock, 5 January 1831; Letter from Mrs Wyatt, 8 December 1830, ibid.; Application of Mrs Harriet Alwyn, 2 July 1833, Minutes of Meetings of the Committee of Management, King's Orphan Schools.

60 Letter from Elizabeth Kenniwell, 8 May 1826; Letter from Robert Foulcher, 30 August 1826; Letter from Mary Ann Caton, 21 May 1827, ibid.

61 Paula Byrne, 'The "Public Good": Competing Visions of Freedom in Early Colonial New South Wales', *Labour History*, no. 58, May 1990, p. 82.

62 This new identity within a family context also defined black women's response after they had gained their freedom from slavery. See Jacqueline Jones, *Labor of Love, Labor of Sorrow: Black Women, Work and the Family: From Slavery to the Present*, New York, Basic Books, 1985, p. 58.

63 Letter from Mary Bolton, 7 May 1831; Letter from David and Ann Patterson to Archdeacon Scott, 6 May 1827; Letter from Catherine Darby, September 1831; Application from Catherine Buck, 15 January 1827, Applications for Children Out of the Orphan Schools.

64 Letter from Edward and Ann Raper to Archdeacon Scott, 18 March 1827; Letter from Margaret Quinn, October 1831; Application from Bridget Walsh, August 1830; Application from Ann Howard, 1 May 1831; Application from Mary Ann Clark, 5 November 1832, ibid.

65 Application of William Guthrie, 5 March 1833, ibid.

Bibliography

PRIMARY SOURCES

Correspondence and Manuscripts

Bonwick Transcripts, 28, CY 1546, ML.
Colonial Secretary Inward Letters, 4/2610.1, AONSW.
Colonial Secretary's Office, 1/902/19161; 5/216/5423; 22/63/943; 5/114/ 2608; 1/855/18093, AOT.
Colonial Secretary Outward Letters, 4/3719; 4/3725 AONSW.
Convict Department Records, 52/7, AOT.
Franklin Papers, NS 279, State Library of Tasmania.
Governor's Office, 33/66, AOT.
Hammersley Papers, A657, ML.
Hassall Correspondence, MS A1677, CY 913, ML.
Marsden Papers, MS 18, ML.
Objects of the Formation of the Proposed Committee of Ladies for the Charitable Superintendence of Female Convicts, ML Dixson Library Add 64.
Piper Papers, vol. 3, CY A256, ML.
Sisters of Charity Archive, Sydney.

Court Records

Bathurst Benchbooks, 1825–6; 1832–3; 4/7573, 4/5626, Reel 662; 2/8324, Reel 663, AONSW.
Bench of Magistrates, Parramatta, January–September 1822, Reel 660, AONSW.
Bench of Magistrates, Police Court, Sydney, 1815–1816, 7/2643, Reel 660, AONSW.
Bench of Magistrates, Stonequarry, 8/6/1829–1/8/1831, 4/7572, Reel 671; 24/6/1837–1/7/1843, 4/5627, Reel 672, AONSW.
Magisterial Records, Launceston Court, 1833–1834, Tasmanian Papers, no. 277, CY 1966, ML.
Magisterial Records, Hobart Branch, 1819–1820, Tasmanian Papers, no. 217, CY 1878, ML.
Minutes of Proceedings in the Court of Quarter Sessions, January 1832–June 1833, LC 216/1/AOT.
Record of Cases Heard in Petty Sessions, September 1836 to April 1837, ML.
Return of Proceedings Taken at the Court House Parramatta for Quarter Ending 30 September 1824, 4/6671, Reel 660, AONSW.
Stonequarry Benchbooks, 4/8/1831–9/12/1833, 4/7573, Reel 672, AONSW.

Police Records

Campbelltown Police Court, 1831–1833, Tasmanian Papers no. 253, ML.
Hobart Town Police Court, September 1836 to April 1837, Record of Charges Laid, AOT.
Oatlands Police Court, 1839–1842, Tasmanian Papers, no. 291, ML.
Police Department, Police Court Records, Minutes 1835–36, Tasmanian Papers, no. 237, ML.
Police Records, 1839–40, Tasmanian Papers, no. 238, ML.
Police Report of Prisoners, 8/7/1828, x821, Reel 660, AONSW.
Richmond Police Court 1838–1839, nos 324, 326, Tasmanian Papers, ML.
Spring Bay Police Court, 1838–1846, no. 334, Tasmanian Papers, ML.
Waterloo Point Police Court, 1834–37, 1837–39, Tasmanian Papers nos 338, 339, ML.

Female Factory Records

Abstract of Punishment at the Female Factory Parramatta for Half Year Ending 31 December 1829, 2/8211, Reel 2278, AONSW.

Parramatta Female Factory Papers, A1813, ML.

Reports of Boards of Inquiries, 1829–1830, 4/2094, AONSW.

Return of Punishments at the Female Factory Parramatta, 1 January to 30 June 1828, 2/8211, Reel 2278, AONSW.

Rules and Regulations for the Conduct of the Female Factory and Recommended by the Committee of Inquiry in their Report, in Governor's Minutes, 1826, 4/990, AONSW.

Orphan School Records

New South Wales

Applications for Admission into the Orphan Schools, 1825–8, 4/330; 1829–1832, 4/331; 1833, 4/332, AONSW.

Applications for Children Out of the Orphan Schools 1825–9, 4/333; 1830–2, 4/334; 1833, 4/335, AONSW.

Black Town Correspondence and Returns of Stock 1826–9, 4/345, AONSW.

Female Orphan Institution Parramatta: Rules and Regulations for the Future Management and Improvement of the Female Orphan Institution, including Minutes of Meetings, 1818–1824, 4/403, AONSW.

Female Orphan School Admission Book, 4/351, AONSW.

Female Orphan School Letters, 1825–9, 4/326; 1830–2, 4/327, AONSW.

Female Orphan School, Medical Reports, 1830–1833, 4/342, AONSW.

Female School of Industry, Annual Reports, 1827, 1828, ML.

Inventory of Documents and Accounts Relative to the Male and Female Orphan Institutions, 1800–1825, 4/7491.1, AONSW.

Male Orphan School Admission Book, 4/353, AONSW.

Male Orphan School Letters, 1825–9, 4/328; 1830–2, 4/329, AONSW.

Male Orphan School Rules and Regulations and Minutes of Meetings, 1819–1823, 4/400, AONSW.

Minutes of Committee of Native Institution, 1821–37, CON 13, FM4/1498, Church Missionary Society Records, ML.

Miscellaneous Papers re Orphan Schools, Native Institution and Agricultural Establishment, c. 1824, 4/7499, AONSW.

Van Diemen's Land

Daily Journal of Admissions and Discharges 1841–1851, SWD 7, AOT.

Minutes of Meetings of the Committee of Management, King's Orphan Schools, 1826–1833, SWD 24, AOT.

Register of Children Admitted and Discharged from the Male and Female Orphan Schools, 1828–1863, SWD 28, AOT.

Journals, Diaries and Accounts

Anderson, William, Journal, *City of Edinburgh*, 1828, PRO 3190, AONSW.

Backhouse, James, and Walker, George, *A Narrative of a Visit to the Australian Colonies*, London, 1843.

Bond, G., *A Brief Account of the Colony of Port Jackson in NSW: Its Native Inhabitants, Productions, etc.*, London, 1809.

Bonwick, James, *Curious Facts of Old Colonial Days*, London, 1870.
Breton, Lieutenant W., *Excursions in New South Wales, Western Australia and Van Diemen's Land, During the Years 1830, 1831, 1832 and 1833*, London, Richard Bentley, 1833.
Bromley, Dr E. Ford, Journal, *Surry*, 1832–1833, PRO 3211, AONSW.
Browning, Colin Arnott, *The Convict Ship: A Narrative of the Results of Scriptural Instruction and Moral Discipline on Board the 'Earl Grey'*, London, Robert Craighead, 1856.
Byrne, J. C., *Twelve Years' Wanderings in the British Colonies from 1835 to 1847*, vol. 1, London, 1848.
Clarke, Thrasycles, Journal, *Kains*, 1830–1, PRO 3199, AONSW.
Collins, David, *An Account of the English Colony in New South Wales*, vol. 1 (1798), Sydney, Reed, 1975.
Crooke, Robert, *The Convict*, Hobart, 1958.
Cunningham, Peter, *Two Years in New South Wales*, vols 1 and 2, London, 1827.
Elyard, William, Journal, *John Bull*, 1821–1822, PRO 3199, AONSW.
Espie, Robert, Journal, *Lord Sidmouth*, 1822–1823, PRO 3201, AONSW.
———, Journal, *Elizabeth*, 1836, PRO 3194, AONSW.
Evans, William, Journal, *Bencoolen*, 1819, PRO 3189, AONSW.
Fairfowle, George, Journal, *Sovereign*, 1827, PRO 3210, AONSW.
Fildon, P., and Ryan, R. J. (eds), *The Journal of Arthur Bowes Smyth, Surgeon, Lady Penthyn, 1787–1789*, Sydney, Australian Documents Library, 1979.
———, *The Journal of Philip Gidley King: Lieutenant R.N. 1787–1790*, Sydney, Australian Documents Library, 1980.
———, *The Journal and Letters of Lieutenant Ralph Clark, 1787–1792*, Sydney, Australian Documents Library, 1981.
Haslem, John, *Convict Ships*, London, Taylor and Hessey, 1819.
Henderson, John, *Observations on the Colonies of New South Wales and Van Diemen's Land*, Calcutta, 1832.
Hughes, Joseph, Journal, *Elizabeth*, 1827–1828, PRO 3194, AONSW.
Instructions for Surgeons-Superintendents and Masters on Board Convict Ships, London, 1838.
Jones, William, Journal, *Aurora*, 1851, PRO 3189, AONSW.
Leonard, Surgeon-Superintendent Peter, Journal, *Atwick*, 1837–8, PRO 3189, AONSW.
Leyson, William, Journal, *Henry Wellesley*, 1837–1838, PRO 3197, AONSW.
Macquarie, Lachlan, *Rules and Regulations for the Management of the Female Convicts in the New Factory at Parramatta*, Sydney, 1821.
Marsden, Samuel, *An Answer to Certain Calumnies*, London, Hatchard and Son, 1826.
Mudie, James, *The Felonry of New South Wales: Being a Faithful Picture of the Real Romance of Life in Botany Bay*, London, Whaley and Co., 1837.
Mundy, Godfrey Charles, *Our Antipodes: or, Residence and Rambles in the Australasian Colonies with a Glimpse of the Goldfields*, London, 1854.
O'Connell, James, *A Residence of Eleven Years in New Holland and the Caroline Islands*, Boston, 1836.
Price, Morgan, Journal, *Almorah*, 1824, PRO 3187, AONSW.
Rae, William, Journal, *Eliza*, 1822, PRO 3194, AONSW.
Reid, Thomas, *Two Voyages to New South Wales and Van Diemen's Land*, London, 1822.
Roylance, Thomas, Journal, *Hadlow*, 1818–1819, PRO 3197, AONSW.
Tench, Captain Watkin, *A Narrative of the Expedition to Botany Bay*, London, 1789.

Therry, Roger, *Reminiscences of Thirty Years' Residence in New South Wales and Victoria*, London, 1863.

Tyerman, Reverend Daniel, and Bennett, George, *Journal of Voyages and Travels*, vol. 2, London, 1831.

Ullathorne, William, *The Catholic Mission in Australasia*, Sydney, 1838.

West, John, *History of Tasmania*, vol. 2, Tasmania, Henry Dowling, 1852.

White, John, *Journal of a Voyage to NSW*, London, 1790.

Newspapers and Gazettes

Austral Asiatic Review
Australian
Blossom
Colonial Times
Hobart Town Courier
Hobart Town Gazette
Sydney Gazette
Sydney Herald
Sydney Monitor
Town and Country Journal
True Colonist

Government Publications, Inquiries and Despatches

British Parliamentary Papers, Colonies: Australia, vol. 4, *Sessions 1830–36*, Shannon, Irish University Press, 1968.

British Parliamentary Papers, Colonies: Australia, vol. 8, *Session 1844*, Shannon, Irish University Press, 1968.

Elizabeth Inquiry 1827–1828, Colonial Secretary Papers, 4/6981, AONSW.

Historical Records of Australia, series 1, vols I–XV.

Historical Records of New South Wales, vols I–IV.

Inquiry into the Reverend Thomas Ewing, CSO 8/2/420, AOT.

'Report of the Commissioner of Inquiry into the State of the Colony of New South Wales, June 1822', in *British Parliamentary Papers, Colonies: Australia*, vol. 1, *Sessions 1822–25*, Shannon, Irish University Press, 1968.

Report of the Committee of Inquiry into Female Convict Prison Discipline, CSO 22/50, AOT.

'Report of the Select Committee on Transportation, 1812', in *British Parliamentary Papers, Crime and Punishment: Transportation*, vol. 1, *Sessions 1810–32*, Shannon, Irish University Press, 1969.

'Report of the Select Committee on Transportation, 1832', in *British Parliamentary Papers, Crime and Punishment: Transportation*, vol. 1, *Sessions 1810–1832*, Shannon, Irish University press, 1968.

'Report of the Select Committee on Transportation, 1837', in *British Parliamentary Papers, Crime and Punishment: Transportation*, vol. 2, *Session 1837*, Shannon, Irish University Press, 1968.

Ritchie, John (ed.), *The Evidence to the Bigge Reports: New South Wales Under Governor Macquarie*, vol. 2, *The Written Evidence*, Melbourne, Heinemann, 1971.

Transcript of Evidence, Tasmanian Papers, nos 93, 107, 111, ML.

SECONDARY SOURCES

Books

Alexander, Alison, *Governors' Ladies: The Wives and Mistresses of Van Diemen's Land Governors*, Hobart, Tasmanian Historical Research Association, 1987.

Alexander, Sally, *Becoming a Woman and Other Essays in 19th and 20th Century Feminist History*, London, Virago, 1994.

Alford, Katrina, *Production or Reproduction? An Economic History of Women in Australia 1788–1850*, Melbourne, Oxford University Press, 1984.

Atkinson, Alan, and Aveling, Marian (eds), *Australians 1838*, Sydney, Fairfax, Syme and Weldon, 1987.

Australian Dictionary of Biography, vols 1 and 2, Melbourne, Melbourne University Press, 1963–66.

Bateson, Charles, *The Convict Ships 1787–1868*, Sydney, Reed, 1959.

Beatty, Bill, *Early Australia: With Shame Remembered*, Sydney, Angus and Robertson, 1962.

Brown, Joan, *'Poverty Is Not a Crime': Social Services in Tasmania 1803–1900*, Hobart, Tasmanian Historical Research Association, 1972.

Buckley, Ken, and Wheelwright, Ted, *No Paradise for Workers: Capitalism and the Common People in Australia 1788–1914*, Melbourne, Oxford University Press, 1988.

Burgmann, Verity, and Lee, Jenny (eds), *Making a Life: A People's History of Australia since 1788*, Melbourne, Penguin, 1988.

Burke, Peter, and Porter, Roy (eds), *The Social History Of Language*, Cambridge, Cambridge University Press, 1987.

Butler, Judith, *Bodies That Matter: On the Discursive Limits of 'Sex'*, London, Routledge, 1993.

Byrne, Paula, *Criminal Law and the Colonial Subject*, Cambridge, Cambridge University Press, 1993.

Chartier, Roger, *Cultural History: Between Practices and Representations*, translated by Lydia Cochrane, London, Polity Press, 1988.

Cohen, Stanley, and Scull, Andrew (eds), *Social Control and the State*, Oxford, Martin Robertson, 1983.

Cornell, Druisilla, *Transformations: Reflective Imagination and Sexual Difference*, New York, Routledge, 1993.

Curtis, L. Perry, *Apes and Angels: The Irishman in Victorian Caricature*, London, David and Charles, 1971.

Daniels, Kay (ed.), *So Much Hard Work: Women and Prostitution in Australian History*, Sydney, Fontana, 1984.

Davidoff, Leonore, *Worlds Between: Historical Perspectives on Gender and Class*, London, Polity Press, 1995.

Davidoff, Leonore, and Hall, Catherine, *Family Fortunes: Men and Women of the English Middle Class, 1780–1850*, London, Hutchinson, 1987.

Davidson, Alastair, *The Invisible State: The Formation of the Australian State 1788–1901*, Cambridge, Cambridge University Press, 1991.

Davis, Kathy, and Fisher, Sue (eds), *Negotiating the Margins: The Gendered Discourse of Power and Resistance*, New Brunswick, Rutgers University Press, 1993.

Dening, Greg, *Mr. Bligh's Bad Language: Passion, Power and Theatre on the Bounty*, Cambridge, Cambridge University Press, 1992.

Diamond, Irene, and Quinby, Lee (eds), *Feminism and Foucault: Reflections on Resistance*, Boston, Northeastern University Press, 1988.

Dickey, Brian (ed.), *The Australian Dictionary of Evangelical Biography*, Sydney, Evangelical History Association, 1994.

Dobash Russell, Dobash, R. Emerson, and Gutteridge, Sue, et al., *The Imprisonment of Women*, London, Basil Blackwell, 1986.

Douglas, Mary, *Purity and Danger: An Analysis of the Concepts of Pollution and Taboo*, London, Penguin, 1966.

———, *Natural Symbols: Explorations in Cosmology*, London, Penguin, 1970.

Finnane, Mark (ed.), *Policing in Australia: Historical Perspectives*, Sydney, University of New South Wales Press, 1987.

Fitzpatrick, Kathleen, *Sir John Franklin in Tasmania 1837–1843*, Melbourne, Melbourne University Press, 1949.

Flax, Jane, *Disputed Subjects: Essays on Psychoanalysis, Politics and Philosophy*, New York, Routledge, 1993.

Fletcher, Brian, *Ralph Darling: A Governor Maligned*, Melbourne, Melbourne University Press, 1984.

Fletcher, J. J., *Clean, Clad and Courteous: A History of Aboriginal Education in New South Wales*, Sydney, 1989.

Foucault, Michel, *Power/Knowledge: Selected Interviews and Other Writings 1972–1977*, Susse, Harvester, 1980.

———, *A History of Sexuality: An Introduction*, Harmondsworth, Penguin, 1976.

———, *Discipline and Punish: The Birth of the Prison*, Harmondsworth, Penguin, 1987.

Fraisse, G. and Perrot, M. (eds), *A History of Women: Emerging Feminism from Revolution to World War*, Cambridge, Harvard University Press, 1993.

Freedman, Estelle, *'Their Sisters' Keepers': Women's Prison Reform in America 1830–1930*, Michigan, University of Michigan Press, 1981.

Fuss, Diana (ed.), *Inside/Out: Lesbian Theories, Gay Theories*, New York, Routledge, 1991.

Gagnier, Regina, *Subjectivities: A History of Self-Representation in Britain*, London, Oxford University Press, 1991.

Gillis, John R., *Youth and History: Tradition and Change in European Relations 1770–Present*, London, Harcourt, Brace, Jovanovich, 1981.

Grimshaw, Patricia, et al. (eds), *Families in Colonial Australia*, Sydney, Allen & Unwin, 1985.

———, et al., *Creating a Nation 1788–1990*, Melbourne, Penguin, 1994.

Grocott, Alan, *Convicts, Clergymen and Churches: Changing Attitudes of Convicts and Ex-Convicts Towards the Clergy and in New South Wales, 1788–1851*, Sydney, Sydney University Press, 1980.

Hall, Catherine, *White, Male and Middle Class: Explorations in Feminism and History*, London, Polity Press, 1992.

Hassam, Andrew, *Sailing To Australia: Shipboard Diaries By Nineteenth Century British Emigrants*, Melbourne, Melbourne University Press, 1995.

Heney, Helen, *Australia's Founding Mothers*, Melbourne, Nelson, 1978.

Hirst, J. B., *Convict Society and Its Enemies: A History of Early New South Wales*, Sydney, Allen & Unwin, 1983.

Hughes, Robert, *The Fatal Shore: A History of Transportation of Convicts to Australia 1787–1868*, London, Pan, 1987.

Ignatieff, Michael, *A Just Measure of Pain: The Penitentiary in the Industrial Revolution 1750–1850*, New York, Columbia University Press, 1978.

Jervis, James, *The Cradle City of Australia: A History of Parramatta 1788–1961*, Parramatta, City of Parramatta, 1961.

Jones, Jacqueline, *Labor of Love, Labor of Sorrow: Black Women, Work and the Family: From Slavery to the Present*, New York, Basic Books, 1985.

Keith, Michael, and Pile, Steve (eds), *Place and the Politics of Identity*, London, Routledge, 1993.

Kerr, J. S., *Design For Convicts: An Account of Design for Convict Establishments in the Australian Colonies During the Transportation Era*, Sydney, Library of Australian History, 1984.

———, *Out of Sight, Out of Mind: Australia's Places of Confinement 1788–1988*, Sydney, Library of Australian History, 1988.

Kirkby, Diane (ed.), *Sex, Power and Justice: Historical Perspectives on Law in Australia*, Melbourne, Oxford University Press, 1995.

Kociumbas, Jan, *The Oxford History of Australia*, vol. 2, *Possessions 1770–1860*, Melbourne, Oxford University Press, 1992.

Mackinolty, Judy, and Radi, Heather (eds), *In Pursuit of Justice: Australian Women and the Law 1788–1979*, Sydney, Hale and Iremonger, 1979.

Maynard, Margaret, *Fashioned from Penury: Dress As Cultural Practice in Colonial Australia*, Cambridge, Cambridge University Press, 1995.

McClintock, Anne, *Imperial Leather: Race, Gender and Sexuality in the Colonial Contest*, New York, Routledge, 1995.

McRobbie, Angela, *Postmodernism and Popular Culture*, London, Routledge, 1994.

Morris, Norval, and Rottman, David J. (eds), *The Oxford History of the Prison: The Practice of Punishment in Western Society*, New York, Oxford University Press, 1995.

Nead, Lynda, *Myths of Sexuality: Representations of Women in Victorian Britain*, London, Oxford University Press, 1988.

Neal, David, *The Rule of the Law in a Penal Colony: Law and Power in Early New South Wales*, Cambridge, Cambridge University Press, 1991.

Nichols, Stephen, et al., *Convict Workers: Reinterpreting Australia's Past*, Cambridge, Cambridge University Press, 1988.

Oxley, Deborah, *Convict Maids: The Forced Migration of Women to Australia*, Cambridge, Cambridge University Press, 1996.

Pateman, Carole, *The Disorder of Women: Democracy, Feminism and Political Theory*, London, Polity Press, 1989.

Peiss, Kathy, and Simmons, Christina (eds), *Passion and Power: Sexuality in History*, Philadelphia, Temple University Press, 1989.

Perrott, Monica, *A Tolerable Good Success: Economic Opportunity for Women in New South Wales 1788–1830*, Sydney, Hale and Iremonger, 1983.

Philips, David, and Davies, Susanne (eds), *A Nation of Rogues? Crime, Law and Punishment in Colonial Australia*, Melbourne, Melbourne University Press, 1994.

Porter, Roy (ed.), *Myths of the English*, London, Polity Press, 1993.

Priestley, Philip, *Victorian Prison Lives: English Prison Biography, 1830–1914*, London, Methuen, 1985.

Ramsland, John, *Children of the Back Lanes: Destitute and Neglected Children in Colonial New South Wales*, Sydney, University of New South Wales Press, 1986.

Reynolds, Henry, *Frontier: Aborigines, Settlers and Land*, Sydney, Allen & Unwin, 1987.

———, *Fate of a Free People: A Radical Re-examination of the Tasmanian Wars*, Melbourne, Penguin, 1995.

Ritchie, John, *Lachlan Macquarie: A Biography*, Melbourne, Melbourne University Press, 1986.

Robinson, Portia, *The Hatch and Brood of Time: A Study of the First Generation of Native-Born White Australians 1788–1828*, Melbourne, Oxford University Press, 1985.

————, *The Women of Botany Bay: A Reinterpretation of the Role of Women in the Origins of Australian Society*, Melbourne, Penguin, 1988.

Robson, Lloyd, *The Convict Settlers of Australia: An Enquiry into the Origins and Character of the Convicts Transported to New South Wales and Van Diemen's Land 1787–1852*, Melbourne, Melbourne University Press, 1965.

Russell, Penny (ed.), *For Richer, For Poorer: Early Colonial Marriages*, Melbourne, Melbourne University Press, 1994.

Ryan, Lyndal, *The Aboriginal Tasmanians*, St Lucia, University of Queensland Press, 1981.

Salt, Annette, *These Outcast Women: The Parramatta Female Factory 1821–1848*, Sydney, Hale and Iremonger, 1981.

Saunders, Kay, and Evans, Raymond (eds), *Gender Relations in Australia: Domination and Negotiation*, Sydney, Harcourt, Brace, Jovanovich, 1992.

Shaw, A. G. L., *Convicts and Colonies: A Study of Penal Transportation from Great Britain and Ireland to Other Parts of the Empire*, London, Faber and Faber, 1966.

Smith, Babette, *A Cargo of Women: Sussanah Watson and the Convicts of the Princess Royal*, Sydney, Sun Books, 1988.

Snitow, Ann, et al. (eds), *Powers of Desire: The Politics of Sexuality*, New York, Monthly Review Press, 1983.

Stallybrass, Peter, and White, Allon, *The Politics and Poetics of Transgression*, Ithaca, New York, Cornell University Press, 1986.

Sturma, Michael, *Vice in a Vicious Society: Crime and Convicts in Mid-Nineteenth Century New South Wales*, St Lucia, University of Queensland Press, 1983.

Summers, Anne, *Damned Whores and God's Police: The Colonization of Women in Australia*, Melbourne, Penguin, 1975.

Tardif, Phillip, *Notorious Strumpets and Dangerous Girls: Convict Women in Van Diemen's Land 1803–1829*, Sydney, Angus and Robertson, 1990.

Van Krieken, Robert, *Children and the State: Social Control and the Formation of Australian Child Welfare*, Sydney, Allen & Unwin, 1992.

Walkowitz, Judith, *City of Dreadful Delight: Narratives of Sexual Danger in Late Victorian London*, London, Virago, 1992.

Watson, Sophie (ed.), *Playing the State: Australian Feminist Interventions*, Sydney, Allen & Unwin, 1990.

Weeks, Jeffrey, *Coming Out: Homosexual Politics in Britain, From the Nineteenth Century to the Present*, London, Quartet Books, 1977.

Wilson, Elizabeth, *The Sphinx in the City: Urban Life, the Control of Disorder and Women*, London, Virago, 1991.

Windschuttle, Elizabeth (ed.), *Women, Class and History: Feminist Perspectives on Australia 1788–1978*, Sydney, Fontana, 1980.

Yarwood, A. T., *Samuel Marsden: The Great Survivor*, Melbourne, Melbourne University Press, 1977.

Articles

Atkinson, Alan, 'The Moral Basis of Marriage', *Push from the Bush*, no. 2, November 1978.

————, 'Four Patterns of Convict Protest', *Labour History*, no. 37, November 1979.

Aveling, Marian, 'She Only Married To Be Free; Or Cleopatra Vindicated', *Push from the Bush*, no. 2, November 1978.

————, 'Imagining New South Wales as a Gendered Society 1783–1821', *Australian Historical Studies*, no. 98, April 1992.

Blair, Sandra, 'The Revolt at Castle Forbes: A Catalyst to Emancipist Emigrant Confrontation', *Journal of the Royal Australian Historical Society*, vol. 64, part 2, September 1978.

———, 'The Felonry and the Free? Divisions in Colonial Society in the Penal Era', *Labour History*, no. 45, November 1983.

Bridges, Barry J., 'The Native Institution, Parramatta and Blacktown, Part II 1820–1829', *The Forum of Education: An Australian Journal of Teacher Education*, vol. XXXI, no. 2, September 1972.

Byrne, Paula, 'The "Public Good": Competing Visions of Freedom in Early Colonial New South Wales', *Labour History*, no. 58, May 1990.

Cooper, Robyn, 'Victorian Discourses on Women and Beauty: The Alexander Walker Texts', *Gender and History*, vol. 5, no. 1, Spring 1993.

Curtin, Emma, 'Gentility Afloat: Gentlewomen's Diaries and the Voyage to Australia 1830–80', *Australian Historical Studies*, no. 105, October 1995.

Damousi, Joy, 'Chaos and Order: Gender, Space and Sexuality on Female Convict Ships', *Australian Historical Studies*, no. 104, April 1995.

———, 'Depraved and Disorderly: The Sexuality of Convict Women', *Labour History*, no. 68, May 1995.

———, 'Beyond the "Origins Debate": Theorising Sexuality and Gender Disorder in Convict Women's History', *Australian Historical Studies*, no. 106, April 1996.

Daniels, Kay, 'The Flash Mob: Rebellion, Rough Culture and Sexuality in the Female Factories of Van Diemen's Land', *Australian Feminist Studies*, no. 18, Summer 1993.

Earnshaw, Beverly, 'The Convict Apprentices 1820–1838', *Push from the Bush*, no. 5, 1979.

Foster, Steven, 'Convict Assignment in New South Wales in the 1830s', *Push from the Bush*, no. 15, 1983.

Gale, Michelle, 'Girls and the Perception of Sex and Danger in the Victorian Reformatory System', *History*, vol. 78, no. 253, June 1993.

Gandevia, B., and Cobley, J., 'Mortality at Sydney Cove, 1788–1792', *Australian and New Zealand Journal of Medicine*, vol. 4, no. 2, April 1974.

Gandevia, Bryan, and Gandevia, Simon, 'Childhood Mortality and Its Social Background in the First Settlement at Sydney Cove, 1788–1792', *Australian Paediatric Journal*, vol. 11, no. 1, 1975.

Garton, Stephen, 'The Convict Origins Debate: Historians and the Problem of the Criminal Class', *Australian and New Zealand Journal of Criminology*, vol. 24, no. 2, July 1991.

Gowing, Laura, 'Gender and the Language of Insult in Early Modern London', *History Workshop Journal*, no. 35, Spring 1993.

Hammerton, A. J., '"Without Natural Protectors": Female Immigration to Australia 1832–36', *Historical Studies*, vol. 16, no. 65, October 1975.

Heath, Laurel, '"A Safe and Salutary Discipline": The Dark Cells of the Parramatta Female Factory 1838', *Push from the Bush*, no. 9, 1981.

Humphrey, Kim, 'Objects of Compassion: Young Male Convicts in Van Diemen's Land, 1834–1850', *Australian Historical Studies*, vol. 25, no. 98, April 1992.

Hutchinson, R. C., 'Mrs. Hutchinson and the Female Factories of Early Australia', *Tasmanian Historical Research Association*, vol. 11, no. 2, December 1963.

Hyam, Ronald, 'Empire and Sexual Opportunity', *The Journal of Imperial and Commonwealth History*, vol. 14, no. 2.

Kent, David, 'Customary Behaviour Transported: A Note on the Parramatta Female Factory Riot of 1827', *Journal of Australian Studies*, no. 40, March 1994.

Kingston, Beverly, 'Women in Nineteenth Century Australian History', *Labour History*, no. 67, November 1994.

Kociumbas, Jan, 'Childhood History as Ideology', *Labour History*, no. 47, November 1984.

Lake, Marilyn, 'Convict Women as Objects of Male Vision: An Historiographical Review', *Bulletin of the Centre for Tasmanian Historical Studies*, vol. 2, no. 1, 1988.

Lemire, Beverley, 'The Theft of Clothes and Popular Consumerism in Early Modern England', *Journal of Social History*, vol. 24, no. 2.

Magarey, Susan, 'The Invention of Juvenile Delinquency in Early Nineteenth Century England', *Labour History*, no. 34, 1978.

McGrath, Ann, 'The White Man's Looking Glass: Aboriginal–Colonial Gender Relations at Port Jackson', *Australian Historical Studies*, vol. 24, no. 95, October 1990.

Nichol, W., ' "Malingering" and the Convict Protest', *Labour History*, no. 47, November 1984.

———, 'Medicine and the Labour Movement in New South Wales, 1788–1850', *Labour History*, no. 49, November 1985.

Oxley, Deborah, ' "Female Convicts": An Accurate View of Working Class Women?', *Labour History*, no. 65, November 1993.

———, 'Packing her (Economic) Bags: Convict Women Workers', *Australian Historical Studies*, no. 102, April 1994.

Payne, H. S., 'A Statistical Study of Female Convicts in Tasmania 1843–53', *Tasmanian Historical Research Association*, vol. 9, no. 2, June 1961.

Poovey, Mary, 'Curing the "Social Body" in 1832: James Phillips Kay and the Irish in Manchester', *Gender and History*, vol. 5, no. 2, Summer 1993.

Robson, Lloyd, 'The Origin of the Women Convicts Sent to Australia, 1787–1852', *Historical Studies*, vol. 11, no. 41, November 1963.

Samuel, Raphael, 'Reading the Signs', *History Workshop Journal*, no. 32, Autumn 1991.

———, 'Reading the Signs II: Factgrubbers and Mindreaders', *History Workshop Journal*, no. 33, Spring 1992.

Scott, Joan, 'Gender: A Useful Category of Historical Analysis', *American Historical Review*, vol. 91, no. 5, December 1986.

Sturma, Michael, 'Eye of the Beholder: The Stereotype of Women Convicts 1788–1852', *Labour History*, no. 34, May 1978.

———, 'Police and Drunkards in Sydney 1841–1851', *Australian Journal of Politics and History*, no. 27, 1981.

Summers, Anne, 'Factory Girls, Refractory Girls', *Refractory Girl*, no. 1, Summer 1972/3.

Vicinus, Martha, ' "They Wonder to Which Sex I Belong": The Historical Roots of the Modern Lesbian Identity', *Feminist Studies*, vol. 18, no. 3, Fall 1992.

Walker, R. B., 'Tobacco Smoking in Australia, 1788–1914', *Historical Studies*, vol. 19, no. 75, October 1980.

White, Shane, and White, Graham, 'Slave Hair and African American Culture in the Eighteenth and Nineteenth Centuries', *The Journal of Southern History*, vol. LXI, no. 1, February 1995.

Williams, John, 'Irish Female Convicts and Tasmania', *Labour History*, no. 44, May 1983.

Windschuttle, Elizabeth, 'Women, Class and Temperance: Moral Reform in Eastern Australia, 1832–1857', *Push from the Bush*, no. 3, May 1978.

———, 'Discipline, Domestic Training and Social Control: The Female School of Industry, Sydney, 1826–1847', *Labour History*, no. 39, November 1980.

Zika, Charles, 'Fears of Flying: Representations of Witchcraft and Sexuality in Early Sixteenth Century Germany', *Australian Journal of Art*, vol. VIII, 1989/1990.

Unpublished Theses

Belcher, Michael, 'The Child in New South Wales 1820–1837', PhD thesis, University of New England, 1982.

Bridges, Barry J., 'The Sydney Orphan Schools 1800–1830', M.Ed thesis, University of Sydney, 1973.

Collins, Paul, 'William Bernard Ullathorne and the Foundation of Australian Catholicism 1815–1840', PhD thesis, Australian National University, 1989.

Heath, Laurel, 'The Female Convict Factories of New South Wales and Van Diemen's Land: An Examination of Their Role in the Control, Punishment and Reformation of Prisoners Between 1804 and 1854', MA thesis, Australian National University, 1978.

Humphrey, Kim, 'The Remaking of Youth: A Study of Juvenile Convicts and Orphan Immigrants in Colonial Australia', MA thesis, University of Melbourne, 1987.

Liston, Carol, 'New South Wales Under Governor Brisbane 1821–1825', PhD thesis, University of Sydney, 1980.

Index